MW00808807

GENDER VIOLENCE IN PEACE AND WAR

CENTER FOR THE STUDY OF
GENOCIDE
& HUMAN RIGHTS

Genocide, Political Violence, Human Rights Series

Edited by Alexander Laban Hinton, Stephen Eric Bronner, and Nela Navarro

Alan W. Clarke, *Rendition to Torture*

Lawrence Davidson, *Cultural Genocide*

Daniel Feierstein, *Genocide as Social Practice: Reorganizing Society under the Nazis and Argentina's Military Juntas*

Alexander Laban Hinton, ed., *Transitional Justice: Global Mechanisms and Local Realities after Genocide and Mass Violence*

Alexander Laban Hinton, Thomas La Pointe, and Douglas Irvin-Erickson, eds., *Hidden Genocides: Power, Knowledge, Memory*

Douglas A. Kammen, *Three Centuries of Conflict in East Timor*

Walter Richmond, *The Circassian Genocide*

Victoria Sanford, Katerina Stefatos, and Cecilia M. Salvi, eds., *Gender Violence in Peace and War: States of Complicity*

Irina Silber, *Everyday Revolutionaries: Gender, Violence, and Disillusionment in Postwar El Salvador*

Samuel Totten and Rafiki Ubaldo, eds., *We Cannot Forget: Interviews with Survivors of the 1994 Genocide in Rwanda*

Ronnie Yimsut, *Facing the Khmer Rouge: A Cambodian Journey*

GENDER VIOLENCE IN PEACE AND WAR

States of Complicity

EDITED BY VICTORIA SANFORD,
KATERINA STEFATOS, AND CECILIA M. SALVI

RUTGERS UNIVERSITY PRESS

New Brunswick, New Jersey and London

Library of Congress Cataloging-in-Publication Data

Names: Sanford, Victoria. | Stefatos, Katerina, 1979- | Salvi, Cecilia M., 1987-
Title: Gender violence in peace and war : states of complicity / edited by Victoria
Sanford, Katerina Stefatos, Cecilia M. Salvi.
Description: New Brunswick, New Jersey : Rutgers University Press, 2016. | Series:
Genocide, political violence, human rights series | Includes bibliographical references
and index.
Identifiers: LCCN 2015047354| ISBN 9780813576183 (hardcover : alkaline paper) |
ISBN 9780813576176 (paperback : alkaline paper) | ISBN 9780813576190 (ePub) |
ISBN 9780813576206 (Web PDF)
Subjects: LCSH: Women—Violence against—Political aspects—History. | Sex
crimes—Political aspects—History. | Political violence—History. | Women and
war—History. | Women's rights—History. | Accomplices—Political aspects—
History. | State, The—History—20th century. | State, The—History—21st century. |
World politics—20th century. | World politics—21st century.
Classification: LCC HV6250.4.W65 G477 2016 | DDC 362.883—dc23
LC record available at http://lccn.loc.gov/2015047354

A British Cataloging-in-Publication record for this book is available from the British
Library.

This collection copyright © 2016 by Rutgers, The State University
Individual chapters copyright © 2016 in the names of their authors
All rights reserved

No part of this book may be reproduced or utilized in any form or by any means,
electronic or mechanical, or by any information storage and retrieval system, without
written permission from the publisher. Please contact Rutgers University Press, 106
Somerset Street, New Brunswick, NJ 08901. The only exception to this prohibition is
"fair use" as defined by U.S. copyright law.

Visit our website: http://rutgerspress.rutgers.edu

Manufactured in the United States of America

This book is dedicated to survivors of gender violence who inspire us each time they speak truth to power.

CONTENTS

ACKNOWLEDGMENTS

The editors wish to thank the Lehman College Center for Human Rights and Peace Studies for bringing together many of the authors in this volume at a 2014 conference entitled "Gender Violence, Conflict, and the State." At Lehman, we especially thank Julissa Alvarez, Yvonne Collazo, Glen Rodriguez, Sonia Rodriguez, Evelyn Katz, Salah Noueihed, Vincent Stefan, Joseph Tirella, and Nyssa Wagner for helping us get this project off the ground.

Marlie Wasserman and everyone at Rutgers University Press, without whose support this book would not have been possible. We especially thank John Raymond for his meticulous copy editing and helpful comments.

Irina Carlota Silber and the anonymous reviewer for their thorough review.

Special thanks to Jonathan Moller for permission to use his photo for the cover.

We also thank our families and friends for their support and encouragement. Victoria thanks: Michael Bosia, Valentina Figueroa-Sanford, Alcira Forero-Pena, Heather Walsh-Haney, Kenneth Haney, Margaret Schink, Kimberly Theidon, and Amira Thoron, Terry Karl and Sophie Pirie. Katerina thanks: Stathis Gourgouris, Karen Van Dyck, Nota Pantzou, Chloe Howe-Haralambous, Dimitris C. Papadopoulos, Mary and Yiannis Stefatos, and Lela Stefatou for all their help, encouragement, and patience; I am grateful to Neni Panourgiá for her everlasting support and constant guidance. For their patient and unending support, Cecilia thanks: Raquel Ackerman, Jo Ann Arriola, Mo and Niní Delmoro (q.e.p.d.), José and Saide Salvi (q.e.p.d.), Ellen DeRiso, ChorSwang Ngin, Jorge and Viviana Salvi, and Khétih Seví.

GENDER VIOLENCE IN PEACE AND WAR

INTRODUCTION

VICTORIA SANFORD, KATERINA STEFATOS, AND CECILIA M. SALVI

Gender Violence in Peace and War: States of Complicity offers an analysis of the role of the state, its mechanisms, and its structures in perpetuating, legitimizing, and facilitating gender violence worldwide. This book documents the nature, extent, and progress made in relation to gender-based violence since the advancements in women's rights that had their zenith in the 1990s, and focuses specifically on state participation in and interventions on gender violence. The authors ask: How is gender violence perpetrated and facilitated by the state to be understood as a worldwide phenomenon? What are the connections and effects of sexism, nationalism, and militarism (as structural and ideological elements of the state) in the victimization of women? In what ways does the state's political agenda not adequately respond to and protect women's rights? What possible interventions exist when the state itself is an agent of gender violence?

The 1990s were an important decade in establishing the character and dimensions of women's rights in the international arena and recognizing them as human rights, initially during the 1993 United Nations World Conference on Human Rights in Vienna. The 1995 Fourth World Conference on Women in Beijing is generally noted for highlighting concerns about human trafficking and domestic violence and revitalizing international social movements against gender violence. At the same time, the ongoing brutal victimization, systematic rape, sexual enslavement, and forced impregnation in Bosnia-Herzegovina and in Rwanda led to the creation of the International Criminal Tribunals for Yugoslavia and Rwanda, which were formally established in 1993 and 1994, respectively. These tribunals handed down the landmark rulings (1998 and 2001) that wartime rape (and sexual enslavement) is a war crime, a crime against humanity, and an act of genocide.

The progress made by national and international feminist organizations and social movements, which are often spearheaded by women, nongovernmental organizations (NGOs), and United Nations entities, has given rise to remarkable action and policy changes on behalf of women's rights on a global scale. Indicatively, in 2011 the International Labour Organization passed Convention 189, which called on governments to set standards for domestic workers, noting the gendered nature of the work, which is carried out almost exclusively by girls and women (see Salvi, this volume). Similarly, the Rome Statute of the International Criminal Court (2002), a number of UN Security Council Resolutions, the UN Action against Sexual Violence in Conflict (2007), and the UNiTE to End Violence against Women campaign (2008) significantly broadened the definition of rape and systematic sexual violence during armed conflict, war, and peace. Each of them stressed at the same time the need to treat all forms of sexual violence (including sexual enslavement, enforced impregnation, and sterilization) and rape, as tools of war, as crimes against humanity, as acts of genocide, and as a form of torture, and to address the culture of impunity (also see Theidon, this volume).[1]

Our cross-cultural, multidisciplinary research indicates that rape and sexual violence are *not* produced by the "chaos" of war, rogue soldiers, or a faulty command structure. Rather, our research in Greece, Guatemala, Ireland, Mexico, Kenya, Kurdistan, Indonesia, and Peru identifies the various ways in which rape and sexual violence were used as weapons and deployed by command structures with strategic political intentions.

In the context of this book, gender violence is approached primarily as conceptualized by feminists: as "an assault on a person's physical and mental integrity," and "violence which embodies the power imbalances inherent in a patriarchal society" (El-Bushra and Piza López 1993, 1, cited in Moser and Clark 2001, 6). In doing so, our aim is to analyze gender violence as a form of discrimination leading to inequality and as a violation of human rights affecting primarily women and girls but also men, boys, transgender people, and others whose gender expressions do not conform to societal expectations.[2] Even though emphasis is placed on the victimization and traumatization of women and young girls, our ultimate aim is to shed light on the power structures and retraditionalization of gender roles within militaristic and hypermasculinized, heteronormative state (often nationalist) frameworks, and on practices that legitimize and reinforce gender-based violence that targets particular groups of people based on their perceived gender identities (see McAtackney; Pohlman; Sanford, Duyos Álvarez-Arenas, and Dill; Stefatos; Theidon; this volume).

In this book, gender violence is examined as an inherent phenomenon of state practices in their continuity and totality, not only during war, but also in relation to patriarchy, racism, sexism, and militarism, practices that lead to the victimization of women during the strife and after, in times of peace and in post-conflict/transitional and democratic contexts (Anastario; Moradi; Pohlman; this volume). While we acknowledge the gains that have been made by international human rights movements, we also shed light on women's everyday realities and lived experiences of violence that are often silenced or marginalized within human rights discourses. Social scientists and feminist scholars (Peterson 1992) have documented state-sponsored violence against women during wartime and times of crisis, and it remains a current topic of interest (Giles and Hyndman 2004; Jacobs, Jacobson, and Marchbank 2000; Lorentzen and Turpin 1998; Moser and Clark 2001; Nikolic-Ristanovic 2000; Vickers 1993; Waller and Rycenga 2001). We build on and add to literature that mainly analyzes the state's role as perpetrator in these atrocities by acknowledging the multiple and varying forms that violence can take with respect to other practices that fall within the state's purview. That is to say, structural and institutional forms of violence are associated with the state, especially during times of conflict and revolt, while violence that is experienced as personal or individual by the victims, such as femicide, human trafficking, or domestic violence, is instead associated with criminal actors and becomes a space for state intervention on their behalf.[3] Even as the state regulates and prosecutes these illicit violations, its own complicity in perpetuating and facilitating personal and individual forms of violence against women often goes unexamined.

States are undoubtedly the most significant actors in defining and addressing the severity of women's rights violations, and many states have responded to social movements through comprehensive legislation in response to feminist interventions and social activism. The recent trials in Guatemala against Efraín Ríos Montt (2013) document the troubling coexistence of racism and misogyny in the atrocities committed against Ixil indigenous villages, as well as the role of command responsibility in granting impunity and immunity for military personnel in terms of authorizing and legitimizing gender violence (Sanford, Duyos Álvarez-Arenas, and Dill, this volume). Despite women's increased sociopolitical activism and feminist contestations, as witnessed in the recent uprisings in Turkey and Egypt in which women protested against authoritarian and repressive regimes and for gender equality, their "threatening" presence in the public sphere places them at risk of sexual harassment and abuse. Particularly in areas where political and socioeconomic crises are pervasive, patriarchal and heteronormative discourses are readily institutionalized in state practices that attempt to reappropriate gender roles and hierarchical relations of power, as demonstrated by the noteworthy rise in cases of domestic violence recently reported in Russia (Jäppinen and Johnson, this volume), the Democratic Republic of Congo (Cosgrove, this volume), Brazil (Bowater and Mores 2015), India (BBC 2013), and Argentina (Goñi 2015).

Gender Violence in Peace and War: States of Complicity concentrates on gender violence in relation to state practices because, as the chapters clearly demonstrate, rape, sexual violence, torture, persecution, socioeconomic exclusion, and domestic violence fall within the purview of the state and its proxies. Additionally, while gender, violence, and the state are frequent and well-analyzed objects of study in social scientific and feminist literature, the full extent of this multilayered relation between all three has not been fully explored in an interdisciplinary context. We build on comparative and transnational studies of sexual violence during war (Cohen 2013; Kelly 2000; Kesic 2001; Nikolic-Ristanovic 2000; Nowrojee 1996; Turshen 2001; Wood 2006), sexual violence as public secret (Baxi 2014; Das 2008), the intersection of transitional justice and sexual violence (Sanford 2008; Theidon 2007), as well as the possibilities and limitations of local and international prosecutions (Burt 2011; Henry 2009). We draw on Kimberly Theidon's work on historical "truths" in the reporting of rape to truth commissions (2007, 458). We underscore that rape and sexual violence are human rights violations and war crimes, not incidental collateral damage of war.

Following Philip Alston (2007), we focus on state responsibility for the commission of gender violence, toleration of gender violence, and omission of its responsibility to investigate and punish gender violence (Sanford 2008, 2014). The chapters in the book explore the relationship between the state and gender violence in three dimensions: as a perpetrator, a facilitator, or a perpetuator, that is, a participant by omission that perpetuates violence in its failure to provide adequate protections in cases where private individuals are actors. Rather than using these as discrete categories of analysis, each chapter demonstrates how these dimensions intersect. For example, the state perpetrates violence against women, primarily through sexual assault and rape, when women are directly targeted by soldiers and agents of the state who are trained to sexually abuse, torture, and humiliate victims. At the same time, it condones and sanctions the sexual violation of women by disregarding soldiers' actions as well as the "brutal military socialization" some of these very soldiers experience at the hands of their peers (see Theidon, this volume). Similarly, in democratic or postconflict contexts, women, transgender, and gender-nonconforming people are not treated as equal citizens within the body politic and are discriminated against, marginalized, and excluded from the judicial system, which further legitimizes their harassment and oppression.

Though gender violence has been explored by feminist scholars and academics, what actually constitutes "gender violence" remains controversial within certain academic and theoretical perspectives. This book engages with these debates by clearly demonstrating that gendered violence is experienced in multiple ways by people around the world, and that investigating state practices in connection to nationalism, misogyny, patriarchy, impunity, and immunity reveals the various and intersecting mechanisms of the state and its deployment of violence against its female citizens. In this framework of analysis, we need to underline that despite many positive advances—feminist and activist interventions, UN and various NGO and human rights resolutions, grassroots and social movements, international and domestic legislation, truth and reconciliation commissions, gender quotas, academic contributions, and increased public awareness—gender-based violence, sexual abuse and torture, domestic violence, persecution, and incarceration is still an everyday reality for millions who are among the world's most vulnerable populations.

Gender Violence in Peace and War: States of Complicity aims at building on the existing and influential research across disciplines that discusses the role of the state, gender, and violence. We emphasize the relation between the state and gender violence, that is, the intersection of violence and gender, as a discrete category of investigation as it manifests in state practices that perpetuate, allow, facilitate, or tolerate violence against women. On this ground, gender is not approached, both theoretically and methodologically, as simply another variable or analytical category in the analyses of the role of the state and its proxies in the perpetuation of gender violence. Instead, gender is the central analytical category in our work. Ultimately, the aim of our work is to provide grounds for visibility, agency, and resistance (Sanford, Duyos Álvarez-Arenas, and Dill; Hoewer; McAtackney; Stefatos; this volume) in ways that call into question state and para-state mechanisms and structures along with the prevailing social power and gender hierarchies that normalize and rationalize gender violence. It is our hope that by investigating state power and practices at the interstitial juncture between gender and violence, the chapters will open up new areas of inquiry for researchers that encourage international and interdisciplinary dialogue. Concomitantly, the phenomenon of gender violence and the gendered characteristics of domestic, political, ethnic, and state violence and oppression are addressed not only during war, sociopolitical uprisings, and ethnic conflicts, but also in postconflict or transitional and democratic settings, and during peace. In doing so the aim is to also shed light on the preexisting ideologies and institutionalized constructions of otherness that are tightly connected to gender violence against already marginalized groups, within a precarious life (Butler 2004), during conflict and turmoil, and during peace.

Gender Violence in Peace and War: States of Complicity analyzes the state's role as perpetrator, facilitator, and perpetuator of gendered violence as an integral part of state functioning and capacity—not as an exception. In line with current literature, it critically analyzes sexual violence during and after wartime, stressing the troubling continuum of gender-related violence and abuse (Anastario; Cosgrove; Moradi; this volume),[4] while at the same time adding to this literature an analysis of other forms of state-sponsored, sanctioned, or initiated violence.

In addition to offering cutting-edge research on diverse topics, unique methods of investigation provide new lenses of analysis. Mike Anastario's work uses medical records to investigate and establish the existence of mass rape. The chapter by Laura McAtackney on women prisoners during the Irish Civil War employs graffiti and diaries to construct a picture of the daily lives of women political prisoners and state repression.

A consistent theme throughout *Gender Violence in Peace and War: States of Complicity* is that of trauma "as a wound inflicted not [only] upon the body but upon the mind" (Caruth 1996, 3) and as "an overwhelming experience of sudden or catastrophic events" (Caruth 1996, 11) of war and conflict, rape and sexual violence, interpersonal violence and socioeconomic ostracism, torture, and incarceration. From the trauma of fear and the physical trauma of violence (Cosgrove; Pohlman; Sanford, Duyos Álvarez-Arenas, and Dill; Stefatos) to the emotional trauma of survival and the official silencing of memory (Cosgrove; Moradi; Pohlman; Sanford, Duyos Álvarez-Arenas, and Dill; Stefatos), each chapter challenges conventional understandings of trauma that seek to demarcate a beginning and an end. From the moral disengagement of the perpetrators (Stefatos) to the breaking of moral codes by perpetrators (Theidon), these chapters demonstrate the myriad ways in which sexual violence traumatizes individual victims, families, communities, and nations (Cosgrove) and the official powerlessness foisted upon victims by states that shame the victim, rather than prosecute the perpetrator (Theidon). The state is a male-dominated and masculine construction (Pettman 1996), and often cultivates a "forgive and forget" (McKay 2000, 565) approach to women's traumatic experiences of suffering and death. However, these traumas and stories of violence, torture, and humiliation through the gendering of memory often take the form of political resistance, as Temma Kaplan reminds us (2002, 180–181, 187). On this ground, Melanie Hoewer shows the power of trauma when harnessed by survivors and redeployed through activism by those it was meant to silence. Traumatic relations are also presented in their messiness wherein survivors of domestic violence may "bond" with their aggressor in the belief that they can "fix" the violence through their relationship. The recording and documentation of these traumatic stories and memories through official and unofficial processes—in the context of truth commissions and tribunals, international organizations and academic research—is not always unproblematic; it is a complex, multidimensional, and political process that brings relief and justice, and healing in some cases, but needs to be engendered and contextualized (Simic 2005, 5). Anastario offers a new path for documenting the traumas of mass rape through forensic evidence without retraumatizing or dehumanizing survivors, enabling a more "gender sensitive" process (Hackett and Rolston 2009, 355, 357; Kaplan 2002; Simic 2005, 5).

It is our collective goal to bring together interdisciplinary theoretical insights and methodological contributions from political science, history, gender studies, anthropology, and legal studies, while employing empirical evidence and analysis in order to provide grounds for comparative approaches. Each chapter draws from these approaches and presents cutting-edge research into areas of investigation that are either new or hard to find. There is scant research into the means used during the Anfāl genocide. Research on domestic violence as a state issue (Jäppinen and Johnson) is a nascent topic. Furthermore, Walsh's chapter on police stations for women in Nicaragua tracks a new trend in law enforcement practices as a response to the recently documented increase in rape and crimes of sexual violence. At the same time, chapters that focus on historical cases in Ireland, Greece, and Indonesia underscore the long-standing subjugation of women in different milieux. *Gender Violence in Peace and War: States of Complicity* demonstrates the ongoing struggles of women and establishes the need for more research and intervention.

Contributors demonstrate vast methodological creativity in their efforts to document and understand gender violence. Contributors use ethnography (Cosgrove; Hoewer; Moradi; Sanford, Duyos Álvarez-Arenas, and Dill; Stefatos; Walsh), archival research (Anastario; Sanford, Duyos Álvarez-Arenas, and Dill; Moradi; Stefatos), linguistic analysis (Sanford, Duyos Álvarez-Arenas, and Dill; Moradi; Pohlman), participant-observation (Cosgrove; Hoewer; Stefatos; Walsh), forensic analysis (Anastario; Sanford, Duyos Álvarez-Arenas, and Dill), and analysis of underused primary sources such as poems and art (McAtackney; Moradi), graffiti (McAtackney), testimony (Sanford, Duyos Álvarez-Arenas, and Dill; Pohlman; Salvi; Stefatos), and messages written in autograph books (McAtackney). These less than conventional methods documenting life experiences with extreme state violence or violence condoned by the state have significant implications for postconflict policy and research practices. In particular, we are reminded that sometimes breaking the silence is empowering (Hoewer; Moradi), but sometimes it is a new form of trauma (Anastario). Together, these methods offer new ways for researchers to engage and bear witness to extreme human suffering caused or tolerated by the state, or both.

Additionally, because of recent highly publicized cases of rape in India and elsewhere, there has been a resurgence in public attention to sexual violence against women and "rape culture" and what responsibility the state bears in preventing such violence. This book directly responds to that interest by highlighting how state power is implicit in seemingly individual crimes in a multilayered fashion. Several of the chapters take on issues such as the current femicide killings and recent trials (Sanford, Duyos Álvarez-Arenas, and Dill) and postconflict sexual violence in the Democratic Republic of Congo (Cosgrove), while other chapters demonstrate the ongoing need for more research into those issues that often receive little to no media attention, such as indigenous women's activism in the Chiapas region of Mexico (Hoewer) and sexual torture in Indonesia in the context of the New Order regime (Pohlman). Besides the focus on the nature and effects of state-sponsored or state-tolerated sexual violence, persecution, and oppression, both in the public and private sphere, the possibility of women's agency and resistance is emphasized (Hoewer; McAtackney; Stefatos).

Although gender violence does suggest an analysis of the relationship between and among genders, this book does not, despite the range of topics covered, explicitly discuss the gender implications of state violence against men, transgender, or gender-nonconforming people. The authors are aware, however, of the victimization, persecution, and sexual abuse of boys, men, and others in war-affected communities, in militarist and highly masculinized contexts (Bosia 2013 and 2015; also see Theidon, this volume), and in migratory contexts (Salvi, this volume). The topics discussed in the book, such as domestic violence, rape, sexual torture, and the prevalence of sexual abuse, overwhelmingly affect women and girls, both statistically and discursively. Concomitantly, some chapters analyze the traumatization, incarceration, torture, and abuse of women (without dismissing or downgrading male victimization) in relation to gender-specific differentiations that are integral to their suffering, and thus need to be contextualized within the role of the state and often nationalist or militaristic practices that control and sanction the bodies, actions, and beliefs of women who are in a position to challenge prevailing gender and power hierarchies. On this ground, sexual abuse against other groups needs to be examined in relation to female victimization, since it is tightly connected to a hierarchical system of power and gender relations.

Part one brings together four chapters that explore state violence, gender, and resistance in Greece, Guatemala, Ireland, and Chiapas, Mexico. In chapter 1, through meticulous archival research complemented by ethnographic interviews, Katerina Stefatos documents the Greek military regime's systematic utilization of torture driven by patriarchal and nationalistic narratives. She makes connections between militarism, masculinity, and militarized masculinity as projects that are never completed. Just as this Greek project of militarized masculinity resonates with the experience of women survivors in Guatemala (Sanford, Duyos Álvarez-Arenas, and Dill), so too does the Greek nationalist ideology resonate with the Guatemalan state's National Security Doctrine. Stefato's chapter provides evidence supporting analysis of military regimes as maternal regimes that militarize women's lives (Enloe 2000) and their reproductive capacity (see Theidon 2014) and simultaneously carry out reproductive warfare. In this rubric, female dissidents are a "double threat" because they challenge the military regime and the moral order of the patriarchy. Thus, motherhood, reproduction, and sexuality are political acts subject to state control (see also Jäppinen and Johnson).

Chapter 2, "Sexual Violence as a Weapon during the Guatemalan Genocide," takes the 2013 genocide trial of General Efraín Ríos Montt as the entry point to explore the Guatemalan army's systematic use of rape as a weapon of war during the genocide. Drawing on decades of collective field research, forensic investigations, and legal casework, the authors provide an analysis of the evidence presented in the court hearings and the way survivors and the general public in Guatemala understood this evidence. Declassified U.S. government documents, leaked Guatemalan army documents, court testimony of survivors and perpetrators as well as testimonies collected by the authors over the past twenty years document state-sponsored sexual violence as ordered by the army high command. As was the case in Greece (Stefatos) and Indonesia (Pohlman), anticommunism fused with patriarchal structures and centuries-old prejudices to produce a climate ripe for the dehumanization of a targeted population—in the case of Guatemala, it was genocide against the majority Maya. Further, the chapter moves from the genocide and rape by soldiers to the army's deployment of forced silence to maintain control over its victims. The chapter explores the power of the rape survivors testifying in the public genocide hearing and rupturing decades of official silence as the hearings were televised throughout Guatemala and the world.

Uncomfortable truths are explored by Laura McAtackney in chapter 3, "Gender, Incarceration, and Power Relations during the Irish Civil War (1920–1923)." Here, the experiences of women political prisoners are explored through the veiled speech of graffiti and autograph books left by women imprisoned by the regime. McAtackney shows that historic silencing of the experiences of women political prisoners leaves a messy and incomplete history, but a history still well worth exploring. And, here again, we find the link between masculinist and nationalist ideologies eliminating, or seeking to eliminate, the subjectivity of dissident women. Nonetheless, the autograph books and graffiti also tell a tale of women's collective agency to resist, contest, and subvert their condition as prisoners and challenge the official "shame" imposed upon them.

Building on the work of Lynn Stephen (2002), Rosalva Aída Hernández (2001), and Shannon Speed (2008), in chapter 4 Melanie Hoewer looks at post-conflict feminist projects and how they relate to states in transition through her investigation of the farmer's movement, Zapatista movement, and women's rights movement in Chiapas. Through historical and ethnographic study of these three different social movements over time, she provides a new lens to analyze the continuum of violence experienced by women in Chiapas, from state-perpetrated violence to domestic violence where the state fails to protect women.

Part two consolidates our focus on the continuum of sexual violence and the role of the state with chapters on Kenyan elections, the Iraqi Ba'thi state's genocidal al-Anfāl operations against the Kurds, and the Indonesian state's consolidation of the New Order regime. Thematically, these three chapters also underscore the anthropological practice of ethnographic research "as a site of witnessing and testimony, to produce knowledge that makes it possible to bear witness" (Baxi 2014, 149). In "Medical Record Review and Evidence of Mass Rape during the 2007–2008 Post-Election Violence in Kenya," Mike Anastario brings his significant research experience to bear on the difficult task of documenting mass rape. His chapter points to the importance of the ongoing development of both theory and methods to better research and understand the state and gender violence. Moreover, Anastario reminds us that gender violence is about power: "Presenting forensic evidence of mass rape, potentially usable in an international jurisdiction, may be one way that discourse can be effectively used to render that power vulnerable." He then demonstrates how evidence can be collected even in the "chaos" of postconflict by drawing on a study he conducted with Kenyan and U.S. researchers for Physicians for Human Rights.

Anastario and his colleagues present an opportunity and challenge to human rights workers by shifting the burden of proof in evidentiary standards. While testimony has become an established psychotherapeutic model for NGOs working with survivors, intending to help them overcome the trauma of state terror, giving testimony in a public forum, whether a court or truth commission, is not a safe therapeutic environment (Henry 2009, 12) and is, at best, a bittersweet catharsis. Thus, finding new ways to "tell" the survivor story of trauma without retraumatizing the victim remains a challenge. By looking for patterns in medical records, Anastario and his colleagues not only validate the testimonies of survivors but also shift the burden of proof. This can prevent retraumatization of the survivors who have already come forward to document their sexual assault, and save them from unnecessary multiple telling and reliving of horrific experiences.

In chapter 6, "The Force of Writing in Genocide: On Sexual Violence in the al-Anfāl Operations and Beyond," Fazil Moradi chronicles the testimonies of Kurdish female survivors of the Iraqi Ba'thi state's genocide. He documents the ways in which women were abducted as "spoils of war" and victims of public sexual assault, only to be silenced after rescue and return to the Kurdistan region. Looking at the experiences of these women through the prism of testimony and writing, Moradi analyzes the way writing establishes and is deployed by the state to silence the victims at the time of the war crimes and in their immediate aftermath. And, thirty years later, we are presented with survivor testimonies that make public the very sexual assaults the official discourses sought to hide.

Annie Pohlman offers compelling testimonies of survivors of Indonesian army sexual violence in chapter 7, "Sexualized Bodies, Public Mutilation, and Torture at the Beginning of Indonesia's New Order Regime (1965–1966)." These Indonesian survivor stories offer a counterdiscourse to the Indonesian regime and to what Marguerite Feitlowitz (1998) calls a "lexicon of terror" in her work on Argentina's Dirty War. Indonesia continues to live with an official lexicon wherein the genocidal murder of some five hundred thousand Indonesians is officially remembered as a necessary and justified extermination of communists. Forty years after the political genocide, Pohlman and a colleague interview three women who were political prisoners of the regime. Their survival stories are stark portrayals of witnessing the torture and murders of other prisoners, as well as their own experiences of violence and survival. While the Indonesian state has never offered an official acknowledgment or apology to these women survivors or any of the other millions of Indonesian citizens who suffered political torture at the hands of the state, Pohlman's chapter advances the survivor quest for justice by exercising her sacred obligation to witness by listening and sharing their stories with the reader.

Part three documents the efforts, possibilities, and limitations of the state to respond to and address gender violence in Nicaragua, Russia, the Democratic Republic of Congo, and the United States. In "Advances and Limits of Policing for Women's Security: Nicaragua in Comparative Perspective," Shannon Drysdale Walsh investigates the structure and efficacy of women's police stations as experienced by Nicaraguan women seeking assistance. She frames her research within the growing literature on the gendering of security and critiques of what constitutes insecurity. She points to the strengths of the international drive to establish women's police stations, but also recognizes the state's limitations in remedying violence against women. She situates her analysis in relation to the structural inequalities that remain unaddressed by the police stations and the state.

In conversation with Walsh's discussion of the policing of domestic violence in Nicaragua, Maija Jäppinen and Janet Elise Johnson make a significant contribution to the topic in chapter 9, "The State to the Rescue? The Contested Terrain of Domestic Violence in Postcommunist Russia." Tracing the history of domestic violence in the Russian Federation over the past two decades, Jäppinen and Johnson demonstrate how the state and activists link domestic violence to gender inequality as well as the ways in which domestic violence was handled by the Soviet authorities as part of their "coercive control over society," only to be privatized after the Soviet collapse. As in Nicaragua, NGOs stepped in to create public awareness and urge the state to respond. Resonating with other chapters addressing patriarchy in state policies, Jäppinen and Johnson chronicle a policy shift from focusing on violence against women to a focus on violence in the family that makes justice even more inaccessible for victims.

In "The Absent State: Teen Mothers and New Patriarchal Forms of Gender Subordination in the Democratic Republic of Congo," Serena Cosgrove asks us to consider postconflict violence and why so much violence is directed toward young women. Her chapter, like others in this volume (Sanford, Duyos Álvarez-Arenas, and Dill; Stefatos) points to militarized masculinity and masculinity in crisis as it is played out where patriarchal structures dominate, from the family to the police to the courts. She moves from the trope of the absent state to identify the ways in which the state is present, much to the detriment of teen victims of sexual violence. Through conversations with survivors of violence in search of justice, she asks us to consider what it means for victims to deal with sexual violence in and outside of the courts. In this way, patriarchy is revealed by "reconciliation" models that solve family issues in favor of maintaining male pride and privilege at the expense of the teen victims. The prevalence of sexual violence before, during, and after war reveals and reinforces patriarchal practice. While there may be variations in sexual violence (Wood 2006), young women and their offspring remain property in a patriarchal and patrilineal structure. Like Walsh, Hoewer, and Jäppinen and Johnson, Cosgrove provides insight into the possibilities and limitations of local and international NGOs to provide services to women victims in the absence of state commitment to ending violence against women.

In chapter 11, Cecilia Salvi analyzes anti-trafficking legislation in the United States through a feminist ethnographic framework against the background of neoliberalism and globalization. Salvi, through the analysis of human rights and legal discourse and state rhetoric, stresses the need to think beyond gender-restrictive, exclusionary, and often racist binaries and categorizations in order to address the invisibility that surrounds not only women and children (primarily in the context of human and sex trafficking), but also men, transgendered people, economic migrants, and irregular workers (labor trafficking), an invisibility that hinders their recognition as citizens and legal subjects.

In the concluding chapter, Kimberly Theidon provides a critical review of the United Nation's Women, Peace, and Security Agenda, the UN resolutions on violence against women, and the significant legislative steps and landmark cases that contributed to a redefinition of sexual violence and wartime rape of women as war crimes, crimes against humanity, and genocidal crimes. In addition, Theidon underlines the limitations of the UN resolutions and the Women, Peace, and Security Agenda in terms of analyzing sexual violence in war and conflict only in relation to the victimization of women, thus downgrading the multifaceted experiences of both men and women, girls and boys. Theidon's analysis, in a dialogue with the authors of this volume and through her research on Colombia and Peru, and especially the Final Report of the Peruvian Truth and Reconciliation Commission, sheds light on the construction of hegemonic, heterosexist, and "militarized" masculinities as cultivated within violent rites of passage in state, para-state, and militaristic settings (also see Sanford, Duyos Álvarez-Arenas, and Dill; Stefatos; this volume) where the lines between perpetrator and victim are often blurred. She also focuses on the often exclusionary emphasis on wartime rape and sexual violence as the sole and primary source of female victimization, which underestimates the traumas and silences related to socioeconomic exclusion, oppression, and racism in the aftermath of conflict and war.

Limiting research on gender violence only to times of turmoil can obscure the everyday violence that women face in other contexts, as well as obscure the state's role, manifested in various practices, mechanisms, and structures that perpetrate, perpetuate, and facilitate the various and multifaceted forms of gender violence, as well as hinder actions against gender violence. *Gender Violence in Peace and War: States of Complicity* engages with current debates across disciplines regarding the nature of the state's role in gender violence. Our work enables comparative approaches and employs a distinct interdisciplinary and international approach. Rather than attempting a comprehensive overview, we offer our work as part of a continuing multidisciplinary conversation about theories and practices of the state with regards to gender violence. We have sought to demonstrate that there is a continuum of violence primarily against women from state-perpetrated sexual violence during times of conflict and political strife to ongoing state responsibility for gender violence by virtue of state toleration or omission of state responsibility to investigate, sanction, and prevent gender violence.

NOTES

1. The basis was set on the landmark cases of the International Criminal Tribunals for the Former Yugoslavia (Kunarac et al. case) and Rwanda (Akayesu case). Similar arguments have been made by the Committee Against Torture and the European Center for Constitutional and Human Rights in reference to Argentina during the Dirty War—especially the atrocities committed at the ESMA detention and torture camp (see Rodríguez Pareja and Al-Khatib 2012). Under international law the rape of a prisoner is considered a method of torture (also see Pohlman's and Stefatos's chapters in this volume). In that respect, the Čelebići trial and the 1998 ICTY judgment have set a precedent in the definition of rape as a form of torture.
2. See CEDAW (1979) and UN Entity for Gender Equality and the Empowerment of Women (2014).
3. On this ground, Wies (2011) and Merry (2003, 2006) have emphasized the need to address these structural frameworks, that socioeconomic inequality, marginalization, poverty, and lack of healthcare are interconnected with the perpetuation of gender violence. For instance, see the case of femicides in Ciudad Juarez, Mexico (González Rodríguez 2012). Tamar Wilson (2014) provides a useful discussion of the different types of gender violence, drawing on a number of case studies in Latin America and a review of the relevant bibliography.

4. In relation to a gendered continuum of violence during armed conflict and peace, indicatively see Moser (2001) and Cockburn (2004).

REFERENCES

Alston, Philip. 2007. "Civil and Political Rights, Including the Questions of Disappearances and Summary Executions: Mission to Guatemala." February 19. A/HRC/4/20/Add.2, 5. New York: United Nations, Human Rights Council.

Baxi, Pratiksha. 2014. "Sexual Violence and Its Discontents." *Annual Review of Anthropology* 43: 139–154.

BBC. 2013. "Viewpoints: What Next after Outcry over Delhi Rape?" January 4. http://www.bbc.com/news/world-asia-india-20904028.

Bosia, Michael. 2013. "Why States Act: Homophobia and Crisis." In *Global Homophobia: States, Movements, and the Politics of Oppression*, edited by Meredith Weiss and Michael Bosia. Champaign: University of Illinois Press.

———. 2015. "To Love or to Loathe: Modernity, Homophobia, and LGBT Rights." In *Sexual Politics and International Relations—How LGBT Claims Shape International Relations*, edited by Manuela Lavinas Picq and Markus Thiel. New York: Routledge.

Bowater, Donna, and Priscilla Moraes. 2015. "Brazil Passes Femicide Law to Curb Domestic Violence." *Aljazeera America*, May 10. http://america.aljazeera.com/articles/2015/5/10/brazil-passes-femicide-law-to-curb- domestic-violence.html.

Burt, Jo-Marie. (2009) 2011. *Violencia y Autoritarismo en el Perú: Bajo la sombra de Sendero y la dictadura de Fujimori*. Lima: Instituto de Estudios Peruanos.

Butler, Judith. 2004. *Precarious Life: The Powers of Mourning and Life*. London: Verso.

Caruth, Cathy. 1996. *Unclaimed Experience: Trauma, Narrative, and History*. Baltimore: Johns Hopkins University Press.

Cockburn, Cynthia. 2004. "The Continuum of Violence: A Gender Perspective on War and Peace." In *Sites of Violence, Gender, and Conflict Zones*, edited by Wenona Giles and Jennifer Hyndman. Berkeley: University of California Press.

Cohen, Dara Kay. 2013. "Explaining Rape during Civil War: Cross-National Evidence (1980–2009)." *American Political Science Review* 107 (3): 461–477.

Convention on the Elimination of All Forms of Discrimination against Women (CEDAW). 1979. http://www.un.org/womenwatch/daw/cedaw/.

Das, Veena. 2008. "Violence, Gender, and Subjectivity." *Annual Review of Anthropology* 37: 283–299.

El-Bushra, Judith, and Eugenia Piza Lopez. 1993. "Gender-Related Violence: Its Scope and Relevance." In "Women and Conflict," edited by Helen O'Connell, special issue, *Gender and Development* 1, no 2 (June): 1–9.

Enloe, Cynthia. 2000. *Maneuvers: The International Politics of Militarizing Women's Lives*. Berkeley: University of California Press.

Feitlowitz, Marguerite. 1998. *A Lexicon of Terror: Argentina and the Legacies of Torture*. New York: Oxford University Press.

Giles, Wenona, and Jennifer Hyndman, eds. 2004. *Sites of Violence: Gender and Conflict Zone*. Berkeley: University of California Press.

Goñi, Uki. 2015. "Argentine Women Call Out Machismo." *New York Times*, June 15. Accessed July 9, 2015. http://www.nytimes.com/2015/06/16/opinion/argentine-women-call-out -machismo.html?_r=0.

González Rodríguez, Sergio. 2012. *The Femicide Machine*. Translated by Michael Parker-Stainback. Los Angeles: Semiotext(e).

Hackett, Claire, and Bill Rolston. 2009. "The Burden of Memory: Victims, Storytelling, and Resistance in Northern Ireland." *Memory Studies* 2 (3): 355–376.

Henry, Nicola. 2009. "Witness to Rape: The Limits and Potential of International War Crimes Trials for Victims of Wartime Sexual Violence." *International Journal of Transitional Justice* 3: 114–134.

Hernández Castillo, Rosalva Aída. 2001. *Histories and Stories from Chiapas: Border Identities in Southern Mexico*. Austin: University of Texas Press.

Jacobs, Susie, Ruth Jacobson, and Jennifer Marchbank, eds. 2000. *States of Conflict: Gender, Violence, and Resistance*. London: Zed Books.

Kaplan, Temma. 2002. "Acts of Testimony: Reversing the Shame and Gendering the Memory." *Signs* 28 (1): 179–199.

Kelly, Liz. 2000. "Wars against Women: Sexual Violence, Sexual Politics, and the Militarized State." In *States of Conflict: Gender, Violence, and Resistance*, edited by Susie Jacobs, Ruth Jacobson, and Jennifer Marchbank. London: Zed Books.

Kesic, Vesna. 2001. "From Reverence to Rape: An Anthropology of Ethnic and Genderized Violence." In *Frontline Feminisms: Women, War, and Resistance*, edited by Marguerite Waller and Jennifer Rycenga. New York: Routledge.

Leydesdorff, Selma, Luisa Passerini, and Paul Thompson, eds. 2005. *Gender and Memory*. New Brunswick, NJ: Transaction.

Lorentzen, Lois, and Jennifer Turpin, eds. 1998. *The Women and War Reader*. New York: New York University Press.

McKay, Susan. 2000. "Gender Justice and Reconciliation." *Women's Studies International Forum* 23 (5): 561–570.

Merry, Sally Engle. 2003. "Constructing a Global Law—Violence against Women and the Human Rights System." *Law and Social Inquiry* 28: 941–977.

———. 2006. *Human Rights and Gender Violence: Translating International Law into Local Justice*. Chicago: University of Chicago Press.

Moser, Caroline. 2001. "The Gendered Continuum of Violence and Conflict: An Operational Framework." In *Victims, Perpetrators, or Actors? Gender, Armed Conflict, and Political Violence*, edited by Caroline Moser and Fiona Clark. London: Zed Books.

Moser, Caroline, and Fiona Clark, eds. 2001. *Victims, Perpetrators, or Actors? Gender, Armed Conflict, and Political Violence*. London: Zed Books.

Nikolic-Ristanovic, Vesna, ed. 2000. *Women, Violence, and War: Wartime Victimization of Refugees in the Balkans*. Budapest: Central European University Press.

Nowrojee, Binaifer. 1996. *Sexual Violence during the Rwandan Genocide and Its Aftermath*. New York: Human Rights Watch.

Peterson, V. Spike. 1992. "Introduction." In *Gendered States: Feminist (Re)Visions of International Relations Theory*, edited by Spike Peterson. Boulder, CO: Lynne Rienner.

Pettman, J. Jan. 1996. *Worlding Women: A Feminist International Politics*. London: Routledge.

Rodríguez Pareja, Mariana, and Alia Al-Khatib. 2012. "Justice for Sexual Violence and Gender Crimes in Argentina." *Justice in Conflict Blog*. May 25. http://justiceinconflict .org/2012/05/25/justice-for-sexual-violence-and-gender-crimes-in-argentina/.

Sanford, Victoria. 2008. "From Genocide to Feminicide: Impunity and Human Rights in 21st-Century Guatemala." In "Human Rights in Conflict: Interdisciplinary Perspectives," edited by John Wallach, special issue, *Journal of Human Rights* 7 (2): 104–122.

———. 2014. "Command Responsibility and the Guatemalan Genocide: Genocide as a Military Plan of the Guatemalan Army under the Dictatorships of Generals Lucas Garcia, Rios Montt, and Mejia Victores." *Genocide Studies International* 8 (1): 86–101.

Simic, Olivera. 2005. "Gender, Conflict, and Reconciliation: Where Are the *Men*? What about *Women*?" *Journal for Political Theory and Research on Globalization, Development, and Gender Issues* 10: 1–13.

Speed, Shannon. 2008. *Rights in Rebellion: Indigenous Struggle and Human Rights in Chiapas.* Stanford: Stanford University Press.

Stephen, Lynn. 2002. *Zapata Lives! History and Cultural Politics in Southern Mexico.* Berkeley: University of California Press.

Theidon, Kimberly. 2007. "Gender in Transition: Common Sense, Women, and War." *Journal of Human Rights* 6 (4): 453–478.

———. 2014. "First Do No Harm: Enforced Sterilizations and Gender Justice in Peru." *ReVista: Harvard Review of Latin America* (Fall): 84–87.

Turshen, Meredeth. 2001. "The Political Economy of Rape: An Analysis of Systematic Rape and Sexual Abuse of Women during Armed Conflict in Africa." In *Victims, Perpetrators, or Actors? Gender, Armed Conflict, and Political Violence*, edited by Caroline Moser and Fiona Clark. London: Zed Books.

UN Women. 2014. "Women's Right to Equality: The Promise of CEDAW." United Nations Entity for Gender Equality and Empowerment of Women. http://asiapacific.unwomen .org/~/media/field%20office%20eseasia/docs/publications/2014/7/the%20promise%20of%20cedaw%20final%20pdf.ashx.

Vickers, Jeanne. 1993. *Women and War.* London: Zed Books.

Waller, Marguerite, and Jennifer Rycenga, eds. 2001. *Frontline Feminisms: Women, War, and Resistance.* New York: Routledge.

Wies, Jennifer. 2011. "Practicing Political Economy: Anthropology and Domestic Violence Advocacy." *Practicing Anthropology* 33 (3): 4–8.

Wilson, Tamar Diana. 2014. "Violence against Women in Latin America." *Latin American Perspectives* 41 (1): 3–18.

Wood, Elizabeth. 2006. "Variation in Sexual Violence during War." *Politics and Society* 34 (3): 307–341.

PART I

STATE VIOLENCE, GENDER, AND RESISTANCE

1 · SUBALTERN BODIES

Gender Violence, Sexual Torture, and Political Repression during the Greek Military Dictatorship (1967–1974)

KATERINA STEFATOS

This chapter analyzes the sexually related torture and abuse of dissidents during the Greek military dictatorship (1967–1974). It shows how sexual torture and terrorization during interrogation and incarceration functioned as a tool of repression and as part of a state-sponsored project of control, regulation, and rehabilitation of "incorrigible," politically active women. In Greece, the 1967 coup d'état initiated a prolonged period of political persecution, social oppression, and incarceration, with communists and leftists or even just politically active, progressive citizens becoming the chief targets. For both men and women (but especially women), the colonels' regime employed calculated mechanisms of torture and abuse based on patriarchal and nationalistic narratives that carried gender-specific markers. Although political violence and state terror against dissidents was not a new phenomenon, state-sponsored violence and sexual torture during the junta were organized and implemented as official state practice, systematized and scientifically performed by agents of the police and armed forces, specially trained torturers, and high-ranking officials.

In this chapter, I focus on the gender dynamics of torture and the micro technologies of power and terror within the interrogation and police centers of the junta period, as the power relations and the nationalist ideology of the military system were effectuated in these places (see Foucault 1991). I investigate the cases of torture and interrogation as a corollary of a nationalist, anticommunist rhetoric and ideological framework, which facilitated and legitimized torture, sexual abuse, and humiliation. I discuss in some detail the physical, sexual, and psychological machinery of terror, the practices of torture against both men and women (mostly young women). In addition, I set the role of the torturers and perpetrators of abuse within the backdrop of extreme militarism and intensified masculinization. Understanding the victimization of the Greek dissidents sheds light on the sexual and institutionalized parameters of the torture of women and men, the nature and ideological framework of the junta, the implications for the state and its proxies (military, police, Greek Orthodox Church, medical establishment, and the judiciary), and the hierarchical system of gender relations. To make my case, I draw on the narratives of junta dissidents, including oral testimonies, memoirs, and archival sources. I conclude with a brief discussion of the construction of political and gendered subjectivities, providing snapshots of resistance, survival, and agency within this state-sponsored, nationalist project of political repression and sexual terrorization.

CONTEXTUALIZING TERROR:
THE SITES AND PRACTICES OF GENDER VIOLENCE

Within a few hours of the military coup, on April 21, 1967, the majority of the political leaders of the Left, Center, and even the Right were arrested, including members of the Greek intelligentsia. According to the 1968 Amnesty International Report on Greece, in the first days of the coup, 8,270 citizens were detained; on the barren, remote island of Yaros alone, political exiles numbered more than six thousand, including approximately 250 women.[1] In addition, a significant number of dissidents were detained and imprisoned without a trial, interrogated, and tortured. According to James Becket, the American attorney representing Amnesty International (of London) in Greece at the time, at least two thousand people were tortured (between 1967 and 1969), this being a conservative estimate (1997, 31).

The main sites of incarceration and abuse of women during the military junta were the Yaros concentration camp, the Alikarnassos prison camp in Crete, the Averof and Korydallos Prisons in Athens, the Greek Military Police (ESA) headquarters, and the Security Police Headquarters (Asfalia), both of which were in the center of Athens, along with numerous specifically designated and designed interrogation centers, camps, prisons, and police stations.[2]

The torture and sexual abuse of political activists, both male and female, was not just tolerated but officially regulated and exercised in a quite scientific way by specially trained agents. The officers, soldiers, and servicemen of the armed and police forces were exposed to anticommunist propaganda and nationalist rhetoric; added to this, the young recruits of the Military Police were often themselves abused as part of their training at the Military Police Training Center.

Within this hypermasculine and militaristic culture, notions of nationalism and anticommunism facilitated their transformation into official torturers (Haritos-Fatouros 2003, 38–65).

The victims of gender violence were, in most cases, politically active women, not limited to communists or leftists, but also centrists or even those of a more conservative political background, as well as students, workers, and professionals. Gender violence and torture during the junta had a strongly sexual nature; the process of sexual torture in particular was transformed into what one of the female political inmates in the Mechanics School of the Argentine Navy (ESMA) described as a "diabolical ceremony" (Actis et al. 2006, 61). In Greece, young women, usually students, were sexually victimized in the specifically designated unit of the Security Police, the so-called Special Students' Division (Spoudastiko). But both women and men were sexually humiliated and assaulted: besides rape or attempted rape, women were victimized by genital penetration with objects and water and electroshocks in the genitals; men suffered excessive beatings, electroshocks in the genital area, and anal penetration with objects.[3]

NORMALIZING TORTURE: THE CONSTRUCTION OF FEMALE AND POLITICAL OTHERNESS

The sexual terrorization of women was a state project that was ideologically envisioned and materialized through distinctive practices and strategies that targeted both the political and gender identities of dissidents. Political otherization was a critical first step in creating the conditions that would allow victimization.

State rhetoric defined communism as an "infectious disease" as early as the mid-1930s during the Metaxas dictatorship (1936–1941). But as the anthropologist Neni Panourgiá (2009) explains, during the Greek Civil War (1946–1949) it became more pronounced and set the basis for the persecution of the Left. The civil war intensified the process of "othering" of the Greek left, and it was reactivated and ethnicized in junta rhetoric to justify persecution, incarceration, and torture. Within the nationalist discourse, the persecutors of leftists excluded themselves from accountability by saying that they were not targeting fellow Greeks, but "Slavs" and potential traitors. Since communism was equated to a contagious foreign disease originating from the Eastern Bloc (Bournazos 1997, 110–112, 116–120), communists and perceived communists were seen as a "miasma," a political and ethnic "other," an enemy of the state. During Amnesty International's investigation of torture in Greece, Minister of the Interior Stylianos Patakos denied the existence of torture, apparently because the victims were communists and, therefore, not Greek: "You force me to say it. The Greek Government has to protect its people against its communist enemies. A communist is not a Greek. We must put our own security first" (Amnesty International 1968c).

Similarly, the designation of communists as "subhuman" (*ypanthropoi*) appears in the public pronouncements of Patakos; when asked by a group of European Socialist MPs about the condition of political prisoners in the Yaros concentration camp, he said they were not human political prisoners but brutes and beasts (Clogg 1972, 146).[4] Panourgiá, in her insightful analysis of the construction and reproduction of the leftist as an "alien," a "radical Other," the "internal danger," and traitor to the nation, argues that the metaphors of "biomedicine" (e.g., miasma) and "pestilence" situate the leftist outside the healthy national body (Panourgiá 2009, 106, 114); through these metaphors and discourses, "the process of extermination of the communist" is materialized and naturalized (Panourgiá 2008, 417–418). Finding the "pharmakon" or cure for the disease calls for the use of all applicable remedies: execution, torture, incarceration, humiliation, forced impregnation, and mutilation (see Panourgiá 2008, 418; 2009, 106).

WOMEN DISSIDENTS: MOTHERHOOD, SEXUAL TORTURE, AND THE NATION

In the context of male nationalist politics, historian Wendy Bracewell argues, "Women . . . can act as a convenient internal 'other'" (1996, 32). It was in fact this alienation of women and the institutionalization of their political, ethnic, and gendered "otherness" within the Greek nation that became the basis for both their oppression and their redemption.

During our interview, Dora Koulmanda, a student imprisoned and exiled during the military junta, noted that women were treated equally with men in the camps and prisons (in terms of deprivation, maltreatment, and the intensity of torture). That said, two notable classifications were imposed by the authorities: "women and children" and "whores" (interview, July 29, 2010), the latter referring to politically active women. The demarcation was employed by the state and articulated in state rhetoric throughout the postwar period and during the junta. Within this nationalist and militaristic framework, the dissident, the enemy of the Nation and the Race, was demonized in the official discourse, with special attention paid to politically active women. In this ideological scheme, female dissidents constituted a double threat: first, to the nation, as political opponents of the regime, and second, to the moral and gender code. Following this logic, the perceived (symbolic) threat to the constituent elements of the *ethnos* (nation), namely, morality, tradition, and religion, had to be eradicated.

The nationalist discourse of the junta made use of a virgin/whore dichotomy. On the one hand, women were projected as the continuation of the nation; on the other hand, they were considered lesser political subjects and circumscribed within the private domain so they could be monitored. Rada Ivekovic and Julie Mostov argue that although "women as mothers" are the "reproducers of the nation," they can also be perceived as possible threats or enemies to the nation (2004, 11).[5] Within nationalist and dictatorial regimes, gender nonconformity provides justification for the sexual abuse, political exclusion, and social marginalization of female dissidents. The symbolism and absurdity of this type of juxtaposition is apparent in the torture of women in the Olimpo (Olympus) detention camp during the Argentinean Dirty War in front of statues of the Virgin Mary; the ostensible goal was to rehabilitate these women, while condemning their violation of acceptable social and gender roles (Taylor 1997, 152).

In this framework of analysis, motherhood was considered integral to the traditional and religious values of Greek society, constituting one of the three elements of the national(ist) triptych of homeland, religion, and family. Ironically, while women dissidents were targeted because they had denied the sanctity of motherhood, opting to play an active role in the political arena, they were tortured in such a way as to deprive them of the ability to bear children.[6] Concomitantly, children were frequently used as a mechanism of control and power during interrogation to extract information and declarations of repentance from otherwise unrepentant political inmates.

For instance, Natasa (Anastasia) Mertika (married name Tsirka) was pregnant at the time of her arrest but was extensively tortured; when she informed the torturers of her pregnancy, they responded: "What do we care? If it's going to be like you, it is better off dead" (1974, 17). In fact, she was thrown down the stairs and had a miscarriage the next morning in her cell; she was ultimately unable to have children due to the extensive torture she endured. In a similar way, Aspasia Karra, who was paraplegic as a result of poliomyelitis, was electrocuted on the navel in order "not to give birth to any communist children" (2006, 25). Maria Angelaki recalls that during her interrogation, the torturers kicked her in the genitals and struck her breasts: "They told me that they would torture me in such a way that I would never be able to become a mother. They tore off my clothes, stripped me naked, and then stood around me talking obscenely, laughing coarsely, and threatening me with shameful innuendos or with unmentionable words. They told me that they would subject me to a torture instrument, which they called 'the little machine'" (referring to torture with electric shock) (1971, 22).

Of course, the Greek case is not unique. Historian Temma Kaplan has discussed the sadistic victimization of pregnant women in Augusto Pinochet's Chile, especially Nieves Ayress, a political prisoner who was brutally tortured in various torture centers and concentration camps of the Directory of National Intelligence, such as Londres 38 and Tejas Verdes, even though pregnant; her pregnancy was the result of gang rape. Interestingly, the doctors and gynecologists present at the interrogation were not only complicit but were experimenting and actively facilitating the torture sessions, making sure they could hear the heartbeat of the fetus for the torture to continue (Kaplan 1999, 7; 2002, 191). The "deployment of medical paradigms" in the words of Allen Feldman—referring to male political prisoners in the Maze prison in Northern Ireland—provided the "medical legitimation for collective violence" (1991, 190). One of the prison gynecologists congratulated Nieves for "being able to bear a child for the motherland" (Kaplan 1999, 7; 2002, 191), but she had a miscarriage due to the extensive abuse and torture.

In these instances, the female body is politicized (and simultaneously depoliticized) and ethnicized; stripped of motherhood and deprived of its reproductive capacity, it is ultimately sexualized. At this point, gender makes its reappearance in a decisive way (see Treacy 1996, 135). Motherhood and reproduction, the reappropriation of femininity and the control of sexuality are transformed into political acts, under the control and "jurisdiction" of the state, the church, and the family (a process that Ivekovic and Mostov call "state fatherhood" [2004, 11]).[7] Concurrently, the sexualized, gendered, and political body, which cannot be perceived as maternal,[8] is transformed through abuse into a colonized body within a "state" that is "acting as a male body politic" (Aretxaga 2001, 1, 18).[9]

In Greece, after torture and interrogation, severely abused and lacking medical attention, the dirty, hungry female political detainees were thrown naked or wearing bloodstained, torn, and wet clothes into dark, flooded, bug- and rat-infested prison cells. Consider the case of Kitty Arseni, arrested in 1967 as a member of the Patriotic Anti-Dictatorship Front and tried the same year by court-martial. During her interrogation and torture in the notorious Terrace (*taratsa*) of the Security Police, she was sexually assaulted with a gun barrel. In her memoir she states:

> A blond one was doing *falanga* (bastinado),[10] while the others jumped on top of me, stepping on my stomach, gripping my neck; they lit matches to burn my eyes. I insisted on seeing while I was tortured . . . so Spanos[11] shouted: "No light, since she wants to see, she will stay in the dark. Burn her eyes" . . . and he started tearing up my dress. My mouth was shut with a mop. They were banging my head. And then they turned on a machine that imitates the noise of a motorcycle. "Don't shout, no-one will hear you, no-one, talk." That was when I got very scared. Only for a moment, Spanos said: "we should throw her off the terrace to tear her in pieces." Then I breathed, I wanted so much to die. (2005, 72)

Through "technologies of power," including sexual abuse and humiliation, moral degradation, nakedness, solitary confinement, fear and despair, the unrepentant female political body is politically disciplined, transforming recalcitrant dissidents into docile and submissive detainees.[12]

FEMINIZING THE MALE BODY:
MILITARISM AND HEGEMONIC MASCULINITIES

In Greece, male political detainees were also physically and sexually assaulted. Two well-known cases are the torture of junta dissidents Pericles Korovessis and Petros Vlassis, who were sexually assaulted with wood and iron pipes by the Security Police.[13] In general, the victimization of men included beating their sexual organs with sacks of sand or pulling them with ropes and iron whips, burning them with cigarettes, mutilation, emasculation, and torture with electric shock.[14]

The sexual abuse of politically active men during the military dictatorship needs to be examined in relation to female victimization, since both were bound up in a hierarchical system of power and gender relations. In Greece, as elsewhere, the male body was disciplined by transforming it into a feminine, vulnerable body through sexual torture.[15] On this ground, as I have argued elsewhere (2016, 82), "by feminizing the male body, the act of torture with the distinct gendered and sexual parameters is normalized and naturalized, while the object of attack is not only the physical body of the victim, whether male or female, but also the political locus that it represents."

Female dissidents were already the "other" in civil society and the envisioned national community; thus, their torture served to guard nationalist ideals and mandatory hierarchical relations (see Peterson 1991, 45). Male prisoners were assaulted to turn them into vulnerable, controllable, and ultimately feminized subjects. The sexual abuse of men was seen as an attack against lesser men. At the same time, their bodies were physically and sexually targeted within a nationalist and extreme militaristic context that identified masculine and feminine "countertypes" (see Nagel 1998, esp. 246). In this discursive scheme, anticommunism, misogyny, and heteronormativity evoked and assigned national(ist) fantasies and gender expectations to the tortured female body and the feminized and tortured male body.

The torturers and perpetrators of sexual assaults on male detainees did not consider these to be homosexual sexual acts, since the men were considered feminine on account of their political identity, and, after the attack, were supposedly feminized as a result of their sexual abuse. For the Greek junta, the "feminized" or perceived as homosexual political detainees represented "subordinated forms of masculinity" (Connell 1987, 186; cited in Nagel 1998, 246). Therefore, male sexual abuse targeted the masculinity of the detainee. For example, Gerasimos Notaras was detained with homosexual common-law prisoners, who were encouraged by the authorities to sexually harass him.[16] Similarly, Mary Jeane Treacy, drawing on Jean Franco (1992, 104–118), discusses how the masculinity of prison guards in various Latin American military governments in the 1970s and 1980s was affirmed by feminizing male political prisoners, for instance, by making them wear dresses (1996, 131).

The sexual torture of men transcended the private and assaulted their "male honor," their family, and their community. Victims were called "Bulgarians" and "traitors," their sexual orientation was questioned, and the female members of their families were characterized as whores. Some common locutions during torture were: "Where are your mother and your wife, the whores?" "Bulgarian traitor, communist, atheist, faggot, tonight you will die," and "Where is your party now?" (Korovessis 2007, 32–38).[17] It was common for torturers to threaten victims by saying they would bring family members to watch the torture or that they would sexually assault their wives, mothers, or daughters. One prisoner revealed that during his interrogation and torture, he was told the torturers would rape his fiancée and send her to the brothel that the dictator Papadopoulos had ostensibly set up for his soldiers (Korovessis 2007).

Militarization seems to go hand in hand with masculinization. Accordingly, in the Greek military regime, the Greek "macho" man resurfaced as the ideal image of masculinity and the image was integrated into state practices and discourse.[18] Interrogation and torture were handled by specially trained members of the Security Police and the Military Police, especially the Special Interrogation Unit (EAT/ESA), under the auspices of the official state apparatus, including the military (army) and police forces. A distinction should be made between the torturers of the Military Police, often young recruits completing their military service, and the officers in the Security Police, usually high-ranking officials.[19] In any case, in both units, the tortures were supervised and occasionally conducted by high-ranking officials trained in military schools and college-educated, in Greece or the United States (especially members of the Security Police).[20] Former political dissident Dora Koulmanda found a difference between the torturer who conducted *falanga* (beating on the feet) and the one who applied electric shocks to the genital areas of victims; in the latter case, the torture was authorized or carried out by a specially trained officer (interview, July 29, 2010).

The Greek military, as an exclusively male institution at the time, had cultivated and appropriated violence through what Kara Martinez calls "institutional indoctrination" (2005, 12). Routine, institutional authority, rigid hierarchy (Robben and Suarez Orozco 2000, 9n6), and "moral disengagement"[21] from torture further facilitated the transformation of the ESA men during their military service and training at the Military Police Training Center into hypermasculinized supermen (Haritos-Fatouros 2003, 23–25, 38–65, 133–134). According to Mika Haritos-Fatouros's seminal study of the psychological origins of institutionalized torture, focusing on the Greek Military Police, the ESA recruits and junior servicemen were exposed to anticommunist propaganda, nationalist indoctrination, brainwashing, humiliation, abuse, and in some cases sexual torture as part of their training (2003, 38–65, 78–83). This undoubtedly played a vital role in their dehumanization and desensitization, ultimately resulting in their transformation from ordinary men into professional torturers (see Haritos-Fatouros 2003, 18–19, 38–65, 78–83).

Notably, during the second Military Police Torturers' Trial in October 1975, the torturers denied torturing women, despite the numerous cases reported by both the victims and by some ESA servicemen. This denial was probably connected to the prevailing gender and social norms whereby the torture of women would be degrading to the ESA men (Haritos-Fatouros 2003, 59, 82). It was not degrading, however, to torture a man if he was considered homosexual, as this ran counter to prevailing gender norms. According to Haritos-Fatouros's respondents (men serving in the ESA), male political detainees were beaten harder because they were seen as homosexuals (2003, 58).

The assault on men was not denied; however, the sexual dimensions of torture were not usually publicly discussed either by male victims or by their torturers. In the case of the young torturers, even though they were transformed into hypermasculine men, and, therefore, their masculinity and heterosexuality was not to be questioned, there was an evident reluctance to admit the sexual victimization of men.[22] One of Fatouros's respondents states: "They made us feel we were such supermen that we could also fuck men. Nobody will be able to stand against you; you will beat and fuck anybody you want, they told us" (Haritos-Fatouros 2003, 59). The hypermasculinization manifested in military settings and authoritarian regimes encapsulates what Spike Peterson calls "heterosexist masculinity" (1999, 40), which, along with hegemonic masculinity, was employed to sustain gender hierarchies.

CONCLUDING REMARKS

The torture, especially sexual torture, of political activists was used to take "a living body" and turn "it into text," sending "a cautionary 'message' to those on the outside" (Taylor 1997, 152). At the same time, as Michel Foucault argues, torture functions as "a policy of terror" to make everyone aware of the absolute source of power, control, and dominance, while turning it into an essential "part of a ritual" (1991, 49, 34). Within this "liturgy of punishment" (Foucault 1991, 34), the materiality of the body is targeted and marked, along with its gendered, political, and ethnic demarcations, to punish and rehabilitate both the socially, politically, and gendered unrepentant and unruly political prisoner and the body politic as a whole. The penalized fe/male body and the political and gender subjectivities of the junta dissidents were transformed through sexual humiliation and harassment, solitary confinement, hunger, and fear, ultimately becoming a "spectacle" (Foucault 1991, 34) of dehumanized, abject, and desubjectified subjects assigned a biopolitical and disciplined existence.[23]

Even in this Agambenian "bare life" (1998), a third space (see Bhabha 1994) emerged between humanity and evil, death and survival, submission and resistance. Despite the mechanisms of alienation and disconnection (see Sayed 2014), the political prisoners, in Greece and elsewhere, called on language and narrative, writing on the walls with their bleeding and swollen hands and fingers, in some cases using their own blood, to send encrypted messages to their tortured comrades, singing political songs and lullabies, or talking to inanimate objects (as Nieves Ayress in Chile; Kaplan 1999, 5). At the same time, they managed to preserve their humanity, political consciousness, solidarity, and comradeship.[24] Argentine poet Alicia Partnoy kept the tooth she lost during torture in a matchbox as her most valuable belonging; it was, in fact, her only belonging, but it was also an artifact of selfhood, "a piece of herself" (1998, 87–88). One of the women political prisoners of the Argentine torture camp ESMA reached out for her torturer's hand during torture, seeking for human contact but also to confirm whether her torturer was a human or a beast (Actis et al. 2006).

By and large, the women and men who were sexually victimized by the junta retained their strong political beliefs and maintained their struggle for justice and freedom, thereby proving the ineffectiveness of sexual violence against political activists.[25] Their main concern was to ensure that they would not confess or "break" under interrogation; they have emphasized how their political ideology (generally communist or leftist) helped them to resist and deal with their sexual victimization. In one extreme case, Dora Lelouda tried to commit suicide by cutting herself with her eyeglasses out of fear of "breaking" during the interrogation.[26]

In the Greek case, the gendered body as a "container"[27] of suffering, memory, and survival becomes a site of resistance and agency, and, ultimately, a performative body. Through these fragmented narratives, the selective silences of sexual victimization, underlying solidarity and comradeship, and politicization, a counterdiscourse or an antiscenario is developed wherein autonomy, selfhood, and agency become consolidated against shame, silence, and fear.[28] As Natasa Mertika says emphatically in Alinda Dimitriou's documentary *Ta Koritsia tis Vrohis* (The Girls of the Rain, 2012):[29] "Natasa Mertika is my name and I want that to be heard; Mertika is my name." In the same documentary, one of her comrades attests: "If I were to start my life again from the beginning, I would have chosen the same life."

NOTES

I would like to thank Victoria Sanford, Cecilia Salvi, Kimberly Theidon, Chloe Howe-Haralambous, and Dimitris Papadopoulos for their words of encouragement, useful comments, and overall support. Special thanks go to Neni Panourgiá for her particularly thorough reading of this chapter and her extremely helpful and detailed comments. I am deeply grateful to the women who shared their life stories and experiences with me. Of course, I am responsible for any errors or oversights.

1. The numbers are provided by Koundouros (1978, 24–30) and Alivizatos (1995, 603–606). Even though the number of women detainees cannot be specified with great accuracy, according to women's written and oral accounts and the lists of the Yaros's Gendarmerie Directorship, the number as of April 26, 1967, seems slightly higher than Amnesty International's claim, probably between 260 and 300.

2. For instance, the notorious Dionysos military camp (505 Naval Unit) and the Boyiati Military Prisons outside Athens, the Piraeus Security Police, and the 401 Military Hospital; the Reform Prisons and the Third Army Corps, a special place of torture of the Central Information Agency, and the Karatassos camp were based in Thessaloniki.

3. See the Amnesty International reports: "Situation in Greece" (1968b) and "Human Rights in Greece" (1973); also see Korovessis (2007), Arseni (2005), and Beikou Archive (Box 9), Contemporary Social History Archives (ASKI), Athens.

4. Marguerite Feitlowitz (1998, 2011), in her seminal study of Argentina's lexicon of terror during the Dirty War, discusses the regime's employment of language both in the official rhetoric and public proclamations but also during torture in order to dehumanize the victims and rationalize their torture through the employment of "germ theories" (2011, 58) and medical, authoritative, and ultraconservative discourses defining the political activists and detainees as "subversives," "demons," anti-Christian, and unpatriotic elements (2011, 43, 321).

5. The employment of women in state, often nationalistic and militaristic, projects is also discussed by Jäppinen and Johnson in this volume, in connection to Putin's Russia and the gradual incorporation of authoritarian and traditionalist policies and rhetoric, especially when it comes to domestic and gender violence, and gender issues in general. In the case of domestic violence in Russia, Jäppinen and Johnson argue that it was often considered and addressed as a private matter, within a gender-blind agenda that emphasized traditional family values and gender roles.

6. Also see Treacy 1996, esp. 135–137.

7. Jäppinen and Johnson make a similar argument in terms of Russian "state paternalism" and the state's responsiveness to incidents of domestic and gender violence, violence against LGBTQ (lesbian, gay, bisexual, transgender, and queer) people, gender inequality, and social services in general, all against the background of increasing authoritarianism, socioeconomic crisis, and militarism; see their chapter in this volume.

8. See Treacy 1996, 135–137, esp. 136; also see Agger 1994 and Feitlowitz 2011, 43–44, 78–80.

9. For the colonization of the female body, see Aretxaga 1997, 131–136, and for the male, see Feldman 1991, 195–209.

10. A common method of torture during the Greek Civil War and the military junta, this involved strapping the prisoner to a bench and beating the soles of the feet with bamboo or a pipe.

11. Odysseas Spanos, a police officer and a notorious torturer of the Security Police.

12. In relation to these modern technologies of power, see Foucault 1991; for more on the ways in which torture is literally and symbolically inscribed on the body, see Aretxaga 2001, 4–5, 8; 1997, 131–136; Feldman 1991, 186; Foucault 1991, 23–24; and Taylor 1997, 151–152.

13. They describe this in their memoirs; see Korovessis 2007 and Vlassis 2009; also see Becket 1997.

14. See Beikou Archive (Box 9), (ASKI), Becket 1997, and Amnesty International Report, *Torture in Greece: The First Torturers' Trial 1975* (1977).

15. Taylor discusses how the individual body is transformed into a feminine, penetrable, and docile social and political body through torture (1997, 152).

16. Notaras's case can be found in the second report by Amnesty International ("Torture of Political Prisoners in Greece"); also see Becket 1997, 88.

17. For more on the nature of threats against male dissidents, see Korovessis 2007, Becket 1997, and Amnesty International Report, *Torture in Greece: The First Torturers' Trial 1975* (1977).

18. Wendy Bracewell (2000, 569–570) has analyzed the ways in which Milosevic's nationalist project in the 1980s instrumentalized the "hysteria over nationalist rape" against Serbs in Kosovo and a supposed crisis of Serbian masculinity within a hypermasculine and heterosexist gender order.

19. There is a clear differentiation that needs to be made between the Military and the Security Police. The Military Police was part of the armed forces and had jurisdiction only over military matters—i.e., military personnel and anything and anyone else whose actions touched upon its jurisdiction. The Security Police, on the other hand, administratively belonged to the civic police and had no jurisdiction over military personnel or military matters. The difference was further recognized during the two "Torturers' Trials" (as they came to be known). The ESA Torturers' Trial in October 1975 concerned the military police torturers whose sentences were considerably heavier than those given to the Security Police torturers at their trial in November 1975. Among the accused in the Security Police Trial were the leadership of the Security Police Intelligence Services, something that created a political risk for the new, postjunta government. According to Nadia Valavani, a former dissident who had been tortured at the Security Police Headquarters, those who formulated the democratic constitution that emerged after the fall of the dictatorship, having reformed the armed forces, realized that the postjunta state did not need the mechanisms of the military, whereas it still had to rely on the police for general policing and surveillance. Therefore, the officers of the Security Police would remain useful and, consequently, they were given lighter sentences (interview with Nadia Valavani, November 30, 2005). At the end only four out of fourteen accused and tried officers were sentenced to a few months' imprisonment.

20. The dissidents have often argued that their interrogators and torturers were trained in the United States; see the interviews with Dora Koulmanda, July 29, 2010, Athens; and Nadia Valavani, June 7, 2010, Athens. This charge is also found in excerpts of a letter written by a woman political prisoner and smuggled out of the Security Police (April 1968), Amnesty International, "Letter from Athens Security Police Station."

21. Mika Haritos-Fatouros uses the term "moral disengagement" (2003, 48, citing Bandura 1990).

22. For more, see Haritos-Fatouros 2003, 58–60.

23. Also see Sayed (2014). Useful connections can be made with Polhman's study (in this volume), which analyzes the spectacular forms and communicative intent of sexualized torture and public mutilations against communist political detainees in Indonesia during the first phase of the New Order regime (1965–1966).

24. Laura McAtackney, drawing on women political internees during the Irish Civil War and focusing on prison graffiti and autograph books, discusses in this volume the survival and resistance mechanisms in prisons through mundane practices and direct physical

confrontations that nevertheless are transformed into significant political contestations and vehicles of agency.

25. See the interviews with Dora Koulmanda, July 29, 2010, and Nadia Valavani, June 7, 2010. Also see Treacy 1996, 138.

26. Maria Karagiorgi narrates the incident in her memoir (2007, 258).

27. Emilia Barbosa (2014, 68) approaches the body as a container of memory in her analysis of Regina Galindo's "279 Golpes" in reference to the 279 female victims of feminicide in Guatemala from January 1 to June 9, 2005.

28. On counterdiscourse, see Hackett and Rolston 2009, 355. See Barbarosa's (2014, 63–64) definition of antiscenario in reference to Galindo's performance "279 Golpes."

29. This is the third documentary in a trilogy on women political detainees and dissidents from the 1940s to the 1970s. *The Girls of the Rain* focuses on women political activists who were imprisoned and tortured during the Greek military junta (1967–1974).

REFERENCES

Actis, Munú, Cristina Aldini, Liliana Gardella, Miriam Lewin, and Elisa Tokar. 2006. *That Inferno*. Nashville: Vanderbilt University Press.

Agamben, Giorgio. 1998. *Homo Sacer: Sovereign Power and Bare Life*. Translated by Daniel Heller-Roazen. Palo Alto, CA: Stanford University Press.

Agger, Inger. 1994. *The Blue Room: Trauma and Testimony among Refugee Women, a Psychological Exploration*. London: Zed Books.

Alivizatos, Nikos. 1995. *Oi politikoi thesmoi se krisi, 1922–1974: Opseis tis ellinikis empeirias*. Athens: Themelio.

Amnesty International. 1968a. "Letter from Athens Security Police Station." April. League for Democracy in Greece. London: King's College Archives.

———. 1968b. "Situation in Greece." January. League for Democracy in Greece. London: King's College Archives.

———. 1968c. "Torture of Political Prisoners in Greece." Second Report. League for Democracy in Greece. London: King's College Archives.

———. 1973. "Human Rights in Greece." March. League for Democracy in Greece. London: King's College Archives.

———. 1977. *Torture in Greece: The First Torturers' Trial 1975*. London: Amnesty International.

Angelaki, Maria. 1971. *The Black Book: The Greek Junta Stands Accused*. Vol 1. N.p.: Central Committee of the Patriotic Anti-Dictatorship Front.

Aretxaga, Begona. 1997. *Shattering Silence: Women, Nationalism, and Political Subjectivity in Northern Ireland*. Princeton: Princeton University Press.

———. 2001. "The Sexual Games of the Body Politic: Fantasy and State Violence in Northern Ireland." *Culture Medicine and Psychiatry* 25: 1–27.

Arseni, Kitty. 2005. *Bouboulinas 18: Martyria*. Athens: Themelio.

The Athenian [Roufos Rodis]. 1972. *Inside the Colonels' Greece*. Translated by Richard Clogg. London: Chatto & Windus.

Bandura, Albert. 1990. "Mechanisms of Moral Disengagement." In *Origins of Terrorism: Psychologies, Ideologies, Theologies, States of Mind*, edited by Walter Reich. Cambridge: Cambridge University Press.

Barbosa, Emilia. 2014. "Regina José Galindo's Body Talk: Performing Feminicide and Violence against Women in 279 Golpes." *Latin American Perspectives* 194 (41) (January): 59–71.

Becket, James. 1997. *Varvarotita stin Ellada, 1967–69*. Athens: Pontiki Publications.

Beikou, Maria Archive. Box 9: Youra. Contemporary Social History Archives, Athens.

Bhabha, Homi. 1994. *The Location of Culture*. London: Routledge.

Bournazos, Stratis. 1997. "O anamorfotikos logos ton nikiton sti Makroniso." In *To Emfylio Drama*, edited by Nikos Kotaridis. A special issue of *Dokimes 6*, Athens.

Bracewell, Wendy. 1996. "Women, Motherhood, and Contemporary Serbian Nationalism." *Women's Studies International Forum* 19 (1–2): 25–33.

Connell, Raewyn. 1987. *Gender and Power: Society, the Person, and Sexual Politics*. Stanford: Stanford University Press.

Dimitriou, Alinda, director. 2012. *Ta Koritsia tis Vrohis* (documentary).

Feitlowitz, Marguerite. (1998) 2011. *A Lexicon of Terror: Argentina and the Legacies of Torture*. New York: Oxford University Press.

Feldman, Allen. 1991. *Formations of Violence: The Narrative of the Body and Political Terror in Northern Ireland*. Chicago: University of Chicago Press.

Foucault, Michel. 1991. *Discipline and Punish: The Birth of the Prison*. London: Penguin.

Franco, Jean. 1992. "Gender, Death, and Resistance: Facing the Ethical Vacuum." In *Fear at the Edge: State Terror and Resistance in Latin America*, edited by Juan Corradi, Patricia Weiss Fagen, and Manuel Anonio Garreton. Berkeley: University of California Press.

Hackett, Claire, and Bill Rolston. 2009. "The Burden of Memory: Victims, Storytelling, and Resistance in Northern Ireland." *Memory Studies* 2 (3): 355–376.

Haritos-Fatouros, Mika. 2003. *The Psychological Origins of the Institutionalized Torture*. London: Routledge.

Ivekovic, Rada, and Julie Mostov, eds. 2004. *From Gender to Nation*. New Delhi: Zubaan.

Kaplan, Temma. 1999. "Truth without Reconciliation in Chile: Testimonies of the Tortured and the Case against Augusto Pinochet." Paper presented at the History Workshop, "The TRC: Commissioning the Past," Center for the Study of Violence and Reconciliation, University of the Witwatersrand, Johannesburg, June 11–14.

———. 2002. "Acts of Testimony: Reversing the Shame and Gendering the Memory." *Signs* 28 (1) (Autumn): 179–199.

Karagiorgi, Maria. 2007. *. . . Kai perimenontas ti Dimokratia*. Athens: Proskinio.

Karra, Aspasia. 2006. "Martyries." In *Gynaikes ston Anti-diktatoriko Agona*, edited by Triantafyllos Mitafidis and Christos Mouchayier. Thessaloniki: Historical Archives Preservation Company.

Korovessis, Pericles. 2007. *Anthropofylakes*. Athens: Electra.

Koulmanda, Dora. 2010. Interview, July 29, Athens.

Koundouros, Roussos. 1978. *I Asfaleia tou Kathestotos: Politikoi kratoumenoi, ektopismoi kai taxeis stin Ellada 1924–1974*. Athens: Kastaniotis.

Martinez, Kara. 2005. "Structures of Violence: The Proliferation of Atrocity Environments under the Brazilian Military Government and the Bush Administration." *Human Rights and Human Welfare* 5: 1–15.

Nagel, Joanne. 1998. "Masculinities and Nationalism: Gender and Sexuality in the Making of Nations." *Ethnic and Racial Studies* 21 (2): 242–269.

Panourgiá, Neni. 2008. "Desert Islands: Ransom of Humanity." *Public Culture* 20 (2): 395–421.

———. 2009. *Dangerous Citizens: The Greek Left and the Terror of the State*. New York: Fordham University Press.

Partnoy, Alicia. 1998. *The Little School: Tales of Disappearance and Survival*. San Francisco: Midnight Editions.

Peterson, Spike V. 1999. "Sexing Political Identities/Nationalism as Heterosexism." *International Feminist Journal of Politics* 1 (1): 34–65.

Robben, Antonius C. G. M., and Marcelo M. Suárez-Orozco. 2000. "Interdisciplinary Perspectives on Violence and Trauma." In *Cultures under Siege: Collective Violence and Trauma*, edited by Antonius C. G. M. Robben and Marcelo M. Suárez-Orozco. New York: Cambridge University Press.

Sayed, Abdulhay. 2014. "In the Syrian Prison: Disconnected and Desubjectified." *Global Dialogue* (newsletter of the International Sociological Association) 4 (2) (May). http://isa-global-dialogue.net/in-the-syrian-prison-disconnected-and-desubjectified/.

Stefatos, Katerina. 2016. "The Female and Political Body in Pain: Sexual Torture and Gendered Trauma during the Greek Military Dictatorship (1967–1974)." In *Gendered Wars, Gendered Memories: Feminist Conversations on War, Genocide, and Political Violence*, edited by Ayşe Gül Altınay and Andrea Petö. London: Ashgate.

Taylor, Diana. 1997. *Disappearing Acts: Spectacles of Gender and Nationalism in Argentina's "Dirty War"*. Durham, NC: Duke University Press.

Treacy, Mary Jane. 1996. "Double Binds: Latin American Women's Prison Memories." *Hypatia* 11 (4) (Fall): 130–145.

Tsirka, Anastasia. 1974. *Vasanistiria, Vasanistes, kai Vasanismenoi stin Ellada tis Hountas*. Council of Europe Report. Company for the Study of Left Youth History. Athens: Mnimon.

Valavani, Nadia. 2005. "Vasanizan, alla ohi epitides." *TA NEA*, November 30.

———. 2010. Interview, June 7, Athens.

Vlassis, Petros. 2009. *Diadromes Zoes: Politiki kai politikoi*. Athens: Epsilon.

2 · SEXUAL VIOLENCE AS A WEAPON DURING THE GUATEMALAN GENOCIDE

VICTORIA SANFORD, SOFÍA DUYOS ÁLVAREZ-ARENAS, AND KATHLEEN DILL

Judge Yasmín Barríos and her tribunal made world history on May 10, 2013, when they found former Guatemalan dictator José Efraín Ríos Montt guilty of crimes against humanity and genocide—the first time ever that a head of state has been convicted of these crimes in a national court. The eighty-year prison sentence was the just conclusion of a court process that was nearly derailed by threats to witnesses, presidential declarations denouncing the trial, and over one hundred appeals by the defense team. Perseverance, courage, and a commitment to the rule of law on the part of the survivors, prosecutors, and tribunal judges repeatedly pushed the case back on track. Although ten days later a corrupt Constitutional Court annulled the verdict on technical grounds,[1] the genocide sentence is an unforgettable moment in the historic struggle for justice in Guatemala. It was also the first time a Guatemalan court recognized the systematic rape and torture to which Maya women were subjected during Ríos Montt's reign of terror.

Beginning on March 19, 2013, the court heard 102 witnesses (94 for the prosecution and 8 presented by the defense) and 68 expert testimonies. The tribunal also reviewed hundreds of documents. The nine lawyers for the defense used every stalling tactic possible to avoid reaching the verdict—filing over one hundred separate appeals. As the trial wore on, Guatemalans read about it in newspapers, watched news coverage on television, and listened to it live on national radio and on the Internet. This brought the testimonies of survivors into the homes of any Guatemalans willing to learn how criminal state violence destroyed hundreds of thousands of individual lives and families, and in hundreds of cases annihilated entire Maya communities.[2]

Like the genocide itself, the organized use of sexual violence by the state was a public secret. Though it was not the central focus of the court case, the information had long been available from human rights reports, survivor testimonies, and truth commission reports. Reports from both the Commission for Historical Clarification (CEH 1999) and the Catholic Church's Nunca Más project (REMHI 1998) documented the fact that the army systematically deployed sexual violence as a counterinsurgency weapon. Sexual violence was ordered by the high command and enshrouded with impunity by official denial. During the war, army soldiers and other security officers were responsible for 94.3 percent of all sexual violence against women (CEH 1999; Rompiendo el Silencio 2006, 32).[3] Of the 1,465 cases of rape reported (CEH 1999, vol. 2, 23), fully one-third of the victims were minor girls (CEH 1999, vol. 2, 23).[4] Women who survived bore the physical and psychological consequences, including pregnancy and sexually transmitted diseases, as well as the social stigma attached to victims of rape (REMHI 1998, vol. 2, 210).

While female witnesses recounted in detail how they were gang-raped by army soldiers, indigenous women observing the trial covered their heads with their shawls in solidarity. Witness Elena de Paz Santiago told the court what Guatemalan soldiers did to her at the army base when she was a child: "I was 12 when I was taken to the army base with other women. The soldiers tied my feet and hands. . . . They put a rag in the mouth . . . and started raping me. . . . I do not even know how many soldiers had a turn. . . . I lost consciousness and blood ran from my body. When I came to, I was unable to stand" (Sentencia por genocidio 2014, 514). The fact that the prosecution called Ms. de Paz Santiago and other women as witnesses, and that their testimonies support claims that sexual violence was systematically used as a genocide strategy, signals a relatively new development in the practice of international law.

Sexual violence has long been explained as an unfortunate outcome of war in which men are placed in extraordinary circumstances that provoke aberrant behavior. This is no longer a tenable theory. The work of the International Criminal Court, the United Nations Special Rapporteur on Violence against Women, feminist scholars, and human rights advocates has done much to reframe the issue. This conceptual shift was clearly expressed by the United Nations Special Rapporteur on Violence against Women, who reported in 2009 that studies of wartime rape "conclusively demonstrate that sexual violence is not an outcome of war, but that women's bodies are an important site of war, which makes sexual violence an integral part of wartime strategy" (Ertürk 2009).

PLANNING A GENOCIDE

When oral arguments in the 2013 genocide trial came to a close, eighty-six-year-old Ríos Montt demanded to speak, breaking the silence he had held since the trial began. Far from displaying any remorse for the genocide committed during his regime, he stated: "I never authorized, I never proposed, I never ordered acts against any ethnic or religious group" (Burt 2013). He also denied that he commanded army troops, despite leading the junta that came to power through a military coup in March 1982. He then asserted that his role was purely administrative. As the Adolf Eichmann trial proved, pushing papers does not excuse responsibility (Arendt 2006). Yet Ríos Montt was much more than an administrator; he had command responsibility of a vertical military organization (Sanford 2014). As the de facto president of Guatemala, Ríos Montt initiated genocide, beginning with propaganda against the indigenous Maya and any other Guatemalan who dared to question repression, inequality, and poverty.

Following the U.S.-sponsored overthrow of democratically elected President Jacobo Árbenz in 1954, successive military governments in Guatemala fought against "the enemy within" as defined by the United States' Cold War era anticommunist National Security Doctrine. The Guatemalan government applied the doctrine to justify eliminating any person who challenged the regime by working to bring sociopolitical change to the nation—it was not necessary to carry a gun to be a target. According to the Guatemalan truth commission (CEH 1999): "The broad concept of enemy wielded by the State was re-launched with particular violence and intensity in the eighties, and included not only those actively seeking to change the established order, but all who might potentially decide to support the struggle at some point in the future."[5] Victims of the doctrine included men, women, and children from all strata: workers, professionals, religious leaders and lay workers, politicians, peasants, students and academics; in ethnic terms the vast majority of victims were Maya.[6] Once the security forces had destroyed the social bases of dissent in the city and assassinated rural community leaders, the war machine focused its full attention on Maya communities.

Anticommunism fused with patriarchal structures and centuries-old prejudices against the majority Maya population produced a climate ripe for the dehumanization of a targeted population. The conflation of Maya identity with guerrilla insurgency was exaggerated by the dictatorship with the intent to deploy this alleged widespread Maya/guerrilla affinity to justify the elimination of present and future members of the Maya population. Genocide ideologues implicitly acknowledged the poverty and exploitation of Maya life as they argued that if the Maya were to join the guerrillas in their demands for social justice, the army would lose the war.[7]

When a *population* is classified as an enemy, as opposed to specific elements within a group, women become primary targets for sexual violence rather than collateral damage. Women are recognized as "reproducers" in both the biological and socioeconomic senses of the term (Meyer 2003, 126). Although women's work is undervalued by general populations, analysts understand that it is essential, especially during times of crisis (Sen and Grown 1987). Because sexual violence harms women's ability to perform their roles, military analysts know that when the goal is to destabilize or destroy a population, targeting women will help them reach that goal.[8]

There is another compelling reason why when a population is the target, sexual violence against women is considered militarily advantageous. Despite the fact that the crime is committed against the actual victims, men experience their inability to protect women as a demoralizing humiliation and perceive it as an attack on *their* own power and dignity. Sexual violence against women committed by an invading army is a potent symbol clearly intended to demonstrate victory over the opposition. As Radhika Coomaraswamy states: "It is a battle among men fought over the bodies of women" (Ertürk 2009, 15).

Thus, the Guatemalan state launched a campaign designed not only to crush communities suspected of resistance but also to debase the reproductive bodies and degrade the sociocultural status of Maya women. Leaked (and authenticated) army documents refer to Ixil women as "cockroaches" and Ixil children as "chocolates" (Dada 2014). Within this idiom, forced displacement, the organized rape of women and girls, systematic slaughter of unarmed men, women, and children, and the burning of hundreds of villages was reduced to a simple order: "Kill the cockroaches and leave no chocolates" (Dada 2014).

TRAINING SOLDIERS TO RAPE

Cynthia Enloe reminds us that historically rape has provided cost-free recompense for soldiers and collaborators, converting captive young women into the "spoils of war" (Enloe 2000; see also Moradi in this volume). However, when rape is used as a weapon of genocide, more is involved than the forfeiture of women to conquering forces. Under the direction of Ríos Montt, the military simultaneously identified the Maya population as the enemy *and* stipulated that soldiers have sexual contact with women. Psychological operations for the troops included "recreation zones designed to maintain the soldier's fighting spirit," which featured "contact with the female sex."[9] Military plans included sexual contact as part of the soldier's "rest and recreation" because the normalization of rape was utilized to maintain control over the troops.

According to testimonies gathered by the CEH, the women used by the army to accustom soldiers to the practice of rape were prostitutes: "The Army took prostitutes to the soldiers who went to the lieutenant before being passed on to the rest of the soldiers." The CEH documents that women identified as "prostitutes or whores were passed from the lieutenant to all the soldiers during one week." Then, the CEH reports that "some [soldiers] passed up to 10 times." It is also noted that the army "changed" the women every three months (CEH 1999, vol. 2, 27).

In its replication of this lexicon, the CEH is shockingly passive and vague in its reporting of sexual violence, utilizing the term "pass" instead of rape. It fails to identify the absolute impunity under which the military operated and, in so doing, the full magnitude of sexual violence against women. Under what conditions would a woman, even if she was a prostitute, willingly go to a military base to be "passed" among dozens of soldiers on a daily basis for three months? The CEH fails to specify the sexual violence to which these women were subjected, despite knowing that the army brought a new group every three months, which suggests the level of physical and psychological battery experienced by these women. Perhaps one of the legacies of genocide is that even those seeking to chronicle the truth of the unimaginable can fall victim to its doublespeak, a phenomenon Marguerite Feitlowitz refers to as "a lexicon of terror" in her magisterial work by the same title (Feitlowitz 1999). What is certain is that this "training" produced the expected outcome.

Maya women survivors interviewed by the authors in four departments of Guatemala reported that they were selected by army officers to provide the service of delivering tortillas to the soldiers each day. It was understood that they would be gang-raped when they made their delivery to the army base, but the women went hoping to protect their daughters from the same fate. In Rabinal, women were forced into rotations at the local military base. Gilberta Iboy[10] described being part of a captive group: "There was so much fear, but by necessity we had to go to the plaza [in Rabinal] because they would not give the men permission to leave the village. In Rabinal, the soldiers captured us and took us to the outpost. We were assaulted. . . . They kept us there for a week and then they let us go" (Dill 2004).

Tomasa Toj[11] was still unable to talk about what happened to her: "They kept us in the military outpost for twenty-five days. We were there with other young women from various villages. The soldiers raped the women and some ended up pregnant . . . [The interview ended there because the woman could not continue]" (Dill 2004). Given the fact that along with other village women Ms. Iboy was held for a week and Ms. Toj for twenty-five days, their testimonies strongly suggest that the women previously identified by the CEH as "prostitutes" were also kidnapped and held on army bases as sex slaves.

A former G-2 (army intelligence) officer recounted rapes to REMHI investigators, making clear the way in which superior officers organized massive sexual violence:

> Some of the guys came and said, "Come on, don't you want to go grab some ass?" I thought to myself, "Wow, just like that?" One said to me, "There are some girls and we are grabbing them." I responded, "We'll see." There were only two girls. They were prisoners. The guys said they were guerrillas, right? And, they were

massively raping them. When I got there, I remember there was a line of 35 or so soldiers waiting their turn. They were surrounding them and raping them. One got up and another *passed* [authors' emphasis] on. Then he got off and another passed on. I calculate that those poor women were raped by 300 soldiers or maybe even more. Sergeant Soto García grabbed them. He was a bad man. He wanted whatever woman we found and he liked to rape them because he knew that we were going to kill them anyway. (REMHI, vol. 3, 212–213)

The G2 officer went on to explain how gang rape was planned to reduce the spread of sexually transmitted diseases among the troops. On another occasion, some seventy men had raped a woman and some of them had raped her two or three times: "There were some soldiers who were sick with gonorrhea and syphilis, so the lieutenant ordered them to wait to *pass* [authors' emphasis] last after the rest of us were done" (REMHI, vol. 2, 213–214).

Guatemalan soldiers were trained to think of gang rape as a bonding exercise among the troops as well as an effective weapon for the extermination of the civilian enemy. Because the troops were not being directed to engage an armed insurgency, but rather to annihilate villages and terrorize civilian communities, the army needed to dehumanize the soldiers as well as their intended victims. *The Counterinsurgency War Manual (Manual de Guerra Contrainsurgente)* states: "The soldier normally has great aversion toward police-type operations and repressive measures against women, children, and sick civilians, unless he is extremely well indoctrinated in the necessity of these operations."[12] One survivor testified to the truth commission: "There were always rapes inside the army bases . . . sometimes by [soldier's] choice, other times by order [from superiors]. They would say: 'We have to break the asses of these whores' or even worse things."[13]

The army prepared its soldiers by subjecting them to brutality, torture, and psychological manipulation. Once their resistance was extinguished and a blood lust established, soldiers were taught that entire communities were "breeding grounds" for subversives. This process would ensure that the fully indoctrinated would carry out abhorrent attacks on women, children, elderly and disabled persons, oftentimes in front of their families—while those who remained appalled by the violence were too afraid to disobey orders.

As the vessels from which new "subversives" would emerge, women's bodies were transformed into primary targets. Jean Franco recounts some of the most horrific CEH testimonies of rape in Guatemala: "Women were mutilated, their breast or bellies cut, and if they were pregnant, fetuses were torn from their bodies. In one case, a woman's breasts were cut off after the rape and her eyes were pulled out. Her body was left hanging on a pole with a stick in her vagina" (Franco 2007, 39). Franco rightly concludes: "Such ferocity can only be explained on the grounds that women represented a significant threat" (ibid., 27).

MODERN-DAY CONQUISTADORS

The prosecutors of the Ríos Montt trial focused on the evidence of state violence against the Ixil Maya; however, the army's genocidal campaign was not limited to that region or that ethnolinguistic group. Rape survivors and witnesses have confirmed that it was common knowledge in Maya villages across the country that the army was committing massacres and that soldiers were raping women. That means that systemic rape was a "public secret" shared by the residents of a village and the army that occupied it. But within the context of military impunity, even if remaining silent might not save your life, speaking out would certainly end it. This further underscores the power and authority with which sexual assaults were deployed by the army.

Power in Guatemala is a racialized phenomenon and the symbolic superiority of white and ladino men over the Maya was a catalyst for genocidal violence. In the same way that racism is a key to understanding the fury with which Ríos Montt's military plans were carried out against hundreds of Maya communities throughout the country, the patriarchal ideology resulted in a misogynist spiral of violence against women. Within this rubric of racist patriarchy, Maya women were objectified as enemy "property" deserving cruel destruction. Thus, the Guatemalan army raped and tortured women with the same ferocity with which they torched fields of sacred maize, burned houses, and slaughtered animals, leaving these signs of destruction to further terrorize any survivors (Sanford 2003).

The state achieved several goals by re-creating and affirming the historic relations in which indigenous women were the property of, and thus subordinate to, masculine white European and *ladino* power. In 1999, the CEH concluded that "massacres, scorched earth operations, forced disappearances and executions of Maya authorities, leaders and spiritual guides, were meant not only to destroy the social base of the guerrillas, but above all were meant to disintegrate cultural values that ensured cohesion and collective action of communities."[14]

Michelle Leiby uses data gathered by truth commission reports to compare the army's use of sexual violence in Guatemala and Peru (Leiby 2009). She points out that in the case of Guatemala, there exists a direct relationship between the perceived threat to the state and the number of rapes committed by soldiers. Although the war continued through December 1996, only 11 percent of sexual violence occurred after 1984, when it was clear that the URNG (Unidad Revolucionaria Nacional Guatemalteca) had been effectively defeated (ibid., 460). Leiby cites testimonies of Guatemalan soldiers that demonstrate that rape and in particular gang rape was as integral to the army's strategy as was the spectacularly violent killing of "subversives": "The commander has his group of killers, and he tells them how they have to kill. Today they are going to behead or hang them; today they are going to rape all the women. Many times, orders are given to the soldiers before they go out. . . . They were also ordered to do the 'percha' . . . where 20 or 30 soldiers would rape a single woman" (ibid., 459).

Other army sources asserted that if soldiers hesitated to rape they were berated by their superiors, and those who refused to rape were punished (ibid., 459). Based on her analysis of the data, Leiby concludes that while the military in Peru targeted actual or suspected guerrillas or other opponents of the state, "sexual violence in Guatemala was an explicit tool of repression, employed indiscriminately against the indigenous peasantry. Victims were not punished for joining the insurgency. Victims were not interrogated for information. Instead, sexual violence was used to spread fear and terror through entire 'communities of interest'" (ibid., 466).

Thus, to be a Maya woman—the heart of a community of interest—was to be at the mercy of a merciless army. Juana Sis[15] described what happened when the army surrounded her settlement near the village of Chichupac, Rabinal: "The soldiers captured us and they tied us up. They marched us to Chichupac and they assaulted us. They threatened us and accused us of being guerrillas and they raped women. It was the same in the Xesiguan community. They raped women in the community and they ordered some to go to the outpost [in Rabinal] and they raped them there. The soldiers respect no one" (Dill 2004).

At the same time, the army manipulated and indoctrinated Maya collaborators so they participated in this attack against their own communities. Dorotea Chen[16] of Buena Vista, Rabinal, was raped by Maya men from the neighboring village. The rapists were members of the local militia instituted by the military and referred to as the Civil Patrols (PACs). The state forcibly recruited Maya men into PACs in order to extend its reach into every indigenous municipality in the country. Like enlisted soldiers, PAC members were brutalized and threatened with death if they did not follow orders. Some indigenous men fled into the mountains to avoid having to serve in the PACs. Some stayed behind and were horrified by what they were forced to do, while still others were eager to take advantage of their newfound power and impunity: "The PAC from Xococ arrived here and dragged young women out of their houses and they took them to Xococ where they raped them. Afterwards, they would send them back home but they always returned [for more] every so often. A great many of the women here have been raped" (Dill 2004).

Almost all cases of mass and organized rape operationalized by the army and their proxies took place in rural Mayan communities, especially during the height of the violence between 1980 and 1983 (CEH 1999). The Guatemalan army's deployment of systematic sexual violence during the genocide devastated individual victims as well as the indigenous groups to which they belonged. Of the twenty-one ethnolinguistic Maya groups in Guatemala, K'iche, K'anjob'al, Mam,

Kekchi, Ixil, Kaqchikel, and Chuj communities were either most often the victims of massive rape or were more recorded by human rights observers. As researchers who have worked with K'anjob'al, K'iche, Kakchikel, Akateco, Achi, Mam, Ixil, and Tz'ujil communities, we have found that the rape of Maya women was intended to terrorize, subjugate, debilitate, and demoralize entire populations. We have not encountered a department in Guatemala where women were not raped.

THE POLITICAL ECONOMY OF RAPE

In addition to the demoralizing spectacle of power and impunity that the "public secret" of mass rapes provided, by aiding, abetting, and promoting rape as a military strategy, the Guatemalan state also achieved some economic goals. Drawing from research conducted in Rwanda and Mozambique, Meredeth Turshen argues: "In civil wars, armies use rape systematically to strip women of their economic and political assets. Women's assets reside in the first instance in their productive and reproductive labour power and in the second instance in their possessions and their access to valuable assets such as land and livestock" (Turshen 2001, 56).

In Rabinal, families that lived in the Chixoy River basin were especially targeted for violence because the state wanted their land for a World Bank–funded hydroelectric dam (Johnston 2010). It is not surprising, then, to learn that the first cases of mass rape in that municipality occurred in the villages located on the banks or on the approach to the river. Hermenegildo Cuxum,[17] a man from Canchún, Rabinal, recalls:

> In March 1980, soldiers assassinated three men from Canchún who were visiting in the nearby community of Río Negro. One man was shot in the hand, but was able to escape and return to the village. Later, more army troops came. Three hundred soldiers entered Canchún, demanded information about the guerrillas and threatened the community. This time, the soldiers raped five women and five young girls before they left. We knew that we had to escape into the mountains to save our lives, but two elderly women were unable to come with us. One woman's body trembled too much to travel and the other woman was blind [so we had to leave them behind]. When we returned to the village, we discovered that in a savage and incomprehensible act, the soldiers had killed them. (Dill 2004)

Across the indigenous highlands of Guatemala, women were raped wherever the army displaced Maya communities, during massacres as they razed villages, in public buildings and churches converted into army detention centers, in military bases, and in so-called model villages where the army forcibly concentrated massacre survivors.[18] For many Maya women, rape and the ensuing loss of their way of life defined how they experienced the war.

CONCLUDING REMARKS

Genocide is an all-consuming type of violence. As researchers, it is impossible to convey the measure of human suffering experienced by its victims. We are often reduced to making lists. All told, we know that the Guatemalan genocide took the lives of some 200,000 civilians, 50,000 people were disappeared, 626 villages were annihilated, 1.5 million people were displaced, and 150,000 people fled to refuge in Mexico (CEH 1999). But we do not know how many women and girls were raped, how many were abducted by the military and forced into sexual slavery, how many gave birth to children who were the product of sexual assault, or how many suffered from the venereal diseases transmitted during the rape(s). Despite real advances in international law, there has been little progress in prosecuting these crimes.

In this chapter, we have touched upon a number of ways in which the Guatemalan genocide operationalized rape: to terrorize the Maya population, destabilize the reproductive role of women, demoralize the enemy, provide soldiers with the spoils of war, and train them to commit hyperviolent acts, usurp land, and to reaffirm historic relations of power between the Euro-American elite and the Maya. Jelke Boesten detangles the various types and intents of sexual violence during war by carefully analyzing what she calls "rape regimes" (Boesten 2014). Because her study focuses on Peru, which like Guatemala is a country with a large indigenous population, Boesten also recognizes that sexual violence can be used to reinscribe racialized socioeconomic hierarchies present during peacetime. During the Ríos Montt regime, the systemized rape of Maya women was a weapon of genocide used to accomplish multiple ends, all of which supported the singular operational goal—breaking emergent Maya communities.

On May 10, 2013, José Efraín Ríos Montt was sentenced to the maximum penalty of fifty years' imprisonment for genocide and thirty years for crimes against humanity. The tribunal found that racism played a key role in the execution of acts of barbarism and ordered the development of concrete measures to provide dignified reparation to the victims. One of the measures ordered was for then president of Guatemala Otto Pérez Molina (who is also implicated in the Ixil genocide)[19] and several ministers to ask forgiveness from the Ixil people and especially Ixil women for the acts of genocide and sexual violence suffered. The verdict offered a modicum of justice for the survivors and opened the possibility that Guatemalan society might reconcile itself with its own history of racist exclusion and genocide.

However, Guatemala's elite quickly seized back control. On May 20, 2013, the Constitutional Court overturned the verdict on the pretext of procedural irregularities. In February 2014, the same court ruled that Ms. Claudia Paz y Paz, the attorney general who indicted Ríos Montt, was to be removed from her post six months early. Then in April 2014, the College of Lawyers in Guatemala suspended Judge Yasmín Barrios. She was able to defend herself and has resumed practice, but these blatantly corrupt maneuvers lend a Kafkaesque quality to the state of governance in Guatemala and remind everyone that the rule of law has yet to be established. Nonetheless, justice continues to move forward under the leadership of Attorney General Thelma Aldana. In January 2016, eighteen former high-ranking army officers were arrested for various war crimes. As this book goes to press, the historic Sepur Zarco sexual slavery case is being tried in Guatemala City, marking the first time a domestic court has heard charges of sexual slavery during armed conflict as an international crime (Burt 2016).

NOTES

1. Ten days later, the Constitutional Court vacated the guilty verdict and ordered that the trial restart from the point reached on April 19, 2013, the day a lower court called for the suspension of the trial due to unresolved appeals by the defense. See Kate Doyle, "Guatemala's Genocide on Trial," *Nation*, May 22, 2013. On January 11, 2016, the defense team successfully delayed the start of the retrial. See Anna-Catherine Brigida, "Retrial of Ex-Dictator Ríos Montt: Will a Changed Guatemala Shine Through?," *Christian Science Monitor*, January 11, 2016.

2. The CEH documented 626 army massacres in Maya villages.

3. CEH 1999, 32.

4. Based on our field experience and conversations with colleagues, we assume sexual violence against men and women was underreported. See Theidon 2016.

5. CEH 1999, vol. 2, chap. 2, p. 381, epigraph 1947.

6. CEH 1999, vol. 5, chap. 4, vol. 5, chap. 4, pp. 24–25, epigraph 15.

7. CEH 1999, vol. 5, chap. 4, p. 29, epigraph 31.

8. Conversely, when the goal is to eliminate individual targets *without* destabilizing and alienating the community, military leaders have an incentive to *prevent* their troops from perpetrating sexual violence.

9. Ejército de Guatemala (1982), *Plan Victoria 82*, appendix B, 39.

10. Pseudonym.

11. Pseudonym.

12. Ejército de Guatemala, *Manual de Guerra Contrasubversiva (resumen)* (1965), Anexo A, p. 10.

13. CEH 1999, Testigo CEH (T.C. 53).

14. CEH 1999, Capítulo Cuarto, p. 29, epigraph 32.

15. Pseudonym.

16. Pseudonym.

17. Pseudonym.

18. CEH 1999, Testigo CEH (T.C. 53).

19. Ex-president Otto Perez Molina was arrested on September 2, 2015, and charged with corruption. He is accused of directing a customs fraud scheme, which eliminated government import taxes in exchange for payoffs. He is awaiting trial in a military prison. See Jan Martínez Ahrens (translation by Martin Delfin), "Guatemala's Jailed Ex-Leader: 'I Didn't Want Any Deaths Just to Save My Skin,'" *El País*, December 15, 2015. In October 2015, Jimmy Morales, a television comedian backed by right-wing military and elite business interests, won the presidential

election with the slogan "Not Corrupt, nor a Thief." See Elizabeth Malkin and Nic Wiritz, New York Times, "Jimmy Morales Is Elected New President of Guatemala," October 25, 2015.

REFERENCES

Arendt, Hannah. 2006. *Eichmann in Jerusalem: A Report on the Banality of Evil*. New York: Penguin.

Boesten, Jelke. 2014. *Sexual Violence during War and Peace: Gender, Power, and Post-Conflict Justice in Peru*. New York: Palgrave Macmillan.

Burt, Jo-Marie. 2013. "Historic Genocide Trial Nears End; Rios Montt Addresses the Court, Declares Innocence." *International Justice Monitor*, Open Society Justice Initiative, May 10. http://www.ijmonitor.org/2013/05/historic-genocide-trial-nears-end-rios-montt -addresses-the-court-declares-innocence/.

———. 2016. "Six Witnesses Recount Atrocities at Sepur Zarco on Day Two of Landmark Trial." New York: International Justice Monitor. http://www.ijmonitor.org/2016/02/six -witnesses-recount-atrocities-at-sepur-zarco-on-day-two-of-landmark-trial/.

CEH (Commission for Historical Clarification). 1999. *Guatemala: Memoria del Silencio, Informe de La Comisión para el Esclarecimiento Histórico*. Guatemala: CEH.

Consorcio de Actoras de Cambio. 2006. *Rompiendo el Silencio: Justicia para las mujeres victi- mas de la violencia sexual durante el conflicto armado en Guatemala*. Guatemala City: F & G Editores and Equipo Comunitaria de Ayuda Psicosocial.

Dada, Carlos. 2014. "Guatemala Se Enjuicia." *El Faro*. Accessed December 13. http://www .elfaro.net/es/201304/noticias/11755/?st-.

Dill, Kathleen. 2004. "Mediated Pasts, Negotiated Futures: Human Rights and Social Recon- struction in a Maya Community." PhD diss., University of California, Davis.

Ejército de Guatemala. 1965. *Manual de Guerra Contrasubversiva (resumen)*. Guatemala City: Ejército de Guatemala.

———. 1982. *Plan Victoria 82*. Guatemala City: Ejército de Guatemala.

Enloe, Cynthia H. 2000. *Maneuvers: The International Politics of Militarizing Women's Lives*. Berkeley: University of California Press.

Ertürk, Yakin. 2009. "15 Years of the United Nations Special Rapporteur on Violence Against Women, Its Causes and Consequences (1994–2009)—a Critical Review." May 27. UN Human Rights Council, Report of the Special Rapporteur on Violence Against Women. A/HRC/11/6/Add.5. Accessed January 24, 2016. http://www.refworld.org/ docid/4a3f5fc62.html.

Feitlowitz, Marguerite. 1999. *A Lexicon of Terror: Argentina and the Legacies of Torture*. New York: Oxford University Press.

Franco, Jean. 2007. "Rape: A Weapon of War." *Social Text* 25 (2): 23–37.

Johnston, Barbara Rose. 2010. "Chixoy Dam Legacies: The Struggle to Secure Reparation and the Right to Remedy in Guatemala." *Water Alternatives* 3 (2): 341–361.

Leiby, Michele L. 2009. "Wartime Sexual Violence in Guatemala and Peru." *International Studies Quarterly* 53 (2): 445–468.

Meyer, Mary K. 2003. "Ulster's Red Hand: Gender, Identity, and Sectarian Conflict in North- ern Ireland." In *Women, States and Nationalism: At Home in the Nation?*, edited by Sita Ranchod-Nilsson and Mary Ann Tetreault. New York: Routledge.

REMHI (Recuperación de la Memoria Histórica). 1998. *Guatemala: Nunca Más, Informe de La Recuperación de La Memoria Histórica*. Guatemala: Oficina de derechos humanos del Arzobispado de Guatemala.

Sanford, Victoria. 2003. *Buried Secrets: Truth and Human Rights in Guatemala*. New York: Palgrave Macmillan.

———. 2014. "Command Responsibility and the Guatemalan Genocide: Genocide as a Military Plan of the Guatemalan Army under the Dictatorships of Generals Lucas Garcia, Rios Montt, and Mejia Victores." *Genocide Studies International* 8 (1): 86–101.

Sen, Gita, and Caren Grown. 1987. *Development Crises and Alternative Visions: Third World Women's Perspectives*. New York: Monthly Review Press.

Sentencia Condenatoria en contra de Jose Efrain Ríos Montt. 2013. *Condenado por Genocidio*. Guatemala City: F&G Editores.

Theidon, Kimberly. "A Greater Measure of Justice: Gender, Violence, and Reparations." In *Mapping Feminist Anthropology in the Twenty-First Century*, edited by Leni Silverstein and Ellen Lewin. New Brunswick, NJ: Rutgers University Press.

Turshen, Meredeth. 2001. "The Political Economy of Rape: An Analysis of Systematic Rape and Sexual Abuse of Women during Armed Conflict in Africa." In *Victors, Perpetrators, or Actors: Gender, Armed Conflict, and Political Violence*, edited by Caroline O. N. Moser and Fiona C. Clark. London: Zed Books.

3 • GENDER, INCARCERATION, AND POWER RELATIONS DURING THE IRISH CIVIL WAR (1922–1923)

LAURA McATACKNEY

Ireland entered a loosely defined Decade of Commemorations around 2012, a time when public and academic consciousness has increasingly cast back to the events that contributed to the formation, and partition, of the state in the early years of the twentieth century. In this context, scholars have argued previously that commemoration in Ireland has as much to do with contemporary societal issues and understandings as it does with the events of the past (Ó Gráda 2001), and therefore can result in "bad history" that promotes particular narratives while excluding others (Beiner 2005). Furthermore, Dominic Bryan and Neil Jarman have argued that, as a result of partition in the early 1920s, commemorations in both parts of the island have taken on overtly political aspects and have become intrinsically connected to contemporary political issues (1997, 211). In a more contemporary setting, Bryonie Reid has shown how a focus on gender is important as the narratives of public, communal commemoration have increasingly followed a normative narrative that places the public domain as fundamentally male and the domestic domain as female (2005). The fact that women were imprisoned en masse for political reasons for the first time by the newly formed Irish state in the early 1920s is something that is often considered best forgotten. In combining these interrelated perspectives, I argue that the distance of time, the ignoble role of the newly formed Irish state in targeting women, and the politicization of communal memory in the intervening period negatively affects how gender is incorporated into these reconfigured (re)rememberings of revolutionary Ireland.

This silence is particularly notable in the lack of acknowledgment of state-perpetrated violence against women.

REVOLUTIONARY IRELAND (C. 1912–C. 1924)

Early twentieth-century Irish society experienced waves of pressure for fundamental societal changes. This pressure often originated from groups that had been marginal to the political mainstream immediately prior to this period: workers, women, and republicans (see Foster 2014). The simultaneous emergence—and often active cooperation—of those demanding greater rights for blue-collar workers, women, and pro-independence nationalists reached a zenith during the tumultuous period now known as "revolutionary Ireland" (commonly dated from the Easter Rising of 1916 to the Irish Civil War of 1922–1923). Through a range of public meetings, social gatherings, pickets, protests, and even violent interactions with police and the army, their demands reached widespread public notice through newspapers reporting on the arrests and hunger strikes of suffragettes (1912 onward), reports and experiences of the Dublin Lock Out of industrial workers (1913), and most famously the devastating, if sporadic, impact of republican rebellion and then guerrilla war against the British forces from the Easter Rising (1916) through the War of Independence (1919–1921).

Building on nationalist narratives of political imprisonment in Ireland that date back in popular memory to the rebellion of the United Irishmen of 1798—and becoming materially entwined with the fabric of Kilmainham Gaol in Dublin from at least the mid-nineteenth century—the political prisoner holds an elevated status as a category of struggle in Ireland (see Arextaga 1997; Feldman 1991). Following Allen Feldman, the status of the political prisoner is not simply (or even usually) designated but is performed; resistance against rules and regulations of imprisonment were considered symbolic or political action by these prisoners through time, space, and across gender (Feldman 1991, 147). However, as we move through the period the growing importance of the nationalist struggle, and associated imprisonment, eclipses the other pressing issues of social justice. Alongside this selective remembering of the period there is also an abiding reticence to include political imprisonment under Irish state forces during the Irish Civil War (which almost immediately followed independence in 1922–1923). Such selective remembering most deeply affects the public memory of women, particularly the experiences of politically imprisoned women, a tendency that has been retained and reinforced through to the current decade of commemorations.

Despite the lack of mainstream recognition, women played a significant role in the "revolutionary period." Documentary and oral evidence from a variety of sources reveals that they held a number of key roles not only in facilitating the actions of the men—who are more publicly remembered for their military exploits and political maneuverings—but in serving as active combatants and politicians in their own right. Countess Constance de Markievicz is one prominent example. She came to wider public notice when she was reprieved as the only female sentenced to death as a result of the Easter Rising in 1916. She became the first elected female MP to the British Parliament in 1918 (but did not take her seat due to abstention by Irish nationalists). She is also one of the first female ministers in Western Europe as minister of labour in the newly formed Dáil Eireann, 1919–1922, the Irish revolutionary parliament (Ward 1995, 137). Markievicz's leadership role, as well as that of other women including Kathleen Clarke and Sighle Humphries, shows that in addition to playing key roles in maintaining vital networks of communications and safe houses and smuggling ammunition and provisions, women at this period were also, at least at the elite level, leaders of military garrisons and elected politicians.

The various roles undertaken by women in the nationalist movements in early twentieth-century Ireland have been addressed by a small group of historians. In particular, the works of Louise Ryan (1995, 2001), Margaret Ward (1995), Ryan and Ward (2004), Ann Matthews (2010, 2012), and Sinead McCoole (1997, 2003, 2014) have enriched our understandings of the variety and complexity of women's roles across various levels and echelons of society. They have argued that women played central roles across all aspects of this period, but their contributions were often underplayed by the male leadership, and this lack of acknowledgment has been self-perpetuating. While Margaret Ward notes that some high-profile contemporary male figures publicly commended the women for their role in supporting and maintaining the fighters, the tradition of "man the leader and woman the auxiliary" (1995, 197) meant that their roles were frequently obfuscated.

With the transition to the Free State, the important roles of women during the revolutionary period were swiftly forgotten. This situation does not reflect public knowledge of the time. Louise Ryan has shown that contemporary newspapers were aware of, and reported on, a variety of women's roles that have since been lost from public memory. The widely circulated and highly influential popular press often contained, and publicized, information on women being arrested, convicted, imprisoned, and denounced in their notices, editorials, and articles. Ryan argues that this later obscuring of the range and variety of female roles can be partially attributed to feminist scholars being uncomfortable with the active role some of the women held in military affairs (2001, 221). However, I argue that this loss of public memory may also relate to discomfiture in remembering the civil war at all, and especially the role the authorities played in imprisoning, and targeting, women at this transitional time. While these omissions are now being corrected by some researchers in women's history, they continue to be excluded from many mainstream narratives, which still depict females as "weeping mothers and wives" (Dolan 2006, 131) and "Easter widows" (McCoole 2014). This exclusion of the variety of roles and experiences of women during the revolutionary period can have other, unintended repercussions. This includes a lack of openness regarding the extent and impact of gender-related violence and sexual assault during the time. Ann Matthews has explicitly tackled underreporting of these incidents, noting that they were often underreported because of societal pressures and the shame of being a victim of common or sexual assault (2010); however, there is an almost complete absence of these uncomfortable realities from narratives of this period.

FEMALE EXPERIENCES OF IMPRISONMENT
DURING THE IRISH CIVIL WAR (1922–1923)

One means of adding to our understanding of the extreme experiences of women during this period is through examining the often forgotten issue of female political imprisonment during the civil war. Mass political imprisonment of women occurred for the first time in Irish history during this particular conflict. This phenomenon can best be explained by the swift transition from the preceding War of Independence (1919–1921) (when nationalist paramilitaries used guerrilla tactics to fight the occupying British forces) to the more embittered realities of civil conflict between those who supported—and those who rejected—the Anglo-Irish Treaty with Britain. In a short timescale recent comrades became bitter enemies, and in a stark change from the preceding conflict they also possessed an intimate knowledge of the workings of their foes. Divisions solidified after the pro-Treaty forces were victorious in ratifying the Anglo-Irish Treaty with Britain, which resulted in partition of the island and restricted freedom for the newly formed Free State. Their anti-Treaty opponents reacted with increasing violence in their rejection of these terms and in turn were interned and imprisoned by their previous allies as the conflict escalated. After the outbreak of civil war in May 1922, less than half a year after the Free State was created, women as well as men began to be interned en masse. Such an action, as well as being an innovation, also reveals a tacit acceptance by the Free State that not only were women important in the functioning and continuation of anti-Treaty paramilitaries but that they would also be treated with equality as combatants.

Cumann na mBan (Council of Women), the female political organization whose members made up the majority of the imprisoned women, was the first national organization to officially reject the Treaty, in early February 1922. This action highlighted to the newly formed pro-Treaty government that Cumann na mBan's members were not only hardliners but were potential recruits and supporters of the anti-Treaty forces. While Sinead McCoole has argued that "in evading arrest they appear to have eluded the historical record" (1997, 10), the substantial rise in the numbers of women imprisoned during the civil war, compared to earlier conflicts, contradicts this statement. Indeed, Margaret Ward claims that at least four hundred women were imprisoned by the Free State during the civil war, in comparison to the some fifty women who were imprisoned by the British during the preceding War of Independence (1995, 190). There was a notable shift in public and political perceptions of women, from being essentially apolitical and domestic to having their involvement officially acknowledged, and publicly criticized, by the Catholic Church, Free State politicians, and the press (Ryan 2001, 213). The acceptance of the significant roles that the women played in facilitating conflict, at the very least, marked their transition from vulnerable figures needing protection to increasingly being conceived as active combatants and legitimate targets. The resultant imprisonment that the women experienced supports this uncomfortable truth when we begin to explore their experiences of harassment, implied and actual violence, and sexual assault.

METHODS, THEORIES, AND SOURCES FOR EXPLORING FEMALE EXPERIENCES OF IMPRISONMENT

Due to the paucity of official sources relating to the female experience of imprisonment during this period, this investigation will utilize underused primary sources and take an overtly material approach. This is partly through necessity, but it is also because engaging with less obvious sources has the potential to locate hitherto unconsidered details of the lived experiences of political imprisonment. Therefore, while textual sources from memoirs will be included, including Margaret Buckley's *The Jangle of the Keys* (1938), evidence will largely come from underused primary sources. These include the extant graffiti located in the older, West Wing of the most important political prison during this period, Kilmainham Gaol, and the contents of autograph books. Such books were relatively inexpensive, mass-produced books of blank paper popularly circulated in the late nineteenth to mid-twentieth century to allow friends to write messages at transitional times, especially on leaving school. Although they were used in individual ways, many of the women held them while imprisoned, passed them among friends and acquaintances to sign and add messages, and retained them on their release.

Kilmainham Gaol is now a heritage site of considerable popularity and significance to the Irish state. It was built in 1796 by the British state as the county jail for Dublin but due to its monumental size and secure perimeter, it was considered inescapable and quickly became utilized, and associated, with the holding of groups of political prisoners. The jail closed for the first time in 1910 due to its outdated design and poor living conditions. It had not held women

FIGURE 3.1 Graffiti (paint over whitewash) located in the cell of Bridget O'Mullane on the top floor of the West Wing of Kilmainham Gaol: "Fortune who betrays us today / Will smile on us tomorrow." (Photo by author, May 2013)

since 1881. However, it was reopened a number of times as an emergency measure, holding British soldiers (barracked and imprisoned for minor disciplinary violations during World War I), rebels from the Easter Rising (1916), the War of Independence (1919–1921), and lastly the Irish Civil War (1922–1923). It closed for the final time in early 1924, and the few remaining prisoners were transferred elsewhere. The prison walls were whitewashed many times over its life; however, the last thorough whitewash was recorded during the War of Independence and there is evidence of only sporadic whitewashing thereafter (O'Sullivan 2009, 74). There continues to exist a huge assemblage of graffiti relating to the period of mass imprisonment of women during the civil war. Coupled with the evidence from autograph books, these will be the two primary sources of this investigation. Although autograph books have been relatively underused in academic studies due to their essentially trivial nature, Hanna Herzog and Rita Shapira have argued that such books are useful in gaining insights into personal opinions and the workings of social networks because they provide "authentic material not created for the purpose of study" (1986, 109).

The types of experiences that we are able to extract from this collection of sources varies considerably and includes evidence of violence and brutality that are infrequently mentioned in other, less contemporary, sources. There is also considerable evidence of the more negotiated realities of the relationship between the Irish state, represented through the prison regime, and this special category of prisoner. As well as being physically intimidated and even assaulted the women had the agency to initiate hugely controversial hunger strikes. There is evidence that they claimed descent from the established nationalist pantheon of heroes and heroines and taunted their captors' immorality and cowardice through the medium of graffiti. The women frequently articulate the innate rightness of their cause, despite being on the wrong side of contemporary politics, including a large slogan displayed in Brigid O'Mullane's cell (see figure 3.1): "Fortune who betrays us today / Will smile on us tomorrow." Embracing the specificity and multiplicity of meanings inherent in these graffiti survivals, I argue that the graffiti from this period at Kilmainham Gaol was utilized in a number of ways, including as a means to negotiate power relations. This multiplicity of meanings ensures that its importance lies not only in its survival but in revealing what Jeff Oliver and Tim Neal call "the social experience of more marginal actors" (2010, 2).

EVIDENCE OF STATE-PERPETUATED GENDERED VIOLENCE DURING THE REVOLUTIONARY PERIOD

Ann Matthews argues in her studies of "revolutionary Ireland" that from the War of Independence onward there existed an effective "war on women" (2010, 266–283). She interprets this policy as a repercussion of the unsettled politics and heightened militarization of the period but also as a reaction to the changing roles of women in wider society (Matthews 2010, 12). From the time of the War of Independence women, especially nonelite women on either side, were actively targeted for verbal, physical, and sexual attack. While officially the British army and administration denied that nothing more than inappropriate and rough treatment of women had occurred, a number of contemporary reports reveal that the use of gendered intimidation, threats, and violence was widespread. The *Report of the Labour Commission to Ireland* (Labour Party 1921), which was prepared and published by the British Labour Party, was particularly important in highlighting and documenting these attacks. The report was based on widespread and long-term fieldwork that included interviews with the British and Irish republican sides, with both combatants and civilians. It noted that attacks on women, particularly in isolated, rural locations, were commonplace, frequently targeting those whose male relatives were thought to be involved in either official military (including the British army) or paramilitary organizations (including guerrilla groups such as the Irish Volunteers). Attacks on women as surrogates for their male relatives and acquaintance were a common thread throughout the revolutionary period (McCoole 1997), and these assaults went largely unreported.

Women suffered abuse on both sides of the conflict. Republicans viewed women as legitimate targets if they came from families that were connected to the various branches of the British forces, or were providing services to them (Matthews 2010, 274–276). Those who were romantically involved with police and army members were often sent letters warning of the consequences of their liaisons, and there is evidence that women were attacked—one particularly popular form was to forcibly shave their heads—merely for holding "anti-Republican views" (DMP [Dublin Metropolitan Police] Reports 1923). Republicans often viewed women suspiciously as potential or active spies, particularly those who were seen to fraternize with any member of the British military establishment. The absence of examples of abuse from public memory reveals the level of public forgetting not only about the active roles women took in the conflicts of this time but also about how they were targeted and assaulted as an aspect of war. As noted by Matthews, "national amnesia in republicans, both male and female, reduced the experiences of many Irishwomen to mere speculation. They were completely forgotten" (2010, 282).

Evidence of physical and sexual assault from both the British forces and republican guerrillas during periods of imprisonment follows a similar trajectory of overarching silence, broken only by hints and a minute number of explicit revelations about threats and violence against female political prisoners. While references to violence are often coded or brief, there is enough candor to undisputedly state that brutality did occur, if sporadically. This chapter will highlight a number of references to the threat or actuality of violence that the women noted while imprisoned, ending with an examination of one particularly notorious incident in detail.

The forms of violence referenced most often take the form of deliberately inducing fear. In particular, the fear of being separated from other women, of being the focus of sexualized intentions by armed soldiers and prison guards, and of forced movements between holding centers being used to instigate violence and sexual assault. Entries within the collection of autograph books, in particular, reveal the remembrances of raids of cells by armed soldiers and guards, gunshots ricocheting through prison wings, and drunken soldiers rampaging through the prison. Perhaps not coincidentally, almost all these overtly aggressive actions occurred in the sinister, and anonymizing, darkness of night.

However, despite the fear of physical and sexual assault articulated by many female prisoners, there remained a mutual awareness of the negotiated relationship between the prison regime and the prisoner. This was much more reciprocal in nature than would have been reported or expected on the outside and is revealed through the autograph books and graffiti of Kilmainham Gaol. The women's circumstances of imprisonment—especially the many nationalist heroines and close relatives of dead nationalist heroes held at this time—were often used by anti-Treaty sympathizers outside the prison to deliberately emotive propagandic affect. This was especially utilized in retelling the women's experiences of the terrible prison conditions and their frequent recourse to individual and mass hunger strikes for what were often presented by their detractors as trivial reasons. This chapter will proceed from detailing the evidence for actual and threatened sexual and physical violence against the women to conclude by highlighting their enduring agency to contest, subvert, and indeed shame their imprisoners.

GENDERED VIOLENCE DURING PERIODS OF POLITICAL IMPRISONMENT

Although the Irish Civil War saw women become political prisoners due to their involvement in republican politics for the first time, they were still a minority of the prison population—the estimated four hundred women imprisoned throughout the course of the civil war was significantly less than the nearly twelve thousand men (Ward 1995, 190). However, their incarceration created an initially unforeseen problem for the new government in not only where they housed the women but also how the wider public would view their imprisonment. They were frequently held collectively, housed in all-female wings or holding centers, but were also sporadically moved in small or large groups between sites. It is difficult to pinpoint the official reasons for these frequent removals or transfers, due to the absence of contemporary government files, but the women clearly believed that this policy was used to unsettle them, break morale, and disrupt established hierarchies (McCoole 1997).

Threats of violence against the women were often implicit in their interactions with the prison regime. Margaret Buckley, in her memoir of imprisonment during the civil war, highlighted the experiences of the high-profile Cumann na mBan member Eithne Coyle. Coyle was captured in the relatively quiet northwestern county of Donegal and was initially held alone. Buckley reveals a common set of circumstances in Coyle's initial imprisonment as a lone female, including a prescient fear of violence and the night being associated with threats from aggressive men: "her [Coyle's] cell was invaded at all hours of the night by members of a drunken guard, an undisciplined mob, until sheer force of terrible and unchristian conditions compelled her to go on hunger-strike for more human conditions there, or for a transfer to Mountjoy [Prison]" (1938, 15). The use of "unchristian conditions" follows a notable trajectory of ambiguous language employed by the women to describe the relationship with the men who imprisoned and guarded them. While the women hint at the fear of imminent assault, and even sexual violence, they also emphasize this deviance from contemporary social norms in being unchaperoned in the company of such men and the potential impact on their respectability. This fear of sexual and physical violence—as well as the knowledge that the hint of inappropriate relations with such men would sully their reputations—ensured that the women became highly communalized and met any attempt to separate them with extreme reactions.

The majority of the women imprisoned at this time were arrested in the capital city, Dublin, or quickly transferred there, and were held together between three holding centers: Kilmainham Gaol, North Dublin Union (a derelict workhouse that had been used previously to house British soldiers), and Mountjoy Prison. Even when housed as a collective, the threat of violence remained with drunken guards left in charge, often with guns, at night. As police and prison officers in the Irish state have never been regularly armed since this time, the menace and threat of these extraordinary actions was clear. A number of messages in the autograph books specifically mention the fear of armed men invading their cells, including an entry in the autograph book of Brigid "Bridie" Reed: "Don't forget Bridie when the soldier raided our dormitorys at 3 in the morning when we were asleep, when they came the next night they got a let down, for we had our doors barracaded [sic] and when they tried to force them in but failed" (KMGLM 2010.0130, August 29, 1923). A similar incident from a month later is referenced in the autograph book of Brigid Brophy: "In remembrance of the night we fought the Drunken Governor & Adj[unct] & Slim Doctor with basins of water, boxes, stools, tables etc" (KMGLM 2010.0129, September 12, 1923). Another entry in the same book states: "Remember the night of 10.9.'23" (KMGLM 2010.0129, undated). Margaret Buckley evocatively reveals the fear that the women experienced during these nighttime raids: "The lights were off, the 'Circle' was pitch dark, except for a fitful glare from the floor, and filled with panic-stricken girls, who shouted and cried in turns, while round about stood soldiers, jeering, and under the command of an officer under the influence of drink" (1938, 98).

While the threat of violence, although not often explicitly stated, was omnipresent, there were a small number of notorious incidents when violent interactions definitely did occur. One such incident resulted from the women's refusal to be removed from Kilmainham Gaol to the North Dublin Union Prison in late April 1923. The intention to transfer the majority of the women was revealed to them on the same day and coincided with a hunger strike undertaken by Mary McSwiney and Kate O'Callaghan reaching a critical stage. The women's response to the news was to barricade themselves in their cells, leading to a series of nighttime raids when they were forcibly, often violently, removed. They

FIGURE 3.2 Cartoon image of a woman stripped of her skirt with a male prison guard in attendance. Located in a photocopy of an autograph book belonging to Susan Ryan. Photo by author, June 2011. (Reproduced with permission of Kilmainham Gaol Archive)

were then processed, alone, by male CID (Criminal Investigation Department, an armed, plainclothes police unit that operated during the civil war) officers and members of the newly formed, pro-State, breakaway group from Cumann na mBan, Cumann na Saoirse (Committee of Freedom). Margaret Ward noted the central involvement of the women of Cumann na Saoirse in facilitating and initiating "sexual abuse in some attacks" (1995, 194). Dorothy Macardle complained of being "manhandled, trampled, carried and 'flung down' in surgery to be searched" (quoted in McCoole 1997). The forced searching of women was a multifaceted and decidedly sinister act. It not only facilitated the prison officers in locating and confiscating whatever they decided was contraband, but, following Begoña Aretxaga (1997), it also allowed the "colonialization" of the female body. Forced searches were a deliberate policy that facilitated the violation and conquest of the physical body of female prisoners in the name of the state and its security (see also Stefatos, this volume). In all, seventy women were dragged from their cells and processed over five hours in one night.

A number of firsthand accounts of this night's events survive in the contemporary autograph books, government reports, and newspaper articles.

The government reports noted that two women had to be treated for injuries received while resisting searches. Máire Comerford required three stitches to her head and Mary McDermott broke her wrist (Matthews 2012, 76). Mary McDermott ensured that a letter was smuggled out of the North Dublin Union, to be published by the *Daily Herald*, detailing her abuse: "I was assaulted . . . by four women employed by the Free State. My dress was taken off, because I resisted. . . . The prison adjutant, a man at least six feet of heavy build, knelt on me while the women assaulted me, beating me about the face and body with my own shoes. . . . I fainted. . . . On my recovering consciousness I found myself outside in the passage among drunken soldiers lying in a semi nude state, my clothing saturated with water" (May 7, 1923).

Alongside the many ambiguous and terse messages to "remember" the so-called NDU (North Dublin Union) riot (Ward 1995, 194), there also exists an entry in the autograph book of Susan Ryan depicting the night. Alongside the simple phrase "In memory of the night of the evacuation" on the facing page, the image presents a snapshot of the evening that alludes to violence as it lingers on the vulnerability of the women and latent threat of the situation. The image (see figure 3.2) consists of a stripped woman standing in her underwear saying "Oh my skirt" being watched by a large man in uniform who is holding her clothing. Under the image is the statement: "Another stripe for Cassidy," evidently referring to the official commendation of officers who were following orders in taking part in such violent actions against women (20 MS ID46 08, undated). Mary MacSwiney would later describe the perpatrators as "demoralised and vile Irishmen" (Buckley 1938, v).

FEMALE AGENCY AND PROTESTING POLITICAL IMPRISONMENT

Women, on entering the prison environment, clearly faced an imminent threat of physical and sexual violence that was acted on, if sporadically, during the course of their confinement. However, it would be wrong to portray this group as cowering objects acted upon by others, and with no agency of their own. The women knew that although their public roles in the civil war provoked ambivalent, if not negative, responses among the authorities and general public due to their "blurring of boundaries between privacy and publicity, between feminine and masculine roles," their imprisonment was equally an uncomfortable prospect for the state (Ryan 2001, 215). Added to the ambiguous nature of the situation was the essentially unlawful nature of their imprisonment. In common with male political prisoners, the vast majority of the women had been interned, rather than processed through court trials. On their arrival in prison, the Free State government refused to officially recognize the political nature of their incarceration. This lack of recognition resulted in the women even more overtly proclaiming and performing the political nature of their imprisonment through

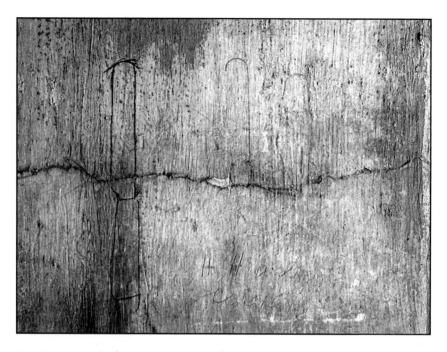

FIGURE 3.3 Graffiti (pencil over whitewash) located in a cell on the top floor of the West Wing of Kilmainham Gaol. (Photo by author, September 2014)

ongoing acts of subversion and defiance. This defiance built on existing foundations that explicitly proclaimed their resilience and steadfastness to the aims of the initial revolutionary period—of complete independence from Britain—and thus provided them with a moral high ground. These dual sentiments were articulated as frequently as possible, regardless of fear of violence.

One of the central power struggles, which structured the prisoners' days and interactions with the regime, emerged from the seemingly mundane realm of physical sustenance. Given the disputed nature of their political imprisonment, food often became a central focus in articulating status for prisoners attempting to utilize and bypass rules and regulations in order to reveal their ongoing, everyday resistance (see Feldman 1991; McAtackney, forthcoming). Food gained this role because it was one of the few essentials that the prisoners needed to survive, but they had to rely on the prison authorities to supply or facilitate access to it. Throughout this period of imprisonment battles over food included contestation regarding its quality and quantity, the provision of suitable crockery and cutlery, the timing of meals, and often the recourse to hunger strike—the self-denial of food for political reasons—which swiftly became the ultimate weapon utilized to protest related and wider issues.

Every autograph book in the Kilmainham Gaol Archive collection holds accounts of the poor quality of the food, and they are often prominently and elaborately detailed. In the autograph book of Brigid Reed: "I hope you will never forget your Holiday in the NDU in the year 1923 when you got boot leather for your dinner and green bulletts [sic] for Potatoes" (KMGLM 2010.0130). Another, more unusual form of entry found in the autograph book of Mary Twamley was a de facto diary detailing the ongoing negotiations of the minutiae of food delivery, quantity, and quality. Alongside information on the exact form and quantity of food, the lack of access to knives became the focus of protests: "Q.M. asks for knife for cutting bread and Seargeant Conlon refuse same. With result that all left Dining Hall and left Dinner there. Ultimatium sent gov that no one would pass gate until knives were given and that everything was settled" (KMGLM 2010.0133). Knives are represented in graffiti (see figure 3.3) where they are located in a number of locations throughout West Wing of Kilmainham clearly traced around rather than a freehand representation. Perhaps these "knives" were being used to taunt the guards, the women victorious in secreting and removing this prohibited utensil from the dining room?

There were a variety of acts of defiance that the women used to communally perform resistance to imprisonment, including the construction of an "escape" tunnel in the basement of the West Wing during 1923, which Margaret Buckley (1938) notes in her autobiography acted as a form of political action defying imprisonment rather than being a real attempt to escape from the prison. However, the use of graffiti to accuse and shame the Free State forces is probably one of the most frequent and telling acts. The huge assemblage of civil war graffiti in the West Wing of Kilmainham Gaol provides a window into many of the experiences of the women. Much of this graffiti follows a template of imprinting or writing names, addresses, and supportive slogans, but there are also a number of examples that directly challenge the authorities who oversee their imprisonment. This includes a number of caricatures of prison staff—often grotesques—and anti–Free State verses such as: "May the harp of olde Ireland / Never want for a string / While there's a gut / In the F[ree] S[tate] Army." These examples are written boldly, located at eye level, and they are in public areas, especially corridors, rather than hidden in the recesses of dark cells. One of the most famous pieces of graffiti is located above a doorway leading to the "1916 corridor" of holding cells of many men who were executed in the aftermath of the Easter Rising (see figure 3.4). It is an edited quotation from the poem "The Rebel," which was written by one of the leaders of the rising, Patrick Pearse: "Beware of the risen people / that have harried and held / Ye that have bullied and bribed."

This slogan is often interpreted in its 1916 context as being anti-British. However, I argue that it was intended to directly challenge the nationalist credentials of the Free State. Its careful editing to bypass lines enumerating the actions of

FIGURE 3.4 Graffiti (paint over whitewash) located above the doorway entering the so-called 1916 corridor on the middle floor of the West Wing of Kilmainham Gaol: "Beware of the risen people / that have harried and held / Ye that have bullied and bribed." (Photo by author, August 2013)

"The Rebel," including "Who shall take what you will not give," to focus instead on the conduct of the unnamed adversary redirect the meaning of the poem to condemn their contemporary imprisoners, not the now-departed British. In this way, the women articulated their claim as champions, and inheritors, of those ideals.

CONCLUSION

The contemporary decade of commemorations in Ireland has already witnessed the Irish state focusing on the triumph of nationalists in establishing their own state in the early decades of the twentieth century. The narratives used to explore this transition often focus on the "big men" and the more comfortable togetherness of the Easter Rising and War of Independence. The civil war is still considered too difficult and divisive to publicly commemorate. Women's increasingly important roles throughout this period—reaching their pinnacle during the civil war—suffer the greatest neglect in not only being communally forgotten but because the multitude of lived experiences of political imprisonment are discarded or bypassed.

Through using the underutilized resources of autograph books, memoirs, and graffiti it is clear that more nuanced and detailed narratives relating to gendered aspects of imprisonment can be located. In particular, these sources begin to fill the void of silence regarding the use of intimidation and the latent threat of physical and sexual violence by the prison forces, often after nightfall and in association with the rampaging of drunken, armed men that sometimes resulted in physical and sexual violence. The transgressing of traditional gender boundaries, which occurred at this time, allowed the women to take on the role of public activists but also resulted in their becoming conceived as legitimate targets in the minds of the Free State leaders. However, it should be remembered that the women continually used their agency to articulate their political status and the rightness of their cause. In providing this short overview of state-perpetrated violence against women, and their actions and reactions to the brutality associated with their imprisonment, we can begin to reveal a richer picture of revolutionary Ireland. This highlights not only of the realities of a "war against women" but their agency in actively resisting and articulating their political status.

REFERENCES

Aretxaga, Begoña. 1997. *Shattering Silence: Women, Nationalism, and Political Subjectivity in Northern Ireland.* Princeton: Princeton University Press.

Beiner, Guy. 2005. "Ireland Ireland: Theme-Parks and Histories Revisited." In *Ireland's Heritages: Critical Perspectives on Memory and Identity,* edited by Mark McCarthy. Aldershot, UK: Ashgate.

Brophy, Brigid. 1923. Autograph book. KMGLM 2010.0129. Collection of Kilmainham Gaol Archive.

Bryan, Dominic, and Neil Jarman. 1997. "Parading Tradition, Protesting Triumphalism: Utilising Anthropology in Public Policy." In *Culture and Policy in Northern Ireland: Anthropology in the Public Arena,* edited by Hastings Donnan and Graham McFarlane. Belfast, Northern Ireland: Institute of Irish Studies.

Buckley, Margaret. 1938. *The Jangle of the Key.* Dublin: J. Duffy & Co.

DMP (Dublin Metropolitan Police) Reports. 1923. Oscar Traynor Collection, Bureau of Military History CD 120/1–4. *Daily Herald,* Letters, May 7.

Dolan, Anne. 2006. *Commemorating the Irish Civil War: History and Memory 1923–2000.* Cambridge: Cambridge University Press.

Feldman, Allen. 1991. *Formations of Violence: The Narrative of the Body and Political Terror in Northern Ireland.* London: University of Chicago Press.

Foster, Roy. 2014. *Vivid Faces: The Revolutionary Generation in Ireland, 1890–1923.* London: Allen Lane.

Herzog, Hanna, and Rita Shapiro. 1986. "'Will You Sign My Autograph Book?': Using Autograph Books for a Sociohistorical Study of Youth and Social Frameworks." *Quantitative Sociology* 9 (2): 109–125.

Labour Party. 1921. *Report of the Labour Commission to Ireland.* London: Caledonian Press.

Matthews, Ann. 2010. *Renegades: Irish Republican Women, 1900–1922*. Dublin: Mercier Press.

———. 2012. *Dissidents: Irish Republican Women, 1923–1941*. Dublin: Mercier Press.

McAtackney, Laura. Forthcoming. "Prison-Issue Artefacts, Documentary Insights, and the Negotiated Realities of Political Imprisonment: The Case of Long Kesh/Maze, Northern Ireland." In *Relationships between Text and Practice: Dissecting Rules and Regulations*. Oxford: Oxford University Press.

McCoole, Sinead. 1997. *Guns and Chiffon*. Dublin: Stationery Office Books.

———. 2003. *No Ordinary Women: Irish Female Activists in the Revolutionary Years (1900–1923)*. Madison: University of Wisconsin Press.

———. 2014. *Easter Widows: Seven Irish Women Who Lived in the Shadow of the 1916 Rising*. Dublin: Doubleday Press.

Ó'Gráda, Cormac. 2001. "Famine, Trauma, and Memory." *Béaloideas* 69: 121–143.

Oliver, Jeff, and Tim Neal. 2010. *Wild Sign: Graffiti in Archaeology and History*. Oxford: Archaeopress.

O'Sullivan, Niamh. 2009. *Written in Stone: The Graffiti in Kilmainham Jail*. Dublin: Liberties Press.

Reed, Brigid. 1923. Autograph book. KMGLM 2010.0130. Collection of Kilmainham Gaol Archive.

Reid, Byronie. 2005. "'A Profound Edge': Performative Negotiations of Belfast." *Cultural Geographies* 12: 485–506.

Ryan, Louise. 1995. "Traditions and Double Moral Standard: The Irish Suffragists' Critique of Nationalism." *Women's History Review* 4 (4): 487–503.

———. 2001. *Gender, Identity, and the Irish Press*. Lewiston, NY: Edwin Mellen Press.

Ryan, Louise, and Margaret Ward. 2004. *Irish Women and Nationalism: Soldiers, New Women, and Wicked Hags*. Dublin: Irish Academic Press.

Ryan, Susan. Autograph book (photocopy). 20 MS ID46 08. Collection of Kilmainham Gaol Archive.

Twamley, Mary. Autograph book. KMGLM 2010.0133. Collection of Kilmainham Gaol Archive.

Ward, Margaret. 1995. *Unmanageable Revolutionaries: Women and Irish Nationalism*. Dublin: Pluto Press.

4 · RESISTANCE AND ACTIVISM AGAINST STATE VIOLENCE IN CHIAPAS, MEXICO

MELANIE HOEWER

Different oppressions determine the life of men and women in Chiapas and inform various social mobilization processes in the Chiapas region of Mexico. The region gained global fame with the uprising of the Zapatista National Liberation Army (EZLN, Ejército Zapatista de Liberación Nacional) on January 1, 1994. This uprising brought to light a new definition of "being indigenous" in Mexico, by questioning the homogenizing incentive of the *mestiza* founding myth and revealing deeply entrenched interconnected inequalities and dimensions of violence (Gutiérrez 1995). Women's organization within the community and their active involvement in the various struggles against state-perpetrated violence brought a gender dimension to the protest agenda of the Zapatistas (Hernández Castillo 2002, 2006; Millán Moncayo 2002a, 2002b; Speed 2006, 2008, 2014; Stephen 2002).

Feminist research has criticized state-centered references to violence (Tripp, Marx Ferree, and Ewig 2013). Discussions of violence in armed conflict contexts are often limited to focusing on state violence as direct military violence by the state's security forces (Jacobs, Jacobson, and Marchbank 2000). By addressing those limitations, feminist researchers have explored the patriarchal nature of state violence (Enloe 2000) and the gendered effects of masculinity, heterosexism, and militarism on state violence (Peterson and Runyan 1993). The feminist slogan "the personal is political" highlights the link between personal experiences of violence and power relations within the state that condition these experiences. A gendered approach to armed conflict and state violence focuses on the different linkages between various forms or dimensions of violence, primarily emphasizing the interconnectedness between the public and the private dimensions of gender violence. Hence, understanding the importance of resistance and activism in women's participation in the armed conflict in Chiapas requires an exploration of the interrelationship of violence at all levels of society; the connections among macro, meso, and micro dimensions of violence; the power relations that inform violence; and the ways that responses to violence relate to inequality (Tripp, Marx Ferree, and Ewig 2013). Rather than regarding the state as neutral, we need to look at the state in gendered terms as privileging power over certain groups. Gender relations are a primary way of signifying power relationships. Patriarchy or culturally institutionalized masculinized hierarchical power relations express themselves through the state, in resistance movements (Enloe 2005; Walby 1990), and in both the private and public spheres. State violence is both gendered and gendering; gender and power relations are constituted and reconstituted through violence (Butler 1994; Shepherd 2008). Gender-related violence and oppression and other forms of abuse and inequality based on ethnic, class, age, and sexual orientation demarcations are buried within the state, and gender relations are at the same time constituted through the state. Concomitantly, the state reflects and informs gender relations and gender violence through the legal and public discourses that emanate from it (Waylen 1996). A gendered perspective on state violence encompasses the physical, social, economic, and sexual aspects of violence. In this framework of analysis, this chapter explores the intersection of different dimensions of violence and oppression that inform the social mobilizations of women in Chiapas. More precisely, the analysis reveals the connection between public violence perpetrated by the state, both of a military and structural nature; violent community structures grounded in patriarchy; and private violence experienced in the family and by intimate partners. It argues that the way indigenous women experience different dimensions of violence is reflected in their social mobilizations and highlights the various positioning and perceptions of women in society. Resistance encompasses the potential for subversion and contestation of established orders (Kandiyoti 1997) that inform the multifaceted dimensions of violence. Different resistances to different dimensions of violence are often parts of armed conflicts, as it becomes evident in Chiapas (Hoewer 2014b; Kampwirth 2004).

EZLN commander Esther famously claimed, while addressing the Mexican parliament in March 2001, that indigenous women are triply oppressed: as indigenous people, as poor people, and as women. Cultural and social violence against indigenous people is deeply entrenched in Chiapas; oppressive colonial policies became embedded in the social structure and formed a part of nation-building after the Mexican War of Independence (1810–1821).[1] Patterns of clientelistic control, introduced during the conquest and the creation of an independent Mexican state, became institutionalized after the Mexican Revolution (1910–1917); it led to the positioning of both indigenous people and women at the margins of society (Gutierrez 2001, 3; Tello Díaz 1995).[2] The state-perpetrated structural violence against indigenous people continues to be an underlying trend in current Mexican modernization and neoliberal state policies. Structural and direct, armed violence conflate in the state's reaction to peasant farmers and the Zapatista mobilizations.

This chapter retraces how women from diverse backgrounds interconnect different dimensions of violence (global, national, and local) in their protest during the farmers' movements (1960s–early 1970s), the Zapatista movement (1983–1995), and women's rights mobilizations (1970s–1995). Based on empirical data gathered in field studies in 2010 in Chiapas, I conducted and translated sixteen semistructured interviews and two focus group discussions, varying from one hour to two-day events over a period of four months in San Cristóbal de las Casas, Ocosingo, and the Selva region with twenty indigenous and fifteen non-indigenous women who have been active in one or more of those mobilization processes. Initial contacts with some of those female activists were established during my previous work in the two regions; I used the snowballing method in order to increase the sample. The sample choice was informed by time and resource constraints. It includes only female activists, although their experiences of conflict and peace cannot be seen in isolation from men's experiences and indeed from the experiences of other women who did not become actively involved.

The theory is introduced in the first part of this chapter, followed by an analysis of the effect of women's collective identity narratives on their involvement in resistance and different social mobilizations against the state and violence in Chiapas, and the meaning this involvement had for them. Looking at women's motivations and the aims of their activism highlights distinctions in the way female activists interrelate state violence with the gender violence they experience in their communities and in their private lives.

ADDRESSING COMPLEXITIES AND DIFFERENCE

Feminist scholars highlight the gendered nature of state violence (Blanchard 2014) and the power relations that inform domestic, community, and state violence, in particular the way experiences and responses of violence are connected to socioeconomic, political, and gender inequalities (Shepherd 2008; Tickner 1992). Social location, including but not limited to positions within patriarchal systems of stratification, shapes violence and victimization in many different ways (Creek and Dunn 2011). Violence is perpetrated both against individuals and against men and women or indigenous peoples as a group; thus agency has both an individual and a collective dimension (Tripp 2013, 6–7). Women are targets of and respondents to violence and therefore act both individually and as a collective. Hence, the analysis of female activists' mobilizations against different forms of violence in Chiapas requires a deconstruction of the categories "women" and "indigenous."

Any attempt to essentialize ethnicity, gender, age, sexuality, or working classness as specific forms of concrete violence inevitably creates narratives and categories that reflect hegemonic discourses of identity politics, obscures the experiences of the members at the margins of the specific group, and constructs a homogenized "right way" of group belonging (Hernández Castillo 1997, 2005; Olivera 2005; Yuval Davis 2006, 195). Therefore, an analysis of women's experiences of violence and mobilizations against violence requires taking into account the complexity within the category "women." Indigenous women have addressed the domestic abuse, social discrimination, and state violence they face as both women and indigenous people—asserting their individual and collective rights (Speed, Hernández Castillo, and Stephen 2006). The difference in the category "women" becomes evident in the way women address those intersecting dimensions of violence in different social mobilizations in Chiapas (farmers', Zapatista, and women's mobilizations).

In contrast to nonindigenous activists, Mayan women activists often make use of strategic essentialism in the way they embrace the ideal of gender complementarity even while acknowledging current gender inequalities (Garza 2000; Hernández Castillo 2005, 2006). A cultural politics of celebrating gender difference along with a Mayan spirituality and worldview allows female indigenous activists to hold their male counterparts to a higher standard and positions women as cultural standard bearers. Further, indigenous women are often essentialized as "indigenous" in activism and in academic analysis, which lack acknowledgment of the diversity of the region's indigenous peoples (Eber and Kovic 2003; Stephen 2002).

Multiple forms of exposure to violence characterize the development of society in Chiapas, which is intertwined with the oppression of indigenous people in Mexico, a result of the Spanish conquest (Harvey 1998, 36). The historic project of subject-making by the Mexican state is based on the official racial state discourse of *mestizaje*, a project of assimilation that celebrates the indigenous past while denying an indigenous present (Blackwell 2011). This cultural structure provides historical meaning and social cohesion to modern Mexico (Gutiérrez 2001, 3) and is central to understanding the connection between state violence and violence in the community and in the family; it provides an ethnic and gender narrative that positions both indigenous people and women at the margins of society. Indigenous women have been particularly affected by existing intersecting dimensions of violence; they are exposed to violence perpetrated by the Mexican state and paramilitaries, as well as to patriarchal community traditions and domestic violence (Garza Caligaris 2000; Rovira 1997; Tello Díaz 1995).

The female activists' collective identity narratives (Ashmore, Deaux, and McLaughlin-Volpe 2004) reveal motivations, strategies, and the complexity of social mobilization, resistance, and activism as a response to state-perpetrated violence, patriarchy, hierarchical power and gender relations, and domestic violence, and the impact on women's everyday lives in Chiapas. The following section explores the ways women connect their traumatization and victimization to their activism in a multilevel analysis that identifies central themes and distinctions in the narratives.

GENDERING EXPERIENCES OF AND RESPONSES TO STATE VIOLENCE

Ana,[3] a Tseltal female activist from Selva region of Chiapas, reveals: "Violence has always been part of our life. There is the state military that threatens our community; the state also keeps us poor. But there is also the violence I have experienced in my community and in my family. Women have to work so hard, but own no land and get beaten in their homes. But, life has changed for me. I could not take the violence at home anymore and started to organize. My activism has allowed me to see my own life differently; I feel strong enough to talk to my partner about the violence, make him understand that it's not good."[4] Ana took part in a two-day active participative workshop with thirteen indigenous (Tseltal) and two mestiza women in Ocosingo, Chiapas. The workshop was organized in collaboration with local human rights, peace, and women's organizations with activists from those organizations. The participants were directly involved in the design of the event; this allowed the creation of a safe and inclusive space in which the participants could freely speak to me and to each other about their experiences of peace and conflict in Chiapas. In the workshop we focused on visual and oral methods such as art work and the theater of the oppressed (Boal 1979). Both the art work (a mapping exercise) and the development of theater plays were based on facilitated storytelling sessions; they were followed by discussions of both process and outcome (visual maps and theater plays).

Many female activists (thirteen of fifteen in the workshop) like Ana highlighted the many conflicts of women in indigenous communities in Chiapas. They interconnected the armed conflict between the Mexican security forces and the EZLN with the violence they experience in their homes, placing a particular emphasis on the latter as a motivator for becoming actively involved in different social mobilization processes (farmers' organizations, Zapatista movement, women's groups). All workshop participants (fifteen of fifteen) underlined the significance of women organizing in order to address violence in the private sphere; however, while for some (four of fifteen) the struggle against gender violence was the beginning of their activism, for others this dimension of activism entered their activism pathway only at a later stage. Of the latter group (eleven of fifteen), some were mobilized in the context of farmers' organizations (seven of eleven), while others became active as part of the Zapatista mobilization process (four of eleven).

References to violence are a central element in all narratives of female indigenous activists, emphasizing the physical military and domestic violence and the inequalities they experience as indigenous people, as poor people, and as women. Female activists' references to violence connect experiences of different dimensions of direct violence to those of structural, rights-based violations such as racial discrimination and marginalization, lack of freedom, lack of access to healthcare and education, the freedom to choose their own husbands and partners, and control over the number of children they would have.

Some activists' reflections on violence (seven of thirty-five women interviewed overall) referred to the *finca* (rural estate or plantation) system in Chiapas, which was both an economic system of land cultivation and a system of domination; it led to the colonization of mostly indigenous peasants in the period after the independence of Mexico from Spain in 1823 (Leyva Solano and Ascencio Franco 2002, 58). The finca system was supported by the state and created a structure of "obedience, fear, and oppression" in Chiapas.[5] Women were particularly affected by this system (Garza Caligaris 2000; Tello Díaz 1995). Female activists (eight of thirty-five) emphasized that indigenous women were obliged to have sexual intercourse with the owners of the fincas the night before their wedding, a rule that formed part of the marriage ritual and was practiced until the 1970s; they were further exposed to sexual abuse while working in the kitchens of the finca and also suffered domestic violence in the home as a result of unequal community structures and their husbands' alcohol abuse; many indigenous men turned to alcohol in order to reassert their masculinity and male honor. The culture of the finca system entailed not only the exploitation of, and ethnic discrimination against, indigenous peoples, but also the institutionalized sexual abuse of indigenous women (Olivera Bustamante 2005, 184).[6]

Horizontal inequality in Chiapas has historical roots; the indigenous population was dominated by a system of colonial rules, which changed in the nineteenth century into a system determined by an ethno-social class of "neo-colonialists" (Olivera Bustamante 2004, 73; Piel 2005). A small minority of local, national, and international *"ladinos"* acquired the great majority of land, which originally belonged to the indigenous population.[7] This development changed the role of indigenous people from small farmer to slave or servant of finqueros[8] (Rus 1983). The coffee plantations—*fincas*—in the Soconusco region, created under the presidency of Porfirio Díaz (1867–1911), lasted until the 1970s and provide important evidence of this development.

In the light of the existing inequalities, indigenous women's image of the state is predominantly determined by feelings of absence, ignorance, and violence.

"We are Mexicans, but are excluded by the state. It [the state] does not respect us and the military often harasses our community," asserts María, reflecting on her relationship to the state as an indigenous woman.[9] Most indigenous female activists (twenty of twenty-seven) perceive the state as being responsible for the poverty of indigenous people and as oppressing indigenous people either directly or indirectly by supporting other oppressors, for instance, the finqueros in the 1970s or the transnational companies in the 1980s and 1990s.

FARMERS' MOBILIZATIONS (1960S TO EARLY 1970S)

Women formed a significant part of the different farmers' mobilizations, which took place in Chiapas in the 1970s; the claim to "land and freedom"[10] was at the center of these violent protests of the indigenous and mestizo farmers against the finqueros and against the state as a protector of the repressive finca system (Tello Díaz 1995; Villafuerte Solís et al. 2002).

Antonia comes from a Tsotsil community and first became involved in a farmers' organization during the struggle for land in the early 1970s. She remembers that she was about thirteen years of age when the fight for land began: "Initially, my involvement was 'desde la casa' (from the house) by providing food and shelter for the male fighters. It was important, because I was listening and learning a lot about politics and injustice. When we prepared food in the kitchen, mestiza women [who supported the farmers' movements] began to talk to me and asked me about my life. I slowly became aware that there is something not right with how women live in my community."[11] This initial contact with mestiza women was significant for Antonia and for many other indigenous women (seventeen of twenty-seven): first, this collaboration created a space for reflection on their lives; and second, it contributed to the development of a deeper understanding of the connection between the gender violence women experience as members of their indigenous communities and in their families.

While indigenous women provided essential support to the 1970s mobilizations through food and shelter, they were not yet "making their voices as women heard within the struggle." However, the social mobilizations of indigenous landless peasants and farmers in the 1970s opened a space for alliance building between indigenous and mestiza women (Kampwirth 2004, 8–9; Millán Moncayo 2006, 77–78). Those collaborations are important stepping-stones for rural women, especially for indigenous women's active involvement in social mobilization processes, and for the development of different social mobilizations on women's issues.

In contrast to indigenous women, most mestiza female activists (eleven of fifteen) highlight in their narratives their commitment to social justice and their support for indigenous and poor women as central motivators for their activism.

A smaller part of the mestiza sample (four of fifteen) highlight direct experiences of poverty and sexual violence in their intimate partnerships as reasons for getting actively involved in the various struggles and activist groups.

Many mestiza women (ten of fifteen) initially became involved in urban social mobilization processes; some began their activism as part of the struggle for socialism (four of ten). Other female mestiza activists (six of fifteen) first joined groups or organizations promoting the principles of liberation theology, in particular the empowerment of the poor. All mestiza activists from an urban background (ten of ten) report that they perceived themselves as part of a wider women's movement and had a strong focus on highlighting sexual and gender-based violence. Mobilizations on sexual and gender-based violence evolving in Mexico in the 1970s were often connected to the student mobilization of 1968, which expressed discontent with the authoritarian Mexican state (Ortiz-Ortega and Barquet 2010). Activism within the student or the farmers' movements not only raised awareness about the repressive nature of Mexican politics but was also a catalyst for growing awareness of discrimination against indigenous people in Mexico (Harvey 1994, 27; Kovic 2013).

One distinguishing feature between female activists is the way they experienced state violence; most indigenous and rural mestiza respondents (twenty of thirty-one) experienced state violence directly as part of a farmers' organization in the 1970s. However, while indigenous women correlate experiences of poverty and racial discrimination in their narratives, mestiza women from a rural background emphasize poverty. Many mestiza activists from an urban background (seven of fifteen) perceived themselves as part of farmers' mobilizations, but drew a boundary between themselves and the indigenous women involved in the farmers' mobilizations by highlighting their supportive role and their lack of direct experience of racial discrimination.

A second distinction emphasized by research participants is the significance of women's issues, in particular sexual and gender-based violence, to their active participation and involvement. All interviewees mentioned women's issues and concerns as integral to their activism. However, only for mestiza activists were women's issues part of their activist agenda during the farmers' mobilizations of the 1970s. Most activists from indigenous communities (nineteen of twenty-seven) report that while they became more aware about women's issues and the gendered experiences and effects of violence on women during the 1970s, they only began to incorporate these concerns into their activist agendas at a later stage.

Third, female activists can be distinguished based on their educational level at the beginning of their mobilization and resistance. Many mestiza activists from an urban background (eleven of fifteen) have a university degree; they became involved in various social mobilization processes during or shortly after completing their studies. Of the indigenous women that took part in this study, only about 20 percent had university degrees and all of them acquired them after they became part of social movements; within the small sample of rural mestiza activists, only one out of four research participants has a university degree, which was obtained, like her indigenous peers, after becoming actively involved in farmers' and women's rights activism.

The collaboration between mestiza and indigenous women evolving from the 1970s mobilizations was a stepping-stone for the politicization of indigenous women and for their organization against the violence they are exposed to in their private lives and outside the community. The involvement of indigenous women in the farmers' organizations in the 1970s began as a response to a necessity: providing food and shelter for other activists. However, once indigenous women became politicized and mobilized, their pragmatic participation changed to a multifaceted activism that linked the fight for land, indigenous rights, and against state violence to the fight for women's rights and against domestic violence. Many women who were active in the farmers' movement describe their support of (fifteen of twenty-seven) or active participation in (fourteen of twenty-seven) the Zapatista movement as a natural progression to their activism.

THE ZAPATISTA MOBILIZATION (1983–1995)

In the 1980s, the modernization process of the Mexican state encouraged a shift from a leftist socialist agenda to an opening of indigenous protest agendas in Chiapas against Mexico's neoliberal development. Neoliberal state policies promoting private land ownership have undermined the strength and culture of indigenous communities, in particular, the traditional cooperative land ownership structure, the *ejido* system (Villafuerte Solís et al. 2002). This provided fertile ground for the Zapatista mobilization that began in 1983. It contests the neoliberal modernization policies of the Mexican state including the country's involvement in international free trade agreements, especially the North Atlantic Free Trade Agreement, or NAFTA (Mattiace 2003). The Zapatista mobilization in the 1980s connected the fight against state violence and for indigenous peoples' rights to the struggle of indigenous women to end domestic violence and to promote shared responsibilities and duties between men and women in their community, in the movement, and in their families.

In this framework of analysis, Antonia, an indigenous women's rights and Zapatista activist, states: "I had the feeling that things were not right for women before I joined the Zapatista movement, but I accepted the violent traditions back then as just how things were. By joining the EZLN, I began together with other indigenous women to divide the traditions I liked from those I saw as violent."[12]

Many female indigenous activists (fourteen of twenty-seven), like Antonia, joined the Zapatista movement in the 1980s to escape violent community traditions or to fight for indigenous peoples' rights—for instance, to collectively own and cultivate the land. However, all Zapatista activists (fourteen of fourteen) remark that their fight against state violence, for land, and for indigenous rights was connected to their demand for a voice for women, to end traditions that justify violence against women, and the imbalance of men's and women's voices, roles, and responsibilities in the community, in the organization, and in the home.

Carmen, an indigenous Zapatista and women's rights activist, stresses her "anger and frustration" when reflecting on her life before she became directly involved in the Zapatista movement and a women's activist group. She continues: "How I lived before [being an activist]? Well, I was sold into marriage as a very young girl. What does that tell you about my life? Well, a lot of sadness and not much joy. . . . My life was worth less than that of an animal."[13] Carmen first became involved in the Zapatista movement in the early 1980s; she stresses that "becoming part of the Zapatista movement was really important as it brought changes to the relationship with my husband. After becoming a Zapatista, my husband supported me leaving the home. I experienced my home, first that of my parents, then that of my husband like a prison since I was a child. Now I was allowed to leave the house and work as part of the movement with other women." Carmen subsequently became involved in the Diocesan Coordination of Women, a network of women's groups set up by religious women of the Catholic dioceses of San Cristóbal de las Casas to reflect on the Bible from a women's perspective. Through her work in this women's group, Carmen "learned . . . to understand that state violence is connected to the violence [she] experienced as a woman." Being Zapatista and part of the Diocesan Coordination of Women brought her an increase in knowledge, self-confidence, and pride for being an indigenous woman.[14]

Anger and the feeling of being constrained by their life circumstances are emotions most indigenous women (twenty-five of twenty-seven) express when referring to their life before mobilization; like Carmen, they interrelate their experiences of state-perpetrated violence with patriarchal and domestic violence and abuse perpetrated at home by their partners. This multilayered experience of insecurity, aggression, violence, and conflict based on ethnic, class, and gender demarcations causes indigenous women to distinguish themselves from both male members of their communities and from mestiza women. All of the mestiza women highlight sexual and gender-based violence as a central aspect of their activism (fifteen of fifteen); rural mestizas also connect poverty to their sexual and gendered victimization (three of four). However, the interplay and interconnectedness of gender, race, class, and ethnicity to gender-based violence clearly distinguishes the experiences and the resulting activism of the indigenous women from that of mestizas.

Indigenous women stress this difference in their references to the Revolutionary Women's Law. Published in 1993, the Women's Law was the "first uprising of the EZLN" and demonstrates a shift in emphasis from the ethnic to the gender boundary. The Women's Law represents the different levels of normative rights of women, from the right to political participation and the inclusion of women in political decision making within the movement and in their communities, to the right to decide over their own bodies (Millán Moncayo 2002a, 204). Furthermore, the Women's Law contributes an internal gender dimension of protest to the Zapatista mobilization process (Millán Moncayo 2006; Speed 2008, 2014).

On this ground, Marga, an indigenous Zapatista and women's rights activist, states: "The consultation process, which resulted in the 'Women's Law,' was the first time indigenous women were expressing 'in public' what they want and what they don't want and all that. That the woman is also free, that she has the right not be beaten, that she has the right to know things and be part of the political decision-making process in her own community. I want to be respected for being indigenous and for being a woman."[15] This quote brings to light the way in which the community and private dimension of violence became part of the public fight of the Zapatista movement against the Mexican state. It illustrates how indigenous women's activism has come full circle from addressing state violence against indigenous communities to addressing the violence they experience as women as part of those communities. By doing so, the Revolutionary Women's Law has institutionalized the transformation of gendered images into social practice within the Zapatista movement (Speed et al. 2006).

Indigenous women resisting soldiers and attacking them by using their bodies as weapons became a famous image of the Zapatista revolt, which shows masked female Zapatista activists raising their fists and pushing against armed soldiers of the Mexican army (Huffschmid 2004; Speed 2008, 2014; Speed et al. 2006). Female activists' narratives highlight a central aspect of the Zapatista mobilization—the increasing visibility of indigenous women, in particular the way female indigenous fighters express their pride in being indigenous and in being a woman in their appearance. While male indigenous fighters' identities disappear behind their military uniforms, female military activists highlight their ethnic and gender identity, for instance by wearing traditional hair ribbons. The public appearance of female Zapatista commanders has real and symbolic meanings for indigenous women; it challenges the image of the oppressed Indian woman by creating agency and space for voicing indigenous women's gender-specific interests. The appearance of female indigenous Zapatista fighters, in particular leadership figures like Commander Ramona or Commander Esther, expresses indigenous women's transformation from silenced victims to survivors and activists (Hoewer 2013, 2014a, 2014b; Millán Moncayo 2008).

The way female activists perceive and position themselves within the various social mobilization processes reflects the multifaceted dimensions of public and private violence. Not only reform but also radical transformation is the basis of the demands of female indigenous Zapatista activists to address the interconnectivity of different dimensions of violence they experience: "Being a Zapatista woman means to me not only to address violence against women and the lack of women's participation in indigenous communities, but to see this as part of wider state violence. Creating autonomous communities is important in order to change the violent state structures that oppress me as indigenous and as a woman."[16]

In the Zapatista movement, as in other contemporary indigenous movements in Latin America, indigenous people have organized through identity politics, emphasizing their differences from the dominant white/mestizo culture that surrounds them (Postero 2007; Seider 2002; Speed 2008; Van Cott 2008). The ways in which indigenous communities "demand the right to maintain an alternative structure of power" do not evolve from some "indigenous cosmovision," but rather are to be found in indigenous practices of collective and consensual decision making, the concept of "rule-obeying," and the assertion of pluriculturality or diversity within the collective (Speed 2008). Women's voices and experiences of violence have informed the collective decision making, which is evident in the inclusion of the demands of the "Revolutionary Women's Law" into the decision-making mechanisms of the autonomous Zapatista communities.

The multidimensional reference to violence (state, community, intimate partnerships) in the Zapatista mobilization process provides evidence for a change in gender roles within both the EZLN and Zapatista communities (Speed et al. 2006; Stephen 2002).[17] The Mexican government officially tolerates the institutionalization of an autonomous government structure of the Zapatista movement at the community level (Burguete Cal y Mayor 2005; Leyva Solano 2005; Rus et al. 2003). At the same time, indigenous people are at risk of being attacked by state-sponsored paramilitaries and experience occasional harassment by security forces.[18] Women play an important role in the Zapatista autonomous structure by being increasingly represented in community leadership, and by being vocal in connecting the need to change direct and indirect state violence to the need to change patriarchal structures and traditions that support violence against women (K'inal Antzetik 1995; Millán Moncayo 2008). Indigenous women in Zapatista communities assert autonomy by "refusing to grant the state the power to decide who are rights bearers and what rights they may enjoy"; by doing so they are articulating "a radically distinct discourse of rights" (Speed 2008, 167).

Mestiza and indigenous women occupy different spaces of participation, and the construction of their subjectivities is problematized by their experiences of violence and oppression. Many mestiza women became mobilized because of women's issues, while for most indigenous women the socioeconomic and cultural rights of their community were initially the focal point of their mobilization. The distinction between indigenous and mestiza activists reveals the multidimensional nature of violence connected to multiple unequal power structures in Mexico that are entangled with the question of ethnic, class, and gendered identity.

Despite their differences, the creation of alliances between indigenous women from different ethnic groups within the various farmers' mobilizations and in the Zapatista movement, and between indigenous and mestiza activists, was central to women's active participation in the various mobilization processes. Alliance building between female activists was facilitated by connecting the public and the private dimensions of violence: state-perpetrated violence in forms that are both direct (armed) and indirect (inequality), and the sexual and gender-based violence women experience in their families and private partnerships. Concomitantly, the way women experience and address the multifaceted nature of gender and state violence, oppression, and marginalization is closely connected to their social, gendered, ethnic positions (as woman, poor people, indigenous/mestiza) within their families, communities, and within the Mexican state as a whole.

CONCLUSION

Based on data from a qualitative, active-participative research project, this chapter has revealed the complexities in the experience of and response to state and gender violence, as experienced by women from different ethnic/racial and social backgrounds in the Chiapas region of Mexico. It has done so by tracing women's diverse positioning, perceptions, and experiences of violence during distinct episodes of social mobilization in the region; for instance, the farmers' mobilizations of the 1970s and the Zapatista movement from 1983.

The chapter reveals the varied experiences of and responses to violence by women from diverse backgrounds by exploring their different positioning and perceptions of the various mobilization processes. While some female mestiza activists played central roles in the farmers' protests, the active participation of indigenous women was limited in this mobilization process. However, the farmers' mobilizations opened spaces for collaboration between indigenous and mestiza women and formed the basis for an evolving awareness and response to the different dimensions of violence indigenous women are exposed to (state, community, domestic). The subsequent Zapatista mobilization connected the public (land rights, indigenous rights, and indigenous autonomy) to the private dimension of violence (sexual and gender-based violence). This transition provided an incentive for further solidarity building and the collaboration of women on women's strategic gender interests across ethnic and class boundaries.

However, those activist spaces are populated by women from diverse ethnic and class backgrounds, and their positioning, motivations, and forms of activism varied depending on their particular experience of violence (military, social, economic, cultural, domestic) and on the contexts in which these processes are situated. Therefore, diverse activist goals and projects evolved within the various social mobilization processes in Chiapas, revealing ethnic and class differences and the multidimensionality of the violence that female activists endured.

Lastly, the chapter explored collaborations between some female activists during social mobilization processes, highlighting the distinctions in their activist work, which evolves from distinct experiences of violence. Women from indigenous communities connect their activism to their experiences of state-perpetrated violence, socioeconomic and cultural marginalization, and the oppressive gendered practices prevalent in their communities. This multifaceted experience of violence distinguished them from both female mestiza activists and from male members of their communities.

NOTES

1. For more information on the history of Chiapas, see Gilly 1998; Olivera and Palomo 2005.
2. Ideologically, the formation of Mexican society after independence has been focused on the mestizo founding myth, based on the assumption that all Mexicans are of common descent going back to the miscegenation of male Spanish conquerors and indigenous native females. See Gutiérrez 2001.
3. Names are pseudonyms to ensure respondents remain anonymous.
4. "Women and the Conflict in Chiapas" workshop, July 13–14, 2010, Ocosingo (Chiapas).
5. "Women and the Conflict in Chiapas" workshop, July 13–14, 2010, Ocosingo (Chiapas).
6. Young indigenous women were sent to the house of the *finquero*, where they were exploited not only in terms of the labor they provided, but the landowners also demanded sexual service, a tradition that was maintained until the early 1990s, and local caciques took advantage of it.
7. A process, facilitated by different legislation passed between 1826 and 1844, which permitted the local elites to claim title for what was previously indigenous people's land.
8. *Finqueros* is the commonly used term for the local elite of big landowners.
9. "Women and the Conflict in Chiapas" workshop, July 13–14, 2010, Ocosingo (Chiapas).
10. Farmers perceive access to land as their entitlement, a result of the Mexican Revolution and further institutionalized by President Lázaro Cárdenas.
11. Interview, July 3, 2010, San Cristóbal de las Casas.
12. Interview, July 3, 2010, San Cristóbal de las Casas.
13. Interview, June 28, 2010, San Cristóbal de las Casas.
14. Interview, June 28, 2010, San Cristóbal de las Casas.

15. Interview, July 17, 2010, San Cristóbal de las Casas.
16. "Women and the Conflict in Chiapas" workshop, Ocosingo (Chiapas), July 13–14, 2010.
17. The EZLN has over 30 percent women in their ranks, some of them in leadership positions at the highest level of the organization; see Kerkeling 2003, 148.
18. For more details, see Centro de Derechos Humanos Fray Bartolomé de Las Casas 2011.

REFERENCES

Ashmore, Richard D., Kay Deaux, and Tracy McLaughlin-Volpe. 2004. "An Organizing Framework for Collective Identity: Articulation and Significance of Multidimensionality." *Psychological Bulletin* 130 (1): 80–114.

Blackwell, Maylei. 2011. *¡Chicana Power! Contested Histories of Feminism in the Chicano Movement.* Austin: University of Texas Press.

———. 2012. "The Practice of Autonomy in the Age of Neoliberalism: Strategies from Indigenous Women's Organizing in Mexico." *Journal of Latin American Studies* 44: 703–732.

Blanchard, Eric M. 2014. "Gender, International Relations, and the Development of Feminist Security Theory." *Signs* 40 (1): 1289–1312.

Boal, Augusto. 1979. *Theatre of the Oppressed.* Translated by Charles A. McBride and Maria Odilia Leal McBride. New York: Theatre Communications Group.

Burguete Cal y Mayor, Araceli. 2005. "Una década de autonomías de facto en Chiapas (1994–2004): Los límites." In *Pueblos indígenas, estado y democracia*, edited by Pablo Dávalos. Buenos Aires: Consejo Latinoamericano de Ciencias Sociales.

Butler, Judith. 1994. "Contingent Foundations: Feminism and the Question of 'Postmodernism.'" In *The Postmodern Turn: New Perspectives on Social Theory*, edited by Steven Seidman. Cambridge: Cambridge University Press.

Centro de Derechos Humanos Fray Bartolomé de Las Casas. 2011. *Gobierno crea y administra conflictos para el control territorial en Chiapas. Informe especial.* San Cristobal de las Casas: Centro de Derechos Humanos Fray Bartolomé de Las Casas.

Cho, Sumi, Kimberlé Williams Crenshaw, and Leslie McCall. 2013. "Toward a Field of Intersectionality Studies: Theory, Applications, and Praxis." *Signs* 38 (4): 785–810.

Collins, Patricia Hill. 1990. *Black Feminist Thought: Knowledge, Consciousness, and the Politics of Empowerment.* Boston: Unwin Hyman.

Creek, S. J., and L. Jennifer Dunn. 2011. "Rethinking Gender and Violence: Agency, Heterogeneity, and Intersectionality." *Sociology Compass* 5: 311–322.

Crenshaw, Kimberlé Williams. 1991. "Mapping the Margins: Intersectionality, Identity Politics, and Violence against Women of Color." *Stanford Law Review* 43 (6): 1241–1299.

Eber, Christine, and Christine Kovic, eds. 2003. *Women of Chiapas: Making History in Times of Struggle and Hope.* New York: Routledge.

Ebert, L. Teresa. 1996. *Ludic Feminism and After: Postmodernism, Desire, and Labor in Late Capitalism.* Ann Arbor: University of Michigan Press.

Enloe, Cynthia. 2000. *Maneuvers: The International Politics of Militarizing Women's Lives.* Berkeley: University of California Press.

———. 2005. "What if Patriarchy Is 'the Big Picture'? An Afterword." In *Gender, Conflict, and Peacekeeping*, edited by Dyan Mazurana, Angela Raven-Roberts, and Jane Parpart. New York: Rowman & Littlefield.

Garza Caligaris, Ana María. 2000. "El movimiento de mujeres en Chiapas: Haciendo historia." *Anuario de Estudios Indígenas* 8. Tuxtla Gutiérrez, Chiapas: Instituto de Estudios Indigenas.

Gilly, Adolfo. 1998. "Chiapas and the Rebellion of the Enchanted World." In *Rural Revolt in Mexico: US Intervention and the Domain of Subaltern Politics*, edited by Daniel Nugent. Durham, NC: Duke University Press.

Gutierrez Chong, Natividad. 1995. "The Culture of the Nation: The Ethnic Past and Official Nationalism in 20th Century Mexico." PhD diss., London School of Economics and Political Science, University of London.

———. 2001. "Mitos nacionalistas e identidades étnicas." Plaza y Valdés, Mexico: Consejo Nacional para la Cultura y las Artes.

Hale, Charles R. 2001. "What Is Activist Research?" *Items and Issues: Social Science Research Council* 2 (1–2): 13–15.

Harvey, Neil. 1994. *Rebellion in Chiapas: Rural Reform, Campesino Radicalism, and the Limits to Salinismo.* San Diego: Center for U.S.-Mexican Studies, University of California at San Diego.

Hernández Castillo, Rosalva Aída. 1997. "Between Hope and Adversity: The Struggle of Organized Women in Chiapas since the Zapatista Uprising." *Journal of Latin American Anthropology* 3 (1): 102–120.

———. 2005. "Between Complementarity and Inequality: Indigenous *Cosmovision* as an Element of Resistance in the Struggle of Indigenous Women." Paper presented at the conference "Indigenous Struggles in the Americas and around the World," February 10–11, at York University, Toronto. Accessed December 15, 2011. http://www.ucgs.yorku.ca/indigenous%20conference/Aida_Hernandez.pdf.

———. 2006. "Between Feminist Ethnocentricity and Ethnic Essentialism: The Zapatistas' Demands and the National Indigenous Women's Movement." In *Dissident Women: Gender and Cultural Politics in Chiapas*, edited by Shannon Speed, R. Aída Hernández Castillo, and Lynn M. Stephen. Austin: University of Texas Press.

Hoewer, Melanie. 2013. "Women, Violence, and Social Change in Northern Ireland and Chiapas: Societies between Tradition and Transition." *International Journal of Conflict and Violence* 7 (2): 216–231.

———. 2014a. "Beyond the Ethno-national Divide: Intersecting Identity Transformations during Conflict." *Identities: Global Studies in Culture and Power* 21 (5): 448–465.

———. 2014b. *Crossing Boundaries during Peace and Conflict: Transforming Identity in Chiapas and in Northern Ireland.* New York: Palgrave Macmillan.

Huffschmid, Anne. 2004. *Diskursguerrilla: Waffenergreifung und Widersinn.* Heidelberg: Synchron Publishers.

Hunter, Rosemary. 1996. "Deconstruction of the Subjects of Feminism: The Essentialist Debate in Feminist Theory and Practice." *Australian Feminist Law Journal* 6: 135–162.

Jacobs, Susie, Ruth Jacobson, and Jennifer Marchbank, eds. 2000. *States of Conflict: Gender, Violence, and Resistance.* London: Zed Books.

Kampwirth, Karen. 2004. *Feminism and the Legacy of Revolution: Nicaragua, El Salvador, Chiapas.* Athens: Ohio University Press.

Kandiyoti, Deniz. 1997. "Gendering the Modern: On Missing Dimensions in the Study of Turkish Modernity." In *Rethinking Modernity and National Identity in Turkey*, edited by Sibel Bozdoğan and Reşat Kasaba. Seattle: University of Washington Press.

Kerkeling, Lutz. 2003. *La Lucha Sigue! EZLN—Ursachen und Entwicklungen des Zapatistischen Aufstands.* Münster: UNRAST.

K'inal Antzetik. 1995. *Mujeres indígenas de Chiapas: Nuestros derechos, costumbres y tradiciones.* San Cristóbal de las Casas, Chiapas: n.p.

Kovic, Christine. (2005) 2013. *Mayan Voices for Human Rights: Displaced Catholics in Highland Chiapas.* Austin: University of Texas Press.

Leigh, Darcy. 2009. "Colonialism, Gender, and the Family in North America: For a Gendered Analysis of Indigenous Struggles." *Studies in Ethnicity and Nationalism* 9 (1): 70–88.

Leyva Solano, Xochitl. 2005. "Indigenismo, indianismo y 'ciudadanía étnica' de cara a las redes neo-zapatistas." In *Pueblos indígenas, estado y democracia*, edited by Pablo Dávalos. Buenos Aires: Consejo Latinoamericano de Ciencias Sociales.

Leyva Solano, Xochitl, and Gabriel Ascencio Franco. 2002. *Lacandonia al filo del agua*. México City: Centro de Investigaciones y Estudios Superiores en Antropología Social.

Marcos, Sylvia. 2005. "The Borders Within: The Indigenous Women's Movement and Feminism in Mexico." In *Dialogue and Difference: Feminisms Challenge Globalization*, edited by Marguerite Waller and Sylvia Marcos. New York: Palgrave Macmillan.

Mattiace, Shannan L. 2003. *To See with Two Eyes: Peasant Activism and Indian Autonomy in Chiapas*. Albuquerque: University of New Mexico Press.

McCall, Leslie. 2005. "The Complexity of Intersectionality." *Signs* 30 (3): 1771–1800.

Mihesuah, Devon Abbott. 2003. *Indigenous American Women: Decolonization, Empowerment, Activism*. Lincoln: University of Nebraska Press.

Millán Moncayo, Márgara, 2002a. "Indigene Frauen in der neuen Politik." In *Reflexionen einer Rebellion: 'Chiapas' und ein anderes Politikverständnis*, edited by Ulrich Brand and Ana Esther Ceceña. Münster: Westphaelisches Dampfboot.

———. 2002b. "Chiapas y sus mujeres indígenas: De su diversidad y resistencia." Accessed February 14, 2014. http://www.ezln.org/revistachiapas/No4/ch4millan.html.

———. 2006. "Indigenous Women and Zapatismo: New Horizons of Visibility." In *Dissident Women: Gender and Cultural Politics in Chiapas*, edited by Shannon Speed, Aída Hernández Castillo, and Lynn Stephen. Austin: University of Texas Press.

———. 2008. "Nuevos espacios, nuevas actoras: Neozapatismo y su significado para las mujeres indígenas." In *Etnografías e historias de resistencia: Mujeres indígenas, procesos organizativos y nuevas identidades políticas*, edited by Rosalva Aída Hernández Castillo. México City: Centro de Investigaciones y Estudios Superiores en Antropología Social and Programa Universitario de Estudios de Género, Universidad Nacional Autónoma de Mexico.

Mohanty, Chandra Talpade. 1995. "Feminist Encounters: Locating the Politics of Experience." In *Social Postmodernism: Beyond Identity Politics*, edited by Linda Nicholson and Steven Seidman. Cambridge: Cambridge University Press.

Molyneux, Maxine. 2001. *Women's Movements in International Perspective: Latin America and Beyond*. New York: Palgrave Macmillan.

Olesen, Thomas. 2005. *International Zapatismo: The Construction of Solidarity in the Age of Globalization*. London: Zed Books.

Olivera Bustamante, Mercedes. 2004. "Una Larga Historia de Discriminaciones y Racismos." In *De Sumisiones, Cambios y Rebeldías: Mujeres Indígenas de Chiapas 1*, edited by Mercedes Olivera Bustamante. Tuxtla Gutiérrez, Chiapas: Universidad de Ciencias y Artes de Chiapas.

———. 2005. "Discriminación Étnica y Genérica de las Indígenas en el Siglo XIX." In *Chiapas: De la independencia a la revolución*, edited by Mercedes Olivera Bustamante and María Dolores Palomo Infante. Mexico City: Centro de Investigaciones y Estudios Superiores en Antropología Social and Consejo de Ciencia y Tecnología del Estado de Chiapas.

Olivera Bustamante, Mercedes, and María Dolores Palomo Infante, eds. *Chiapas: De la independencia a la revolución*. Mexico City: Centro de Investigaciones y Estudios Superiores en Antropología Social and Consejo de Ciencia y Tecnología del Estado de Chiapas.

Ortiz-Ortega, Adriana, and Mercedes Barquet. 2010. "Gendering Transition to Democracy in Mexico." *Latin American Research Review* 45: 108–137.

Peterson, V. Spike, and Anne Sisson Runyan, eds. 1993. *Global Gender Issues*. Boulder, CO: Westview Press.

Piel, Jean. 2005. "Nacionalismos sin nación: El siglo 19 Latino-Americano, entre utopias nactionalistas y realidades regionals." In *Chiapas: De la independencia a la revolución*, edited by Mercedes Olivera Bustamante and María Dolores Palomo Infante. Mexico City: Centro de Investigaciones y Estudios Superiores en Antropología Social.

Postero, Nancy Grey. 2007. *Now We Are Citizens: Indigenous Politics in Postmulticultural Bolivia*. Stanford: Stanford University Press.

Rovira, Guiomar. 1997. *Mujeres de maíz*. Vol. 272 of *Biblioteca Era*. Mexico City: Ediciones Era.

Rus, Jan. 1983. "Whose Caste War? Indians, Ladinos, and the 'Caste War' of 1869." In *Spaniards and Indians in Southeastern Mesoamerica*, edited by Murdo MacLeod and R. W. Wasserstrom. Lincoln: University of Nebraska Press.

Rus, Jan, Rosalva Aída Hernández Castillo, and Shannon L. Mattiace, eds. 2003. *Mayan Lives, Mayan Utopias: The Indigenous Peoples of Chiapas and the Zapatista Rebellion*. Lanham, MD: Rowman & Littlefield.

Seider, Rachel, ed. 2002. *Multiculturalism in Latin America: Indigenous Rights, Diversity, and Democracy*. London: Palgrave Macmillan.

Shepherd, Laura J. 2008. *Gender, Violence, and Security: Discourse as Practice*. London: Zed Books.

Speed, Shannon. 2006. "At the Crossroads of Human Rights and Anthropology: Toward a Critically Engaged Activist Research." *American Anthropologist* 108 (1): 66–76.

———. 2008. *Rights in Rebellion: Indigenous Struggle and Human Rights in Chiapas*. Stanford: Stanford University Press.

———. 2014. "Zapatista Autonomy, Local Governance, and an Organic Theory of Rights." In *The World of the Indigenous Americas*, edited by Robert Warrior. New York: Routledge.

Speed, Shannon, Aída Hernández Castillo, and Lynn Stephen, eds. 2006. *Dissident Women: Gender and Cultural Politics in Chiapas*. Austin: University of Texas Press.

Stasiulis, Daiva, and Nira Yuval-Davis, eds. 1995. *Unsettling Settler Societies: Articulations of Gender, Race, Ethnicity, and Class*. London: Sage.

Stephen, Lynn. 2002. *Zapata Lives! Histories and Cultural Politics in Southern Mexico*. Berkeley: University of California Press.

Tello Díaz, Carlos. 1995. *La rebelión de las cañadas*. Mexico City: Cal y Arena.

Tickner, J. Ann. 1992. *Gender in International Relations: Feminist Perspectives on Achieving Global Security*. New York: Columbia University Press.

Tripp, Aili Mari. 2013. "Towards a Gender Perspective on Human Security and Violence." In *Gender, Violence, and Human Security: Critical Feminist Perspectives*, edited by Aili Mari Tripp, Myra Marx Ferree, and Christina Ewig. New York: New York University Press.

Tripp, Aili Mari, Myra Marx Ferree, and Christina Ewig, eds. 2013. *Gender, Violence, and Human Security: Critical Feminist Perspectives*. New York: New York University Press.

Van Cott, Donna Lee. 2008. *Radical Democracy in the Andes*. Cambridge: Cambridge University Press.

Villafuerte Solís, Daniel, Salvador Meza Díaz, Gabriel Ascencio Franco, María del Carmen García Aguilar, Carolina Rivera Farfán, Miguel Lisbona Guillén, and Jesús Morales Bermúdez. 2002. *La tierra en Chiapas: Viejos problemas nuevos*. Tuxtla Gutiérrez, Chiapas: Plaza y Valdés and Universidad de Ciencias y Artes de Chiapas.

Walby, Sylvia. 1990. *Theorizing Patriarchy.* Oxford: Basil Blackwell.

Waylen, Georgina. 1996. *Gender in Third World Politics.* Buckingham, England: Open University Press.

Yuval-Davis, Nira. 1997. *Gender and Nation.* London: Sage.

———. 2006. "Intersectionality and Feminist Politics." *European Journal of Women's Studies* 13 (3): 193–209.

———. 2011. *The Politics of Belonging: Intersectional Contestations.* London: Sage.

PART II THE CONTINUUM OF SEXUAL VIOLENCE AND THE ROLE OF THE STATE

5 • MEDICAL RECORD REVIEW AND EVIDENCE OF MASS RAPE DURING THE 2007–2008 POSTELECTION VIOLENCE IN KENYA

MIKE ANASTARIO

The mechanisms of the state can be explicitly used to commit mass crimes against its citizens, including mass rape. Mass rape is one type of crime that includes an element of systematic attack, typically under conflict-related conditions. When mass rape is perpetrated these conditions may include the terrorization, destabilization, and subjugation of communities, the sexual abuse of individuals held in captivity, and the creation of opportunistic conditions that erode the rule of law (Agirre Aranburu 2010). When it is perpetrated under opportunistic conditions, the general social and physical infrastructure may be diminished to the point that the ensuing environmental "chaos" makes defining incidents of mass rape difficult. Survivor accessibility to healthcare facilities and adequate forensic examinations becomes disrupted, and biological forensic evidence may not be properly collected.

The mechanisms of state power can make establishing a mass rape challenging. Michel Foucault (1991) reminds us that power is possible in part due to its complexity, and that the state can exercise complex mechanisms to leverage its power. Through systematic complexities it becomes easier to ignore than to establish and enter into the public record crime such as a mass rape that implicates the state. Presenting forensic evidence of mass rape, potentially usable in an international jurisdiction, may be one way that discourse can be effectively used to render that power vulnerable.

For anyone who has studied, provided services to, or simply interacted with a population affected by mass crimes, it is a known challenge to ascertain information about events that have occurred. In resource-constricted settings where crimes such as mass rape have allegedly occurred, there is the additional challenge of the availability of limited viable biological forensic evidence. This chapter describes the background, methods, and forensic science implications of one study that documented changes in case characteristics of sexual assault that occurred during a complex humanitarian emergency—in this case, a period of postelection violence. The use of social science research methods to provide evidence of an incident is emphasized. The study, funded by Physicians for Human Rights, was conducted by several Kenyan and American researchers (Anastario et al. 2014) who tested for alterations in case characteristics that occurred during a three-month period of postelection violence in Kenya.

THE 2007–2008 PERIOD OF POSTELECTION VIOLENCE IN KENYA

Following the declaration that President Mwai Kibaki was the winner of the Kenyan presidential election held on December 27, 2007, there was a period of postelection violence. The violence was documented as occurring over a fifty-nine-day period until February 28, 2008, when the National Accord and Reconciliation Act was signed following mediation efforts by the African Union Panel of Eminent African Personalities. The government-sponsored Commission of Inquiry into the Post-Election Violence (also referred to as the Waki Commission) described this period as "the most deadly and the most destructive violence ever experienced in Kenya" (2008). Anecdotal reports suggested a rise in the number of sexual assaults, a rise in gang rapes, and an increase in the overall physical violence associated with sexual assaults during the postelection period.

While international courts of law and truth commissions attempt to obtain testimonies from survivors, compelling survivor testimonies can also be methodologically challenged given that testimonies may rely upon methods that emphasize subjectivity, locality, and standpoint. As such, it can become difficult to establish the occurrence of "mass rape." It is important to consider additional methods for testing for an occurrence of mass crimes, adding objective data to the historical record and providing useful evidence to both defense and prosecutorial cases in international courts of law.

Research methods such as population-based surveys can be used to establish the occurrence of mass rape, but they are costly, time consuming, and prone to producing error during implementation if not well executed. Population-based surveys can exhibit the prevalence, incidence, and correlates of sexual assaults during a given period, but they are challenged by assumptions of representation (which are particularly difficult to manage in fielding population-based surveys in resource-limited settings), are dependent upon survivor recall, and have the potential to retraumatize survivors during the data collection process. Further, these methods typically rely upon cross-sectional sampling designs, which make it difficult to eliminate error in testing for time-sensitive effects.

While population-based surveys remain one method that can be used to establish the occurrence of mass rape, it is important that researchers consider and examine other methods that can also be used, and which minimize retraumatizing survivors of sexual assault in the process of data collection. Here, I describe how medical records, when treated as "artifacts" of a society's healthcare system, can be used to test for evidence of time-sensitive changes in the case characteristics of rapes during a time of conflict. Below, I describe a study that was funded by Physicians for Human Rights that aimed to examine changes in sexual assault characteristics during a three-month period of post-election violence following the declaration that President Mwai Kibaki was the winner of the 2007 election. I discuss how medical records were identified, reviewed, coded, and analyzed to test for systematic alterations in the pattern of Kenyan sexual assault during that period. While the findings are specific to Kenya, they have implications for using this type of research method to define case characteristics of mass rape, which may be useful to both defense and prosecutorial efforts.

METHODS

Epistemology and Methodology

Before providing an in-depth description of the methods used, it is important to call attention to the epistemological assumptions underlying this research endeavor. For this project, a positivist epistemological paradigm was used—one where the research team aimed to uncover patterns and produce knowledge from objects (medical records) that would elucidate sexual assault case characteristic alterations associated with the period of postelection violence. The methodological assumptions of this research are grounded in the practice of positivism, where it is assumed that a knowable reality can be elucidated through scientific investigation by researchers, informed by the collection and objective analysis of empirical data (Babbie 2000; Hesse-Biber and Leavy 2006). It is important to explicitly state these assumptions as these are the epistemological assumptions that underlie the forensic sciences that are used to establish evidence in courts of law (e.g., latent prints, trace evidence, toxicology), and which underlie the practice of gathering evidence for a court.

Purpose and Research Questions

One strength of social science is that it can be used to describe patterns within populations. As such, social science can also be used to exhibit systematic alterations in sexual assault characteristics that occur during a temporal period of interest—in this case, the 2007–2008 Kenyan period of postelection violence.

Rape is addressed in the Rome Statute (Article 7 (1) (g)-1) as a crime against humanity. The third element of Article 7(1)(g), the crime against humanity of rape, specifies that "the conduct was committed as part of a widespread or systematic attack directed against a civilian population." Defining whether an attack was widespread or systematic can be a challenge in itself. Sexual assaults occur regularly under conditions of peace, and thus testing for changes in sexual assaults can be used to ascertain if there has been a systematic alteration in a population's pattern of sexual assaults.

The purpose of this study was to test whether the Kenyan period of postelection violence was associated with systematic alterations in the characteristics of sexual violence cases in affected Kenyan locations. Under nonconflict conditions, there may be patterns in the perpetration of sexual assault that show a trend in perpetration—such as a general percentage of cases where the perpetrator assaults a known individual or engages in drug-facilitated sexual assault. There would be other forms of sexual assault that may occur (such as gang rapes), but these types of sexual assaults may not be as quantitatively prevalent. During periods of conflict, the pattern of perpetration may alter from the "normal" pattern. This alteration may be associated with different types of rape in frequencies that vary markedly from nonconflict periods (e.g., more frequent gang rape, more frequent rape by an unknown person) that characterize the type of rape committed during that period. These case characteristics of perpetration would be reflected in the experiences of sexual assault survivors, which are partially documented in the medical records of survivors who present to a healthcare facility.

One major challenge in identifying preconflict patterns of rape versus conflict period and postconflict period patterns of rape is the data available to illustrate those changes. Patterns of perpetration of sexual assault vary by society, and it is difficult to generalize known "constants" across different populations' sexual assault patterns and case characteristics. However, if medical records for sexual assault survivors in one affected location were sorted by date relative to the mass crime incident, statistical models could be used to test for deviations from "normal" sexual assault patterns.

Medical Record Review

Medical records are part of the normal business records of a clinic or hospital. However, medical records vary by country, quality, and information contained within the record. Medical records can be particularly problematic to review in resource-limited settings, as the quality of the record and lack of standardization remain issues that challenge their representativeness. Regardless, it can be assumed that medical providers perform occupational tasks with some degree of pattern. The medical record can thus be examined as a contemporary artifact of a single patient's health at a given moment in time, moderated by the medical provider or healthcare facility that produced the record. Across multiple individuals presenting to a healthcare facility, the *population* of medical records can be examined to examine trends in specific types of diagnoses and health issues. Using this logic, the population of medical records documenting sexual assault case characteristics can be used to provide temporal indicators of the population of sexual assault survivors who were affected by a population of perpetrators during a given time period.

In this study, the medical records of sexual assault survivors were sampled for periods before, during, and after the period of postelection violence. Medical records were examined over time at three facilities: Moi Teaching and Referral Hospital, Nakuru Provincial General Hospital, and Naivasha District Hospital. Figure 5.1 illustrates how medical records were sorted by time to examine systematic changes in sexual assault cases during the postelection period.

The medical records for all patients seen at each of three facilities in the Rift Valley region with a diagnosis of sexual violence from January 2007 to December 2011 were extracted from hospital records, and 600 records were sampled per site. Sampling intervals were used to select sexual assault case records for each year and site. A structured data collection guide was developed and used to extract, code, and quantify case characteristics from the medical record regarding the

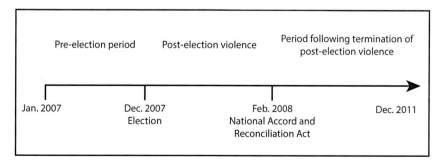

FIGURE 5.1 Arrangement and analysis of Kenyan medical records over time

LOCATION_____   CODER'S NAME_____   DATE CODING TOOK PLACE_____

Var. #	Variable	1	2	3	4
1.1	Patient #				
1.2	Date presented to medical unit				
1.3	Time pres. Med. Unit				
1.4	Gender				
1.5	Marital Status				
1.8	Alleged Perp. Known				
1.9	Number perp.				
1.1	Date of Assault				
1.11	Time of Assault				
1.12	Location of assault				
1.13	Type of Sexual Assault				
1.14	Weapons Used				
1.15	IF Weapon used, type				
1.16	Condom Used				
1.18	Witness/report of rape by other individuals				
1.19	Attended other health facility				
1.2	Treated other health facility				
1.21	History previous rape				
2.1	Injury to Perineum				
2.2	Hymen				
2.3	Vagina				
2.4	Penis				
2.5	Anus				
2.6	Head				
2.7	Neck				
2.8	Upper limbs				
2.9	Chest				
2.1	Back				
2.11	Abdomen				
2.12	Lower Limbs				
2.13	Skin				
3.1	Emotional health/mental health				
4.1	Treatment/Management				
4.2	Referrals				
4.3	General comments/Obs.				

FIGURE 5.2 Medical record entry form used to extract sexual assault case characteristics from patient medical records

sexual assault. An example of the medical record entry form is shown in figure 5.2. All patient records were anonymized and de-identified prior to analysis. Data collectors were trained to individually examine and code patient medical records (figure 5.2). Data collectors were provided codes for each field entered into the medical record review form, so only numbers would appear in the medical record entry sheets.

Once entry sheets were complete, they were entered into a Microsoft Excel database and checked for accuracy.

Measures

Several measures were developed for analysis. First, a series of dichotomous (0,1) measures were created to capture the case characteristics when documented in the medical record. To test the hypothesis that case characteristics would be altered during the postelection period, a postelection violence assault variable was developed for cases where the reported date of the assault fell within the three months during which the postelection violence took place (December 2007, January 2008, February 2008). All other sexual assault cases outside of these three months were coded as 0 and treated as the comparison group. To conduct the time series analysis, data would have to be "collapsed" by month, and thus all cases occurring within this three-month period were defined as postelection cases.

Data Analysis

Data were analyzed using STATA 10 statistical software (2007). Logistic regression was used to estimate odds ratios (ORs) for specific case characteristics in postelection violence cases as compared to non-postelection violence cases, and adjusted odds ratios (aOR) were used to control for sex of the survivor, the number of days lagged between the assault and presentation to a health facility, and the location of the health facility. Time series analysis was used to examine trends relative to the 2007–2008 period of postelection violence. Sensitivity analyses were also conducted.

RESULTS

Descriptive Characteristics of the Sample

In total, the cases that would produce the time series analytic sample included 1,615 medical records with sexual assault diagnoses, with 569 cases derived from Eldoret, 534 cases from Naivasha, and 512 cases from Nakuru. Table 5.1 exhibits descriptive characteristics of the sample by cases falling into postelection violence (n = 95) and non-postelection violence (n = 1,520) periods.

TABLE 5.1 Case characteristics for sexual assaults occurring during the postelection violence period and non-postelection violence period, N = 1,615

Case characteristics	Non-postelection violence period (n = 1,520)	Postelection violence period (n = 95)	P
Gender (male), %	6.6%	8.4%	0.504
Lag between assault and presentation dates, mean (SD)	13.3 (45.1)	64.3 (97.6)	<.001
Did not know perpetrator, %	23.5%	47.4%	<.001
More than 1 perpetrator, %	12.6%	34.4%	<.001
Type of assault:			
Oral	0.5%	1.1%	0.512
Vaginal	88.4%	85.3%	0.355
Anal	7.0%	11.6%	0.097
Weapon used	9.5%	11.6%	0.500
Condom used	5.5%	4.2%	0.585
Rape was witnessed	61.1%	52.6%	0.102
History of previous sexual assault	8.4%	3.2%	0.083
Injury:			
Anogenital	71.8%	63.2%	0.073
Head/neck	8.6%	5.3%	0.266
Limbs	8.2%	5.3%	0.317
Chest	1.9%	1.1%	0.555
Back	2.6%	2.1%	0.782
Abdomen	3.2%	7.4%	0.033
Skin	2.3%	1.1%	0.435
Emotional distress	27.5%	35.8%	0.082

Upon preliminary examination, statistically significant differences in case characteristics were observed when sexual assault cases that took place during the period of postelection violence were compared with non-postelection cases (significant results are highlighted in table 5.1). Postelection cases showed a greater overall number of days in lag between the date that the individual was assaulted and the date the individual presented to a healthcare facility, a greater percentage of cases where the perpetrator was unknown to the assaulted individual, a greater percentage of cases where more than one perpetrator was involved in the assault, and a greater percentage of cases with documented abdominal injuries. Taken together, these patterns illustrate higher rates of assault by a stranger and multiple perpetrators, with a specific type of injury (abdominal injury), which are distinct from cases occurring outside of the postelection period.

When data were subset to cases where the patient reported to the healthcare facility on the day of the assault, injuries indicative of more severe physical violence were observed in postelection violence cases. In this subset of cases, head/neck injuries were more prevalent during the postelection violence period (21.4% vs. 11.7%) as well as injuries to the limbs (14.3% vs. 9.2%) and abdomen (14.3% vs. 2.9%). However, only injuries to the abdomen remained statistically significant ($p<0.050$).

Adjustment for Potential Confounding Effects

Within this preanalytic sample, adjustment for sex of the survivor, number of days' lag between the assault and presentation to a health facility, and location of the health facility showed that these specific case characteristics remained statistically significant.

Time Series Analyses

In addition to simply grouping sexual assault cases by whether they occurred during the postelection violence period, cases were also sorted by date of assault and collapsed by month in which the assault occurred to examine the case characteristics as time series, observable over sixty months (January 2007 to December 2011). Here, tests were conducted for significant deviations associated with the three-month period of postelection violence in the series. An example of a time series for a sexual assault case characteristic is provided in figure 5.3, which presents, by month, the cumulative number of assaults where *the perpetrator was not known*. It is apparent that a "spike" in the series occurs during the three-month period of postelection violence, signified by the arrow pointing to the observation for December 2007 (the month of the presidential election that initiated the period of postelection violence).

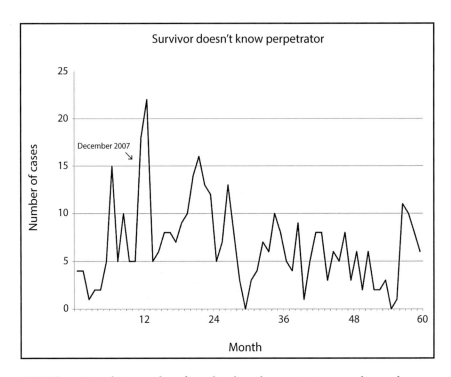

FIGURE 5.3 Cumulative number of assaults where the perpetrator was unknown, by month (January 2007–December 2011)

After adjusting for sex of the survivor and lag between date of assault and presentation to the health facility, the Prais-Winsten estimate of the coefficient for cases where *the perpetrator was not known* (figure 5.3) was highly significant for the postelection violence period, indicating that the postelection violence period was associated with a 24-percentage-point increase in cases where the survivor did not know the perpetrator.

Next, the time series for sexual assault cases by *more than one perpetrator* was examined (figure 5.4). After adjusting for sex and lag between date of assault and presentation to the health facility, the Prais-Winsten estimate of the coefficient of the postelection violence period was highly significant, indicating that the postelection violence period was associated with a 20-percentage-point increase in cases where the survivor reported more than one perpetrator.

Abdominal Injury

The time series for having a documented *abdominal injury* is shown in figure 5.5, with the most elevated spike occurring during the three-month period of

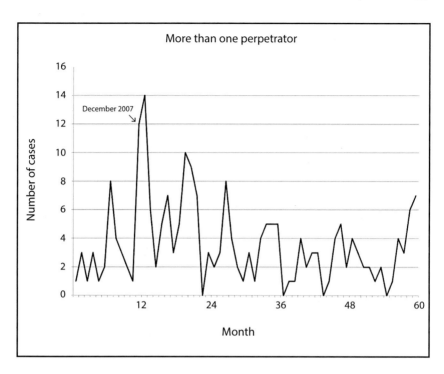

FIGURE 5.4 Cumulative number of assaults with more than one perpetrator, by month (January 2007–December 2011)

postelection violence. After adjusting for sex and lag between date of assault and presentation to the health facility, the estimated coefficient of the postelection violence period was significant, indicating that the postelection violence period was associated with a 4-percentage-point increase in cases with a documented abdominal injury.

Days' Lag between Assault and Presentation to Health Facility

Although this variable was treated as a potential confounder in models for per-petration characteristics and injuries, it is also worth noting the time series in the number of days' lag between the date of the sexual assault and the date of presen-tation to a health facility itself is a case characteristic of sexual assault cases. This time series is shown in figure 5.6, and illustrates a spike in the series occurring during the three-month period of postelection violence. The estimated coeffi-cient of the postelection violence period was significant, indicating that the post-election violence period was associated with an 18-percentage-point increase in cases showing a greater-than-one-month lag in presentation to a health facility.

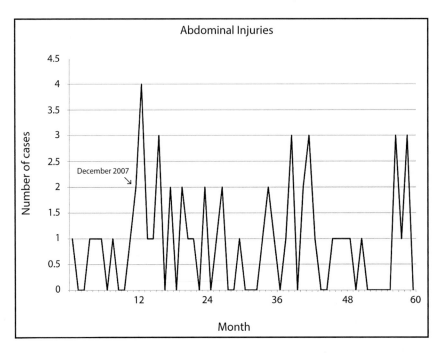

FIGURE 5.5 Cumulative number of abdominal injuries, by month (January 2007–December 2011)

Sensitivity Analyses

It is important to note that the findings presented above are grounded in medical records, which are artifacts of the Kenyan healthcare systems from which they were derived at the time documentation occurred. As such, the argument could be made that findings associated with the period of postelection violence reflect historical trends in documentation, and that the postelection findings above reflect the time period that medical records were collected. To test whether this was a possibility, sensitivity analyses were conducted to test whether findings were specific to the three-month period of postelection violence. This was done by defining a "dummy period" for the three-month period immediately *preceding* the period of postelection violence (see figure 5.7), thus representing cases derived from a similar historical period relative to the series.

All models where the period of postelection violence showed significant association with sexual assault case characteristics were rerun, but this time cases occurring during the dummy period were substituted for the variable that would have represented postelection cases. In these models, the postelection period was allocated to the control group along with the other time periods occurring

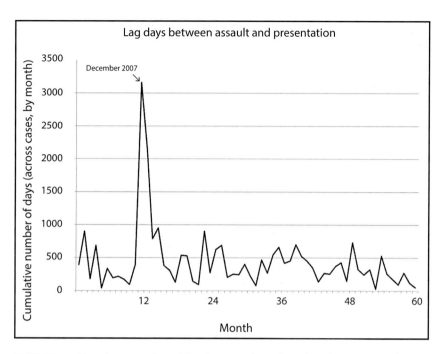

FIGURE 5.6 Cumulative number of days between date of assault and presentation to health facility, by month (January 2007–December 2011)

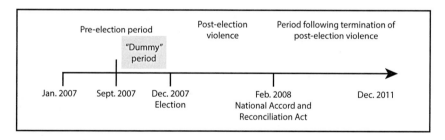

FIGURE 5.7 Defining the "dummy period" to conduct sensitivity analyses

outside of the dummy period. After rerunning each model, no statistically significant differences were observed for cases drawn from the dummy period for the case characteristics that were significantly associated with the postelection violence period in the logistic regressions or Prais-Winsten models.

DISCUSSION

The study shows evidence of alteration in Kenyan sexual assault case characteristics during the period from December 2007 to February 2008. The alterations observed were documented in medical records at three healthcare facilities in Kenya. The characteristics of these sexual assaults that differentiated them from the group of sexual assaults occurring during other time periods include an increased likelihood of assaults where the survivor did not know the perpetrator, had more than one perpetrator at the time of assault, had documented abdominal injuries in the medical record, and waited more than one month to report to a health facility. These findings have implications not only for characterizing the sexual assaults that took place during the postelection violence but for establishing the occurrence of mass rape in future investigations.

First, this is the first study to use medical record review to illustrate systematic alterations in sexual assault case characteristics during the Kenyan period of postelection violence. There was one study conducted at Kenyatta National Hospital that examined medical records and established an increase in the number of sexually abused persons treated at the hospital in the year 2007 compared to the years 2006 and 2008 (Kuria et al. 2013). However, this study did not specifically isolate the postelection violence period. Using thorough medical record review, and time series analyses, the study described in this chapter illustrated highly specific deviations in sexual assault case characteristics during the Kenyan period of postelection violence.

Conflict-related features of mass rape that have been documented elsewhere include the use of racial epithets used during attacks in which sexual assaults took place, a relatively high male victimization rate, gang rape, and the reported victimization of other individuals (Hagan, Rymond-Richmond, and Palloni 2009; Tsai et al. 2012). Other than qualitative and anecdotal evidence of sexual assaults that are specific to conflict periods, very little is scientifically documented regarding the behavior of perpetrators or the characteristics of sexual assault cases during times of conflict. The findings in this study of Kenyan postelection sexual assaults corroborate the narratives of survivors who testified before the Waki Commission, where a number of sexual assault survivors reported gang rape during the postelection period. The explicit details of these assaults can be found in the Waki Commission report (2008). Regarding deviation from "nonconflict" sexual assault cases, research suggests that survivors of sexual assault generally know the perpetrator, and there is also evidence that the more intimate the relationship between a survivor of sexual assault and the perpetrator, the more likely a case is to be processed (Bouffard 2000; Ingemann-Hansen et al. 2008; Janisch et al. 2010; McLean et al. 2011; McGregor, Du Mont, and Myhr 2002). Taken together, an increase in the prevalence of sexual assaults by strangers and multiple perpetrators, and a lack of accessibility to healthcare facilities during the postelection period, suggests that linking perpetrators to all victims of the mass rape would be challenging.

One finding that carries several implications for forensic investigations includes the elevated lag time between date of assault and presentation to a healthcare facility. A forensic exam occurring within seventy-two hours of a sexual assault can provide valuable biological forensic evidence that may be probative in a court of law. There is a critical window in which valuable biological forensic evidence can still be collected using techniques available to crime laboratories, and obtaining a full semen donor profile beyond forty-eight hours postcoitus is not possible (Hall and Ballantyne 2003). The difference in the lag for postelection cases versus non-postelection cases was appreciable (on average, 64.3 days longer for postelection cases) and highly statistically significant at $p<0.001$. The reasons for this lag in postelection cases are numerous, and anecdotal evidence suggests that it was in part due to dysfunctional infrastructure (road shutdowns, law enforcement blockades), inability to physically access the clinic, a lack of knowledge about what to do, and fear of reprisal. This lag period also seriously complicates the ability of this endeavor to detect specific injuries associated with postelection assaults, as sixty-four days provides ample time for wounds such as lacerations and bruises to heal, in part reducing the ability of healthcare practitioners to document the injury characteristics of postelection sexual assault cases. An extended lag period between date of assault and presentation to a medical facility has also been documented in another resource-restricted setting affected by armed conflict—the Democratic Republic of the Congo (Bartels et al. 2012). In the present study, lasting infections, fears surrounding HIV and sexually transmitted infections, and even pregnancy could cause survivors to return at a later date. A post-hoc analysis of the research data in this study also revealed that 23.2 percent of postelection assault survivors arrived at the clinic seven to nine months following their postelection violence assault—the time period that would correspond with the third trimester of pregnancy. In comparison to the 23 percent of postelection assaults who waited seven to nine months to present to a healthcare facility, only 0.4 percent of non-postelection assaults exhibited this same waiting period. It is thus probable that children conceived as a result of postelection sexual assaults carry perpetrator DNA.

Courts of law typically rely on forensic evidence derived from standard disciplines in the forensic sciences, which utilize methods grounded in positivistic assumptions. In practice, courts rely upon methods that reduce quantitative error to inform whether an incident (e.g., sexual contact) can even be established. We are in a nascent phase of using social science research to make determinations about the occurrence of mass crimes in international jurisdictions, and it was deemed important that this research endeavor to utilize methods grounded in the practice of positivism to produce data that could be exhibited in numbers, that could exhibit quantitative patterns, and that could produce probability values matched to findings.

Grounding observations in the medical record, as opposed to survivor interviews, has several benefits. The first is that this method relies upon "normal business records" that were collected as part of routine clinical practice before, during, and after the postelection violence. For cases where the survivor was assaulted but waited weeks to present to a healthcare facility, this method allowed for the documentation of sexual assault by medical professionals versus relying on survey data or survivor testimony. Further, conducting medical record review does not retraumatize survivors who already came forward and who had their sexual assault documented. This strength also leads to a limitation: lack of representativeness of the findings.

Using medical record review, the findings are limited to the sexual assault survivors who presented to the healthcare facilities and who, under non-research-related circumstances, disclosed their experience of sexual assault to a clinician. Thus, there was a high "self-selection" criteria for the cases that were analyzed in this study. Using data from this study, we cannot make conjectures about the population-based prevalence of sexual assault or the nationwide case characteristics that defined survivors who did not present to a healthcare facility.

In conclusion, this study used time series analysis of medical record data to test for systematic changes in sexual assault characteristics for cases presenting to health facilities in the Rift Valley region. It showed that cases of assault during the postelection period were associated with an increased likelihood of survivors waiting to present to a health facility following the assault, not knowing the perpetrator, reporting more than one perpetrator, and evidence of abdominal injury in the medical record. These results were obtained using social science research methods that may be informative to future investigations of mass rape.

REFERENCES

Agirre Aranburu, Xabier. 2010. "Sexual Violence beyond Reasonable Doubt: Using Pattern Evidence and Analysis for International Cases." *Leiden Journal of International Law* 23: 609–627.

Anastario, Mike, Monica Adhiambo Onyango, Joan Nyanyuki, Karen Naimer, Rachel Muthoga, Susannah Sirkin, Kelle Barrick, Martijn van Hasselt, Wilson Aruasa, Cynthia Kibet, and Grace Omollo. 2014. "Time Series Analysis of Sexual Assault Case Characteristics and the 2007–2008 Period of Post-Election Violence in Kenya." *PLoS ONE* 9 (8): 1–6. e106443.

Babbie, Earl. 2000. *The Practice of Social Research*. Belmont, CA: Wadsworth Publishing.

Bartels, Susan A., Jennifer A. Scott, Jennifer Leaning, Jocelyn T. Kelly, Nina R. Joyce, Denis Mukwege, and Michael J. VanRooyen. 2012. "Demographics and Care-Seeking Behaviors of Sexual Violence Survivors in South Kivu Province, Democratic Republic of Congo." *Disaster Medicine and Public Health Preparedness* 6 (4): 393–401.

Bouffard, Jeffrey A. 2000. "Predicting Type of Sexual Assault Case Closure from Victim, Suspect, and Case Characteristics." *Journal of Criminal Justice* 28: 527–542.

Commission of Inquiry into the Post-Election Violence (Waki Commission). 2008. *Report of the Findings of the Commission of Inquiry into the Post-Election Violence in Kenya.* College Station, TX: Stata Corporation.

Foucault, Michel. 1991. *Discipline and Punish: The Birth of a Prison.* London: Penguin.

Hagan, John, Wenona Rymond-Richmond, and Alberto Palloni. 2009. "Racial Targeting of Sexual Violence in Darfur." *American Journal of Public Health* 99 (8): 1386–1392.

Hall, Ashley, and Jack Ballantyne. 2003. "Novel Y-STR Typing Strategies Reveal the Genetic Profile of the Semen Donor in Interval Post-coital Cervico-vaginal Samples." *Forensic Science International* 136: 58–72.

Hesse-Biber, Sharlene, and Patricia Leavy. 2006. *The Practice of Qualitative Research.* Thousand Oaks, CA: Sage.

Ingemann-Hansen, Ole, Ole Brink, Svend Sabroe, Villy Sorensen, and Annie V. Charles. 2008. "Legal Aspects of Sexual Violence—Does Forensic Evidence Make a Difference?" *Forensic Science International* 180 (2–3): 98–104.

International Criminal Court. 2012. "Summary of Decision in the Two Kenya Cases." Press release. January 23. http://www.icc-cpi.int/NR/exeres/7036023F-C83C-484E-FDD-0DD37E568E84.htm.

Janisch, Stefanie, Hildrun Meyer, Tanja Germerott, Urs-Vito Albrecht, Yvonne Schulz, and Anette S. Debertin. 2010. "Analysis of Clinical Forensic Examination Reports on Sexual Assault." *International Journal of Legal Medicine* 124 (3): 227–235.

Kuria, Mary W., Lilian Omondi, Yvonne Olando, Margaret Makanyengo, and David Bukusi. 2013. "Is Sexual Abuse a Part of War? A 4-Year Retrospective Study on Cases of Sexual Abuse at the Kenyatta National Hospital Kenya." *Journal of Public Health in Africa* 4 (e5).

McGregor, Margaret J., Janice Du Mont, and Terri L. Myhr. 2002. "Sexual Assault Forensic Medical Examination: Is Evidence Related to Successful Prosecution?" *Annals of Emergency Medicine* 39 (6): 639–647.

McLean, Iain, Stephen A. Roberts, Cath White, and Sheila Paul. 2011. "Female Genital Injuries Resulting from Consensual and Non-consensual Vaginal Intercourse." *Forensic Science International* 204 (1–3): 27–33.

Tsai, Alexander C., Mohammed A. Eisa, Sondra S. Crosby, Susanah Sirkin, Michele Heisler, Jennifer Leaning, and Vincent Iacopino. 2012. "Medical Evidence of Human Rights Violations against Non-Arabic-Speaking Civilians in Darfur: A Cross-Sectional Study." *PLoS Medicine* 9 (4): e1001198.

6 · THE FORCE OF WRITING IN GENOCIDE

On Sexual Violence in al-Anfāl Operations and Beyond

FAZIL MORADI

How is sexual violence rendered public in the aftermath of genocide, in a world saturated with the political, social, and religious order of female physical intactness? This chapter explores the testimonies of Kurdish female survivors of the Iraqi Ba'thi state's genocide, that is, the al-Anfāl ("spoils" in Arabic) operations of 1987–1991,[1] the treatment of captured women as "spoils," and the silencing of their traumatic experiences. I analyze the ways in which testimonies of female abduction and sexual violence enter the public realm, only to be silenced again in the Kurdistan region. In examining the writing of the state and the question of who writes and what such writing is capable of doing, I draw on anthropological theory and genocide studies. The focus is on the force of writing, taken to cover state constitutions, decrees, laws, documents, communiqués, screenplays, bureaucracy, political ideology, the science of military technology, and the Qur'ān. Thus, I discuss how these writings formed the Iraqi state and the genocide, and how they are translated into testimonial and legal evidence. These in turn, together with the testimonies of siblings of abducted females, recorded almost thirty years later, render public the experiences of sexual violence and rape during the al-Anfāl.

IRAQI STATE-WRITING

The force of state writing has not been an important focus of anthropological studies of genocide. Max Weber (1978, 957) analyzed writing as central to modern bureaucracy. In reiterating Weber's analysis of bureaucracy as dehumanizing, Zygmunt Bauman writes, "Bureaucracy is intrinsically capable of genocidal action" (2002, 131). This is also found in Ben Kafka's *The Demon of Writing*, where "modern political thought" materializes in "paperwork" (2012, 10). Furthermore, the force of writing harkens back in history. The Babylonian Empire, in the third millennium BCE, was fused with lists as "written knowledge" (Rottenburg 2009, 137) that commanded its representation and ways of operating in society at large (Vismann 2008, 6). Through its commands deposited in files and their dissemination in multiple languages, the Roman Empire was inexorably merged into different writing systems (ibid., 47–60). Writing has also been indispensable to the colonial powers' mode of governance. In his report on India, philosopher John Stuart Mill, then a colonial agent, observed writing as *the* most pervasive mode of colonial governance: "The whole Government of India is carried on in writing" (cited in Hull 2012, 7). This is equally applicable to the Nazi operations or those of the communist German Democratic Republic. The latter is now preserved in the form of documents in the Stasi Archive in Berlin, and regulated by the Stasi Files Law.[2] The Holocaust Archive in Baden Arolsen alone preserves 30 million documents, from "transportation lists" to "death books."[3] Documentation and their iterations were fundamental to the Nazi state's operational plans and acts of extermination in the Holocaust. During his trial in Jerusalem, Adolf Eichmann, a Nazi SS commander and the major organizer of the Holocaust, repeatedly insisted that he "always carried out his duty to the letter" (Swift 2009, 66). The secret archive of the Guatemalan National Police, "eight million documents," Kirsten Weld writes, was discovered by human rights activists and used as evidence to prosecute police for human rights violations. These documents were thus translated into people, rights, and justice, and were seen as fundamental to the configuration of a postwar state (2014, 2, 248). The matter of concern in this chapter is translation, in pursuit of justice, as an act of rendering public the silencing, memory, and writing of the genocidal state.

According to Jacques Derrida, "to write is to produce a mark that will constitute a sort of machine which is productive in turn" (1988, 8). To wit, "every sign linguistic or nonlinguistic, spoken or written" is "repeatable" and has the tendency to "break with every given context," and thus extend throughout time and space (ibid., 12). In this context, I discuss how siblings of abducted women are engaged in an act of iterability. That is, how they translate or reiterate a specific document of the Ba'thi state, identity cards, photographs, and a film script into testimony and legal evidence, and thus in contemporary Iraq render public their demands for justice and the silenced experiences of sexual violence during the al-Anfāl. Before doing so I want to briefly lay out the broader context in order to highlight how this single document is attached to other state writings that have been introduced as legal evidence in the Iraqi High Tribunal in Baghdad.

Although the Socialist Arab Baʿth (lit. Resurgence) Party gained total control of the Iraqi state in 1968, within the context of the Cold War, it was already configured during the Second World War. The political authors of Baʿthism privileged the Nazi state and its ideologies as the only way of pushing the British and the French out of the Middle East. The effort to do so was backed by the Nazi state, which also spread its ideologies and plans through the Arabic broadcast of Radio Berlin and its Deutsches Nachrichtenbüro (press agency) (Dieterich 2005). Michel ʿAflaq, one of the leading authors of Baʿthism, who had closely followed the Nazi rise to power while attending the Sorbonne in Paris in the 1930s, translated the vision of "Aryan exceptionalism" into an exceptional Arabism, with Islam as its Spirit (Makiya 1998, 197). Sāmī al-Djundī, another Baʿthist, writes: "We were racialists, admiring Nazism, reading its books and the source of its thoughts. . . . We were the first to think of translating *Mein Kampf*" (cited in Wild 1985, 131). Apart from the Arabic translation that appeared in the Iraqi newspaper *Arab World* in October 1933, *Mein Kampf* had also been a topic of discussion for Iraqi nationalists in Baghdad. Fritz Grobba, the German consul at the time, played a central role in spreading Nazism by participating in different discussion forums. In short, the Baʿth Party, as a reiteration of the Nazi *Weltanschauung*, was founded on April 7, 1947, in Syria and then in Iraq in the beginning of the 1950s. ʿAflaqʾs writings lived on through the Iraqi Provisional Constitution, and as the principles of "A single Arab Nation with an Eternal Message" and "Unity, Freedom, Socialism" (Articles 1 and 4 of the constitution). As president, Saddām Hussein maintained a personal relationship with ʿAflaq, who occasionally visited him in Baghdad, until his death in June 1989. The reiteration of international political writings transformed the Iraqi Baʿthi state into a modern genocidal state with a sophisticated bureaucracy.

THE WRITING OF AL-ANFĀL

In order to materialize ʿAflaqʾs vision, as embodied in Iraqʾs constitution, the Iraqi Baʿthi state embarked on an Arabization campaign in the 1970s, which developed further in the 1980s as a radically different political and social order. The Iraq-Iran War that raged between 1980 and 1988 forced a shifting alliance among the two main Kurdish political organizations—the Patriotic Union of Kurdistan (PUK) and the Kurdistan Democratic Party (KDP)—and the Iranian state. The Iraqi state therefore classified the two organizations as "subversives, agents of Iran, and traitors," and planned to systematically eradicate them. This was made official with the issuance of decree No. 160 (March 29, 1987), which, bearing the signature of President Saddām Hussein, declared 'Ali Hassan al-Majid the secretary general of the Northern Bureau, the governing authority for the Kurdish region of Iraq, and thus the man who became responsible for al-Anfāl. The Islamic phrase "In the Name of God, the Compassionate, the Merciful" is inscribed at the top of the decree, followed by "In the Name of the People." Subsequently, almost all state decrees end with the note, "the decree shall be published in official newspapers and sent to all Ministries and state institutions." In this manner, the Iraqi constitution, the Islamic phrase, and the signature of the president are introduced as the legitimization of the state authority, producing the state as the central codifying power. This practice created and transformed the Iraqi state into "a spectral presence materialized in documents" (cf. Das 2004, 250–251). Thus, the Iraqi state enters the world of the Kurdish rural population. Iraqi state agents received intelligence equipment and training from the Stasi of the German Democratic Republic throughout the 1980s (Sassoon 2014) and learned how to control the population through writing.

Al-Majid, as the new secretary general of the Northern Bureau, replaced Sa'di Mahdi Sāleh, who had already in June 1985 declared an absolute ban on the distribution of food, electricity, water, and transport in and out of certain Kurdish rural areas. The entire region, including security, military, and civil institutions, became subject to al-Majid's sovereign authority. Al-Majid set off the organization of the al-Anfāl by issuing two written extermination orders, which had to be coordinated with the Office of the President inside the Republican Palace in Baghdad and the Iraqi Ministry of Defense. The first, No. 3650 (June 3, 1987), declares the rural areas to be "outlawed areas and villages." This is in line with the Guatemalan army's declaration in the 1980s of the living spaces of the Maya population as "illegal villages," subjected to exterminatory violence (Sanford 2004, 174). The entire Kurdish rural population was designated as the backbone of the PUK and KDP, and the rural areas as the bases of their political operations. Thus, the depopulation and complete destruction of villages within these areas were claimed as fundamental to the stability and security of the political and national order in Iraq. The order states: "The military force is absolutely entitled to kill any human or animal found in these outlawed areas" and commands the collection and transport of the population to "collectives," "where they shall receive their punishment." Around twenty-five "collectives" were established throughout the northern region for the purpose of collection, control, and interrogation. Survivors whom I interviewed referred to them as "camps of pure violence," some of which, although transitory, consisted of nothing more than desert encircled by earthen walls. As the operations developed al-Majid realized the limit of the time frame set in the first order. Therefore he issued extermination Order

No. 4008 (June 20, 1987). It states that the outlawed villages "shall be regarded as operational zones strictly out of bounds to all persons and animals . . . in which the troops can open fire at will. . . . The Corps shall carry out random bombardment, using artillery, helicopter and aircraft . . . in order to kill the largest number of persons in the outlawed areas." Numerous copies of both orders had to travel through the labyrinth of the state hierarchical bureaucracy to authorize and command the armed forces as well as Kurdish collaborators (known by Kurds as *Jāhsh*, lit. donkey's foal), to collect and transport the Kurdish rural population to specified incarceration camps and prisons, and to kill with impunity.

More fundamental to the overall systematic plan of extermination was the relationship of the order to the role of devastating weapons, "the remarkable achievement of advanced science" (Bauman 2002, 111). The Iraqi state resorted to the calculated effects of "special [chemical] strikes," which are inscribed in exchanged documents between the Republican Palace and the military Corps in March-April 1987. In a recorded audio al-Majid described his plans: "I will kill them all with chemical weapons. . . . I will bury them with bulldozers," and "I will publish one million copies of [an amnesty] leaflet and distribute them." Offering amnesty meant that the state granted its promise of forgiveness to those who would voluntarily submit themselves to the Iraqi army. The Kurdish collaborators played an essential role in transmitting this promise to the population or even to individual Peshmerga (lit. "before death," Kurdish guerrillas) of the PUK and KDP. The deployment of modern chemical weapons, whose precursor components had been imported from European corporations, from the Netherlands, Switzerland, the United Kingdom, Austria, France, and fourteen German companies (Kelly 2013, 366-379; Brzoska 1987; Tripp 2007), and dissemination of the false offer of amnesty were central to the capture of those with intelligence information, depopulation, and absolute destruction of villages and towns in the Kurdistan region. The Balisān valley, Gūptapa, Askar, and Halabja (which is now known as "the Kurdish Hiroshima" in the region), among others, were bombarded with chemical weapons, leaving thousands dead and survivors with lifelong injuries. "Piove cianuro su Halabja, nuova Pompei" (Cyanide rains on Halabja, the new Pompeii) is the title of an article in an Italian newspaper. It was published after the attacks and is now archived in the Halabja Museum. The article includes a photograph of a dead young woman and her dead child. The woman is lying on her back with open arms and closed eyes, and her child with knees bent on her/his chest, and with face buried in his/her hands, while seeking refuge under the right arm of the dead mother.

Written documents reveal that the al-Anfāl was an eight-stage aerial and ground military operation that changed over time, adapting as needed to new conditions.[4] Although the operations started in April 1987, the name al-Anfāl was introduced around February 1988. The Iraqi state had to convince the military as well as the rest of the Iraqi population that it not only defended national security and acted on the basis of the constitution but that it also followed the divine order, the *Sūreh al-Anfāl*, inscribed in the Holy Qur'ān. In reiterating *Sūreh al-Anfāl* the Iraqi state produced the rural population as non-Muslim and enemy (like the Guatemalan army produced the Maya as enemy; see Sanford, Duyos Álvarez-Arenas, and Dill, this volume). It is true that Christians, such as Assyrians and Chaldeans, and Ezidis (Yazidis), were also subjected to the al-Anfāl. The twelfth verse of *Sūreh al-Anfāl* speaks of a divine call to "cast terror into the hearts of those who disbelieve," while the first verse states: "They ask you about the spoils, say: The spoils belong to Allah and to the Messenger" (Fakhry 2000, 175–177). The Iraqi state's al-Anfāl, or "spoils," in this case were women, children, and livestock, which are outlined in the Order No. 4008 as rewards: "Everything seized by the [Kurdish collaborators] advisers and [Iraqi] troops . . . shall be retained by them." The conventional and chemical attacks were followed by the collection and deportation of the surviving population to Tūpzāwā Army Camp, where they were registered, and had their identity cards and all personal belongings such as marriage rings, gold, wristwatches, money, prayer beads, lighters, and cigarettes confiscated. The population was then separated on the basis of gender and age. Men between the ages of fifteen and fifty-five were singled out for execution and burial in mass graves, and women, children, and the elderly were transported to the infamous Nūgra Salmān, Dibs, and Nezārkeh camps, where they were subjected to starvation, death, arbitrary killing, torture, female abduction, sexual violence, and secret and public rape. The al-Anfāl also resulted in mass forced migration to Turkey and Iran. A woman (b. 1941) who had lost all members of her family except a daughter, and lived alone, told me: "Among everything, things they took from us, two things were important to me: the prayer beads and the identity card. The first was my life. It was my relation to the creator [God], and the second my nationality. They took our souls" (interview, August 2012, Rezgāri).

From April 1987 until the release of the general amnesty decree No. 736 on September 6, 1988, an estimated 2,000 to 3,000 villages were razed, an estimated 50,000 to 100,000 people were disappeared or killed, and 1.5 million people were forcibly displaced (Hardi 2011; Kelly 2008). Yet, the extermination Order No. 4008 remained in force. Those released from the military-controlled incarceration camps and the returnees from Turkey and Iran were deported to the military-controlled "collectives" in the region. This "containment" introduced what I call the ninth stage of the overall plan, which was extended until 1991. Those "contained," mostly women and children, had to survive on their own and were kept there until the Kurdish uprising in March 1991. Although the Kurdish uprising resulted in Kurdish control over the "outlawed areas," with the

Kurdish Parliament established in 1992, many survivors did not return to their villages before 1993 or 1994, and others still to this day remain in what were once military-controlled "collectives." The internal war between the PUK and KDP, which lasted from 1994 to 1998, extended the sufferings of the al-Anfāl survivors. Moreover, the uprising resulted in the seizure of 18.25 metric tons of secret documents, which were airlifted to the United States for safe storage in 1992 and 1993 (Montgomery 2012). It is important to note that the Iraqi state denied the legitimacy of these documents.

CAPTURED WOMEN AS ANFĀL

The al-Anfāl as military operations also turned Kurdish women into transactional spoils of genocide, over which state institutions and the armed forces exercised exceptional rights. Kanan Makiya, as one of the first to record testimonies of al-Anfāl, writes:

> I had begun hearing some very strange stories before entering northern Iraq. About Kurdish women, for instance, being sold in a *white slave trade* that was reaching all the way down to the Gulf. A Kurd I know received a letter in April 1989 from a friend who drove a freight truck between Aman and Baghdad. On one of his trips, his truck broke down near the town of Ramadi. While waiting for it to be fixed, two women approached him, pleading to be taken to Sulaimaniyya. Realizing they were fellow Kurds, he entered into a conversation with them, only to find out that they had been captured during the Anfāl operations of 1988 and sold by a relatively junior army officer to the shaikh of a local tribe in the Governorate of Anbar. The man had turned down their request and was *writing the letter* because he was feeling ashamed of himself. (Makiya 1993, 158, emphasis added).

Female survivors used the term *Kārasāt* (Catastrophe) to explain what they had witnessed and experienced. "Saddām's regime would do anything" was a common response to my question about the possibility of a trade in women. Kurdish women held at the incarceration camps explained that the guards did not show respect nor did they have mercy on them, and that everyday life consisted of forcing women to drink tea mixed with the guards' urine; tearing off their already torn clothes, without any clothes and unable to wash; tied to iron electric pillars in the sun for hours; while some were tortured to death. A woman in her forties, who had lost one of her four children in Dibs camp, where only women and children were detained, testified to me, "The most shameful moment was when the guards entered at night and took the beautiful girls away, and did to them as they desired. I am ashamed when I talk about it now. At the end not a single young girl could be seen among those detained" (interview, July 2012,

Chamchamāl). She also stated that the guards would hold children hostage until the "beautiful mothers" met their demands and that some women who gave birth "threw their children away," or watched them die. Since the military guards knew that the Kurdish woman's body constitutes the foundation of family and social life among the Kurds, sexual torture and rape were introduced as a fundamental destruction of individual and social life and as a way of spreading horror among the detainees (see also the contributions of Stefatos and of Sanford, Duyos Álvarez-Arenas, and Dill in this volume). Rāzyeh Hassan, ten years old at the time, remembered a poem stitched together by women in Nūgra Salmān. She told me that I was the first outsider for whom she had recited the poem:

Through Kirkūk and Rahīmāwā
My body was taken to Tūpzāwā
Closer to the one, whose corpse is left behind
It is a while since it was taken away from me
My sight lost pursuit
As I reached south of Samāwa [Nūgra Salmān]
Where old people are left alone
There are no youngsters to be seen
Everyone is starving
Only given two pieces of samūn [Iraqi bread]
Humiliation and misery rule
Electricity cut off at night
Rooms turn into ovens because of the heat
Rooms where women's dresses are ripped off.

She continued by saying that female survivors' suffering did not end even when they were released and forcibly resettled in the "collective" in the region (interview, August 2013, Kalār). They came to be named "*barallā*" (sluts) in the Kurdish communities, as they were seen to be on their own, living without men. Adālat Omar, an independent researcher and activist to whom forty-four women had confirmed everyday rape at the incarceration camps, explained to me that female survivors were told: "If you opened your legs for the Arabs, why should you reject the Kurds?" (interview, August 2013, Erbil). She also stated that the Iraqi High Tribunal was the first space where sexual violence against Kurdish females was rendered public. In fact, in *The Dark Days*, a documentary film directed by Najmaddīn Faqī, the author of the renowned book *Death Chamber*, another woman narrates the testimony of a woman (in her forties) about constant rape of young females at the fort of Nūgra Salmān. "We could not show her face or voice," Faqī affirmed. "This would have had inevitable consequences for her. We screened it in April 14, 1994, to also declare the date as a day of commemoration. It was the first time one could hear about rape of incarcerated women during the Anfāl" (interview, July 2012, Sulaimānī).

THE DOCUMENT AS TESTIMONY

The establishment of the Iraqi High Tribunal, which was first formed by the Coalition Provisional Authority in 2003, became the first legal measure to prosecute those accused of genocide, crimes against humanity, war crimes, and crimes against the Iraqi criminal code committed between July 17, 1968, and May 1, 2003. Article 12 (7) and 13 (22) of the Iraqi High Tribal Statute defines sexual violence—rape, sexual slavery, enforced prostitution, forced pregnancy—as a crime against humanity and a war crime. During the legal proceedings of al-Anfāl trial, copies of thousands of previously classified state documents were presented as legal evidence. The two orders of extermination became key evidence in al-Majid's trial. There was also a copy of a "secret and urgent" document from the Foreign Intelligence Agency of Kirkūk Province, dated December 20, 1989, that testified to sexual violence. Carrying the Islamic phrase at the top, it states the execution of an order: "After receiving immediate authorization from the political leadership and carrying out the First and Second al-Anfāl operation, a group of different people were captured, among them a group of girls, whose ages range between 14 and 29. We have, in accordance with your orders, sent a number of those girls to the brothels and nightclubs in the Arab Republic of Egypt. Attached is a list of the names of those girls and their ages, for your reference."

Abdūllā Karīm, a journalist, put the document into circulation in the region as he published it in *Kurdistani Nwe*, a PUK newspaper, in 2003. When I asked for the original version of the document, Abdūllā said a "patriotic friend gave me a copy," and that he does not doubt its originality (interview, July 2013, Sulaimānī). Omar Muhamed, an al-Anfāl researcher, told me, "the document does not lie" (interview, August 2013, Sulaimānī). What is of importance here is not the authenticity of the document but rather its translation. Abdūl-khāleq (b. 1956), brother of one of the girls whose name is listed, who had saved a copy, told me: "As testimony at the Tribunal [in 2006], I showed the *Balgenāmeh* (lit. letter of evidence), but chief judge Mohamed Uraibi declared it to be a forgery. How can it be forged?" The document and the experiences of sexual violence were presented as testimonies directed at Saddām Hussein during his trial, who furiously dismissed the legitimacy of the Iraqi High Tribunal and trade in women and girls and the testimony of rape. "I can never accept the claim that an Iraqi woman was raped while Saddām was president. . . . Kurdish women are being raped at the time of Saddām Hussein, and still Saddām Hussein grows a mustache and speaks with big words?" This was to say that the rape of Kurdish women is against his manhood and presidential responsibility. Abdūl-khāleq remembered this scene vividly: "I could not stand him. I told him, if you could kill children, bomb villagers with chemical weapons, how could you not do this?" By writing off the document as forged, the chief judge also legally hid, occulted the whereabouts of the girls and women, whose names are listed. The al-Anfāl trial resulted in the execution of al-Majid by hanging and in a verdict that recognized the al-Anfāl as genocide, and sexual violence and rape as crimes against humanity and war crimes.

However, it is only in 2013 that the document once again enters the public realm. An Egyptian soap opera, Nīrān Sadīqa (lit. Friendly Fire), premiered on the MBC satellite television in the entire Middle East in July 2013. Three male characters in two scenes of one episode discuss what to do with the Kurdish women who are abducted during the al-Anfāl and sold to one of the owners of a cabaret in Egypt. The owners (father and son) have conflicting views: while one claims that the cabaret saves them from falling prey to the al-Anfāl, the other wants them removed. The film script was translated into Sūrānī Kurdish, and continuously circulated through local mass and social media in the region. In an act of simultaneous screening of the film script, the document, the testimonies of the family members, the photographs and identity cards of some of the names listed, and the testimonies of local survivor organizations and activists' mass media formed what the siblings and activists called a "collection of testimonial evidence." Since testifying "is always to render public" (Derrida 2000, 30), the repeated screening took on a life of its own and each screening testified to the veracity of the abduction and experiences of women during the al-Anfāl. Thus it enabled the siblings to claim moral justice and to demand that the Kurdistan Regional Government (KRG) take political responsibility. The prime minister of the KRG, Nechirvan Barzani, with its Ministry of Martyrs and Anfāl Affairs, formed a committee and promised to investigate the case in August 2013. Almost a year later, in July 16, 2014, Mala Yassin, the KRG representative to Egypt, announced that the case is a "fiction," and demanded that the KRG Council of Ministers take legal measures against whoever spreads wrong information about female abduction. As a result, the Kalār Primary Court issued an arrest warrant for Abdūllā Karīm in April 29, 2015. This has further buttressed the document as evidence, and has extended it into the future. The local branches of the Kurdistan Union of Journalists and the Union of Kurdish Writers in Sulaimānī, satellite TV stations such as Rigā and NRT, local radio stations and newspapers, associations such as Kurdocide Watch, and lawyers have spread the news about the document, and declared support for Abdūllā, who is now awaiting trial.

THE SIBLINGS' TESTIMONIES

The families of the listed women currently live in villages and towns in the Germyān region and in Kirkūk. I had my first meeting with Nāzem (b. 1957), brother of a woman whose name is on the list. He is a lieutenant colonel in the KRG army and lives in Rizgāri (literally, liberation), inhabited mostly by those who survived the al-Anfāl. I went with Nāzem, his son, and Baleen, a research assistant, to Nawjūl, where fifteen of the listed women once lived, in late August 2013. While driving, he told me how in the beginning of April 1988, the Iraqi troops encircled the area: "After people left their homes in search of safety, the bulldozers entered and demol-ished the district. . . . People could not live without water and food, therefore they submitted themselves to the military intelligence. Our sisters and daughters were then taken and sold to Arab countries. I swear by God, the Arabs are not Muslims. How can you trade in human beings?" He also talked about women being sold in Kirkuk, and explained to me that during the time he was serving in the Iraqi army south of Baghdad, in 2008, an officer had told him about a Kurdish woman living in his village. Nāzem recalled: "He told me that during Anfāl an officer hid her in his car and took her home. She is married to one of his brothers and has three children now." The Ministry of Martyrs and Anfāl Affairs is aware of this, but "does noth-ing," he told me. After an almost two-hour drive we arrived in Nawjūl. The families of the women listed had left the ruined village. Therefore we moved on toward Tūz Khūrmāto, about thirty kilometers away, to meet with Kharāmān (b. 1958), sister of a woman whose name is on the list. At the time of the al-Anfāl, the town had been under strict surveillance of the Special Security Organization, the Foreign Intel-ligence Agency, and the national police, and the Kurds were only "allowed to live a life faithful to the state authorities," Kharāmān told me. When I asked whether she thinks that the document is a "fiction," she said: "If the document is a forgery, what about the film? What about the photographs? What about the national identity cards of our sisters? And, what about us? Are we lying, too?" She narrated what she had witnessed in 1988, when her sister together with her children and many other people were captured in the proximity of Nawjūl and transported to the police station in Tūz Khūrmāto and from there to an unknown destination. "They [Iraqi military] brought the captured people to the police station here in Tūz. We were waiting just outside the station, and my sister asked us to go back home. She said, 'I swear by God we will never return.' It was me and my two brothers. . . . I never saw her again. I got a phone call just some time ago, and I was told that they [the KRG] are going to [attempt to] return my sister. I swear by God, my heart was about to stop, because I was so happy [weeping]. I have no one; just two brothers and her. I don't know what to do. I cannot do anything" (interview, September 2013, Tūz Khūrmāto).

It was perplexing for Kharāmān and Nāzem that the KRG did not rely on individual testimony of the female abductions. Jalāl (b. 1971), brother of a woman listed on the document, therefore told me: "It is thanks to the Egyptian soap opera that the KRG has come to listen to us." He showed me a photograph of himself with his sister, shot in early 1988, and said that he is sure it will one day be useful as testimonial evidence. The photographs and the national identity cards are preserved as testimonies of injustice, sites of memory, as well as claims for a justice that is yet to come. All four interlocutors, including Abdūl-khāleq, who spoke about the original list of abductees, insisted that the high-ranking Kurdish collaborators too can testify to the abduction of all those listed in the document, and that they must be held accountable for what they have done. A female survivor who had been among those detained at the police station in Tūz described abduction as a common practice. She explained to me that the Kurds and Turkmen from Tūz had protested and some of the detainees managed to escape. She added, "One night some Kurdish collaborators led by a [Kurdish] adviser, Jabār the tall, entered the police station and only took the young girls. They knew that otherwise the Arabs would take them. My mother said it is better that the Kurds take them than the Arabs" (interview, September 2013, Rizgāri). Therefore, she left her children and her mother behind in the police station and escaped when the protest was at its peak. Her seven-month-old daughter later died, and her two sons together with one of those "young girls" are now living with her. The fate of the other girls who were allegedly "saved" by the collaborators remains unknown.

CONCLUSION

The analysis of iterability of state writings and their translation into testimonial and legal evidence can enable researchers to account for what reduces genocide to human actions, that is, perpetrators or victims. The writings of the state and its translation of religion and law are irreducible to human actions as they render public the formation of the modern state and its bureaucracy, acts, and modes of justification. In addition, the iterability of the collection of testimonial evidence broke the established frontier of silence set by the political, social, and religious order in the Kurdistan region. It rendered public and shaped the narrative about sexual violence, rape, and, in particular, abduction of women during the al-Anfāl. Although the KRG has silenced the demands of the siblings, survivors, and activists, which they understand as denial and political impunity, the struggle of those who have been silenced rather suggests an attempt at rewriting the al-Anfāl.

NOTES

I would like to thank Victoria Sanford, Katerina Stefatos, Cecilia Salvi, and the Law, Organization, Science and Technology research group in Halle, Germany, for their comments and critical interest.

1. A code name that is drawn from Sūreh al-Anfāl, the eighth Sūreh of the Qur'ān.
2. See the Federal Commissioner for the Records of the State Security Service of the former German Democratic Republic. http://www.bstu.bund.de/EN/Home/home_node.html. Accessed January 10, 2015.
3. For more information, see the International Tracing Service webpage: https://www .itsarolsen.org/en/homepage/index.html. Accessed January 10, 2015.
4. Al-Anfāl maps are available at http://www.rightsmaps.com/html/anfalful.html. Accessed January 25, 2015.

REFERENCES

Al-Anfāl Campaign (maps). Accessed January 25, 2015. http://www.rightsmaps.com/html/ anfalful.html.
Bauman, Zygmunt. 1989. *Modernity and the Holocaust.* Ithaca, NY: Cornell University Press.
Brzoska, Michael. 1987. "Profiteering on the Iran-Iraq War." *Bulletin of the Atomic Scientists* 43 (5): 42–45.
Das, Veena. 2004. "The Signature of the State: The Paradox of Illegibility." In *Anthropology in the Margins of the State,* edited by Veena Das and Deborah Poole. Santa Fe, NM: School of American Research Press.
Derrida, Jacques. 1988. *Limited Inc.* Evanston, IL: Northwestern University Press.
———. 2000. *Demeure: Fiction and Testimony.* Stanford: Stanford University Press.
Dieterich, Renate. 2005. "Germany's Relations with Iraq and Transjordan from the Weimar Republic to the End of the Second World War." *Middle Eastern Studies* 41 (4): 463–479.
Fakhry, Majid. 2000. *An Interpretation of the Qur'an: English Translation of the Meanings.* New York: New York University Press.
Federal Commissioner for the Records of the State Security Service of the Former German Democratic Republic. Accessed January 26, 2015. http://www.bstu.bund.de/EN/ Archives/AboutArchivesOfBStU/inhalt.html.
Hardi, Choman. 2011. *Gendered Experiences of Genocide: Anfāl Survivors in Kurdistan-Iraq.* Farnham, UK: Ashgate.
Hull, S. Matthew. 2012. *Government of Paper: The Materiality of Bureaucracy in Urban Pakistan.* Berkeley: University of California Press.
International Tracing Service (ITS). Accessed January 26, 2015. https://www.its-arolsen.org/ en/about-its/index.html.
Kafka, Ben. 2012. *The Demons of Writing: Powers and Failures of Paperwork.* New York: Zone Books.
Kelly, Michael J. 2008. *Ghosts of Halabja: Saddam Hussein and the Kurdish Genocide.* Westport, CT: Praeger Security International.
———. 2013. "'Never Again'? German Chemical Corporation Complicity in the Kurdish Genocide." *Berkeley Journal of International Law* 13 (2): 348–391.
Makiya, Kanan. 1993. *Cruelty and Silence: War, Tyranny, Uprising, and the Arab World.* New York: W. W. Norton.

———. 1998. *Republic of Fear: The Politics of Modern Iraq.* Berkeley: University of California Press.

Montgomery, Bruce P. 2012. "Saddam Hussein's Records of Atrocity: Seizure, Removal, and Restitution." *American Archivist* 75 (2): 326–370.

Rottenburg, Richard. 2009. *Far-fetched Facts: A Parable of Development Aid.* Cambridge, MA: MIT Press.

Sanford, Victoria. 2004. *Buried Secrets: Truth and Human Rights in Guatemala.* New York: Palgrave Macmillan.

Sassoon, Joseph. 2014. "The East German Ministry for State Security and Iraq, 1968–1989." *Journal of Cold War Studies* 16 (1): 4–23.

Swift, Simon. 2009. *Hannah Arendt.* London: Routledge.

Tripp, Charles. 2007. *A History of Iraq.* Cambridge: Cambridge University Press.

Vismann, Cornelia. 2008. *Files: Law and Media Technology.* Stanford: Stanford University Press.

Weber, Max. 1978. *Economy and Society.* Berkeley: University of California Press.

Weld, Kirsten. 2014. *Paper Cadavers: The Archives of Dictatorship in Guatemala.* Durham, NC: Duke University Press.

Wild, Stefan. 1985. "National Socialism in the Arab Near East between 1933 and 1939." *Die Welt des Islams* 25 (1): 126–170.

7 · SEXUALIZED BODIES, PUBLIC MUTILATION, AND TORTURE AT THE BEGINNING OF INDONESIA'S NEW ORDER REGIME (1965–1966)

ANNIE POHLMAN

Ibu Sri, Ibu Nana, and Ibu Lani are three women who survived the violence that swept across Indonesia following an aborted coup on October 1, 1965.[1] In the aftermath of that coup, the Indonesian military rose to power and, together with co-opted civilian militias, wiped out their mass-supported political rivals, the Indonesian Communist Party (Partai Komunis Indonesia, or PKI).[2] An estimated five hundred thousand people were killed during this mass violence for their membership in or association with the PKI, while more than a million others were rounded up and held in political detention where many were tortured, starved, or worked to death (see Cribb 1990, 11–14). These three women witnessed the killings and all had spent time as political prisoners in West Sumatra. All had also lost family members or friends during the massacres. To this day, there has yet to be any kind of official acknowledgment or apology by the Indonesian state to these three women or to the millions of other victims and their families for these mass atrocities. The eradication of communists, and leftist ideology and politics more broadly within Indonesia, is remembered by elites and most of the population as a necessary and justified massacre (Heryanto 2006).[3]

More than forty years after these events, Ibu Sri, Ibu Nana, and Ibu Lani sat with me and a colleague, Narny Yenny, and recounted stories about the violence of 1965: about people who had been killed, murders they had witnessed, prisoners who had been tortured and killed, and about their own experiences of violence and survival. Ibu Sri and Ibu Lani had been helping us to locate and interview women survivors of the massacres in West Sumatra. The three women knew one another from their time together in a detention center in a nearby town. Together, they told stories and reenacted events, describing people and places. Some of these stories were hilarious, such as when Ibu Sri and Ibu Nana together described making fun of one of the guards at the detention center. Other stories were horrific and revealed the cruel and inhuman ways in which perpetrators had degraded, humiliated, maimed, and murdered their victims. Their stories also exposed the sexualization of this violence as they recounted what had happened to men and women whose bodies were targeted and destroyed in ways meant to attack their sexual organs and sexual identities. Here, I quote part of their stories at length:[4]

IBU LANI: In [this] region, [pregnant] women were stabbed from here [she indicated her stomach] so then the baby would be pierced through, and then out the other side [she reenacted a type of spear going through her abdomen]. Or from here [she reversed the action], getting stabbed from the back. They'd be killed like that with bamboo.

IBU NANA: If there was a woman who was cut like that and then died then the baby would die too. So if she were pregnant then the little baby she carried would [die] as well. If [the mother] were stabbed from behind then it [the bamboo spear] would come out of here [she indicated her stomach].

IBU LANI: Some men were cut here [she drew her hand across her throat], cut like this. There were all sorts of ways that [victims] were killed. Many were tortured first, in [detention]. Some had their genitals pulled repeatedly. That's what would happen. All sorts of things like this happened.

IBU NANA: Some were dragged behind cars. Some were sliced here, here, and here, like this [she mimed having a large knife in her hand and sliced it into different parts of her body], with a machete. From here to here with a machete [she mimed being cut in a vertical line from her genitals to her throat]. And after that, they would be dragged behind a car, destroyed like that. That was how some were killed. That happened in ____ town.

IBU SRI: Yes, like what happened to that girl, N___. That girl, [she was] raped and then hung.

IBU LANI: After being raped, hung! . . . There are many [victims] buried near [here]. They would do terrible torture first, cutting of fingers and other parts. Some were buried alive. That's what it was like here. . . . The heads [of victims] were cut off. Decapitated, then taken about like this [she mimes carrying a stick held upright] in the market. All over the place.

ANNIE: Around the marketplace?

IBU NANA: Yes, in the market, paraded about and carried all over the place, like this [she stood up and mimed carrying the stick around us in a circle], the head of someone who'd been decapitated.

Ibu Lani, Ibu Nana, and Ibu Sri's stories are but some of the testimonies given, by survivors and witnesses to the mass killings of 1965–1966, over the past two decades since the end of the military regime that rose to power during the massacres, the New Order (1966–1998). Their descriptions of the many ways in which victims were harmed pre- and postmortem reveal the deeply dehumanizing and sexualized violence enacted against men and women during the anticommunist purges that began in October 1965 and continued on, in some parts of Indonesia, through to 1968. The impalement and disemboweling of pregnant women in order to kill both the mother and fetus; the rape and sexualized torture of women and men; the wounding, mutilation, and disarticulation of bodies through cuts and stabs, lacerations, and other forms of blunt or penetrating trauma; the dragging of victims behind cars, causing skin excoriations on rough road surfaces and deep abrasions to soft tissue, bones, and organs; and the removal and display of body parts, particularly victims' heads, to create spectacles of paraded flesh were all modes of expression whereby the bodies and remains of alleged communists were hung up, left out, or purposefully posed in public areas (see also Anonymous 1990; Siregar 1993). Those victims whose bodies were made into these spectacularized displays on the roads, in the marketplaces, and in other areas of public exhibition, however, made up but a small proportion of the overall number of victims who experienced torture and other forms of extreme violence against their bodies and minds during the anticommunist purges. In the detention centers that sprung up across Indonesia to hold hundreds of thousands of political detainees, similar forms of violence were perpetrated as part of "interrogations"; in many ways the spectacular and the secret forms of torture and mutilation were mirrors for each other.

In this chapter, I examine these stories by Ibu Lani, Ibu Sri, and Ibu Nana, and a number of secondary witness reports as but a handful of accounts about sexualized mutilation and torture perpetrated during the mass violence of 1965–1968. I make two main arguments in relation to these forms of violence. The first relates to the sexualization of torture and public mutilation by state agents and their co-opted militia counterparts in Indonesia; the second, to the communicative intent behind this violence. In this analysis, I contrast examples of sexualized mutilation and trophy-taking during the massacres with gendered forms of humiliation and torture during interrogations in the detention centers. The first part of my argument highlights how acts of state-perpetrated violence in these spectacular and secret forms in Indonesia were sexualized. I argue that the sexualization and fetishization of victims' bodies were fundamental parts of both public mutilations and interrogational torture. As such, this sexualization of violent acts must be seen as central to both forms of violence.

The second part of my argument relates to the communicative intent of both public mutilations and torture in the detention camps across Indonesia during this period. The majority of scholarly work on torture posits it as secretive acts practiced by state agents as part of coercive interrogations. The violence perpetrated at the beginning of the New Order state, however, reveals the broader practices and essentially communicative elements of torture. In my analysis of sexualized forms of this violence, I first examine purposefully inflicted suffering and related forms of coercive treatment and interrogation perpetrated against political prisoners. Second, I examine acts of intentional display killings and mutilation or dismemberment in public places with the purpose of intimidating or terrorizing the local population. Both the secret torture of the interrogations and the spectacular display torture of public mutilation were forms of terror and constituted victims as "bare life"; life that was necessarily eradicated with impunity (Agamben 1998). To argue this, I explore the connections between the torture perpetrated against tens of thousands in the interrogation centers and the public display of torture and mutilation across Indonesia during this period of violent social upheaval (see Pohlman 2012).

THE SEXUALIZATION OF MUTILATION AND TORTURE

The violence perpetrated during the mass killings and during the political detention of alleged communists in Indonesia following the 1965 coup was frequently sexualized in its forms and intent. This violence took many forms, including sexualized humiliation and intimidation, sexual assault and rape, gang rape, mutilation, and torture. The period of time over which sexual violence was perpetrated against individuals also ranged widely, from singular cases of assault, to multiple assaults over days, weeks, and months, to prolonged and protracted cases of ongoing abuses, including enforced prostitution, sexual enslavement, and forced marriage. There were also some cases of forced abortion, particularly when women were held in conditions of sexual enslavement. Of those killed or detained, men in their late teens to early fifties appear to have made up the majority of victims, though women of the same age group, children of both sexes, and older men and women were also killed and detained. While there were some reported cases of sexual violence against men and boys, particularly during public mutilations and torture sessions, this violence was predominantly perpetrated against women and teenage girls during killings, as part of detention, and in the women's homes and communities more generally (see Pohlman 2015; see also McAtackney, this volume).

In accounts about mutilations and dismemberments, which were central aspects of public execution killings, such as in the descriptions given by Ibu Lani,

Ibu Sri, and Ibu Nana, it is clear that sexualized violence played a key role. When contrasting these forms of sexualized violence as part of public mutilations with the forms of violence perpetrated against the hundreds of thousands of political detainees tortured during the years following the 1965 coup, the similarities are often striking. In particular, sexual violence was a frequent feature of both public mutilations and torture against political detainees during interrogations. I argue that, given the pervasive use of sexualized violence as part of torture and public mutilations and how men's and women's bodies were so clearly attacked and disarticulated in ways that distinguished their male and female parts, the sexualization of these forms of violence was fundamental to this violence—seen in the apparent intent behind these acts, in the chosen techniques used against victims, and in the communicative aspects directed at those who witnessed these atrocities.

The sexualization of the violence of public mutilations and torture as part of interrogations was fundamental to both partly because they were two halves of a whole. In the latter part of this chapter, I explain how the spectacular violence of public mutilations must be seen as intimately connected to the torture of detainees in the interrogation rooms. It is estimated that tens of thousands were rounded up in mass arrests and detained every week in the six months that followed the October coup. The prisons, police stations, and military quarters were soon filled well past capacity and so detention and interrogation centers were set up across Indonesia on an ad hoc basis, with confiscated schools, shops, and even libraries converted to hold the many, many detainees in often squalid and inhuman conditions (see Margiyono and Yunanto 2007). Women and any children they had with them were often kept in separate cells from the male prisoners. In these places, detainees were often confined in overcrowded cells, with little or no bathing or toilet facilities, and with very little food. Many starved to death. Others disappeared and were executed en masse, their bodies thrown into mass graves, rivers, or caves. Others succumbed to their injuries from the many torture sessions, which most detainees endured as part of their interrogations. As time went on, these detainees were also increasingly used for forced and unpaid labor. Interrogations were most frequently carried out in the first weeks and months of a detainee's imprisonment, though there were cases where these interrogation sessions continued over a period of years. While the massacres and public mutilations were mostly concluded by mid-1966, the Indonesian military and police worked for years, together with their co-opted civilian counterparts drawn from the ranks of religious and nationalist organizations, to interrogate the men, women, and sometimes children arrested for their alleged communist links. Frequently, interrogation escalated into torture: hundreds of thousands are estimated to have been tortured during the mid-to-late 1960s (Roosa 2008).

Torture against women detainees in the interrogation centers across Indonesia habitually involved sexualized forms of violence meant to inflect pain and to violate the victim's sexual autonomy and identity. As Ximena Bunster-Burotto found in her study of torture against women in Latin America, sexual torture against women is "consciously and systematically directed at her female sexual identity and female anatomy.... [It is a] 'radical disorientation' of her self-respect, dignity, physical integrity" (1994, 166). Interrogation sessions for women detainees routinely began with being forced to strip partially or completely naked. The enforced exposure of a woman's body, often before two or three male, uniformed policemen or soldiers, was a commonly described method to humiliate and intimidate her (see Pohlman 2015; see also Stefatos, this volume). This humiliation and intimidation were clearly sexualized in women's accounts of this abuse; the unwilling and violent forced nakedness exposing breasts, pubic hair, and buttocks, all parts of the body normally covered, were described as ways to deliberately humiliate them as dirty, promiscuous, shameless women. This process of forced nakedness and exposure was an essential part of the radical disorientation of detention; being forced to undress in those rooms with those men was described as an integral part of making detainees feel powerless. The sexualization of this disempowerment was clearly marked in women's stories in which they recounted feelings of vulnerability and their dread of further violence and, in particular, of rape.

This dread was well founded. In most cases, the forced undressing was followed by sexual assault. In interviews with women across Sumatra and Java over the past decade, there were frequent descriptions of how interrogation sessions began with forced nakedness and then rapidly escalated into other forms of violence, including sexual assault, rape, and gang rape, in addition to other forms of torture, such as beatings and other methods of physical assault. Returning to my interview with Ibu Sri, Ibu Nana, and Ibu Lani in West Sumatra, they also described this pattern of abuse:

IBU LANI: Our clothes would be taken off.

IBU NANA: Most of us had to take our clothes off, then they would straddle us, between our legs, with our legs forced open.

IBU LANI: All of [your] clothes were stripped off so there would maybe only be [your] underpants left. All of this [she touches her clothes], this was taken off. And then, then [you would be] beaten, electrocuted. [Your] breasts [she clutches at her breasts and performs the motions] were pulled up, like this, pulled. Your legs were pulled apart. Maybe only with your underpants on, maybe. It was like that, every time it was like that. [You would be] taken in the middle of the night ... then the next night, it would happen again. Every night! And some of them, some of them were raped every night.... The abuse, the sexual abuse, was so common....

IBU NANA: In the interrogations, they'd beat you . . . your body would be black and blue from the beatings, but he wouldn't only torture you. It would also be a way for [the interrogator] to satisfy his base desires. When it was over, when he was finished, you'd be thrown out of the room. There was no kindness, nothing. It was like we were just animals.

In this joint testimony by Ibu Nana and Ibu Lani, they described the pattern of sexual, mental, and physical abuse perpetrated against themselves and the other women at the detention center where they were imprisoned in a town in West Sumatra. In interviews with women across Indonesia, this pattern was often repeated, the descriptions of the wide range of techniques of abuse used against women detainees revealing the profound sexualization of torture aimed at denigrating and destroying women's bodies and sexual identities. These patterns of sexualized abuse were also strongly reminiscent of the violence done to women's bodies and identities in other conflicts and periods of state repression (see Taylor 1997; Treacy 1996; Stefatos, this volume).

To illustrate how some of these techniques used against women detainees were unmistakably intended to attack them based on the sex of their bodies and their sexuality as women, I recount here the experience of Ibu H. Arrested shortly after the coup, Ibu H was interrogated and tortured repeatedly at a military post in East Java. As she recalled:

In front of the interrogator [a soldier], I saw that cable that was attached to an electricity generator. They attached the cable to the ends of my fingers and toes, but I wasn't trembling because of that. What made me stiff [with fear] was when they attached the end of the cable to my nipples and, God help me, they also put one into my vagina. When they connected the end of the other cable to the generator, I fell down and fainted. I don't know what happened after that, but when I came to, I was back in one of the cells again. My breasts were burnt and my vagina was swollen and bleeding. I felt unbelievable pain. (cited in Komnas Perempuan 2007, 57)

Ibu H's testimony about her experience is an example of the highly sexualized techniques used against some women detainees during torture. Electric shock was a type of torture used often against both men and women imprisoned during this period; cables were usually attached to fingers or toes and electric currents passed through the body at increasingly frequent and intense intervals, as was the case for Ibu H. It was, however, Ibu H's most visible physiological organs that mark sexual difference, her breasts and vagina, which differentiates this sexualized torture against her. Instances whereby women detainees were beaten on their breasts and stomachs, raped and gang-raped (penile and with a range of sharp or blunt instruments), whipped, stabbed, or had cigarettes put out on their breasts or on their genital area, had their hair cut or shaved, their pubic hair cut or set on fire[5]—all were recounted in women's testimonies about the violence perpetrated against them during interrogations, which reveal how these forms of violence were fundamentally aimed at sexually denigrating, humiliating, and harming them as women.

In these and other accounts and testimonies by eyewitnesses and survivors of the Indonesian killings, body parts are dissociated from the individual men and women from which they were cut or burnt off, or whose bodies were impaled, torn open, and disarticulated in other ways. The organs and other body parts were removed, reified, and displayed to stand for those being eradicated as part of the anticommunist purges (see Feldman 1991, 63–64). These techniques were not accidental; they were specific forms of brutality meant to harm, desecrate, and dehumanize the sexualized, even fetishized, enemy bodies of victims. These forms of highly sexualized mutilation were intimate, elaborate, and highly symbolic. While the specific intent of individual perpetrators is unknown, these were acts of profound depersonalization and dehumanization to desecrate victims' bodies or perhaps to interfere with mortuary practices and beliefs. Cases of mutilation may also have been intended to accumulate objects of display and dominance, to acquire trophies for individual perpetrators, or as proof of murders carried out; in each case, creating "possessable" items from the bodies of enemies but also the sexualization of those body parts (see Harrison 2012). It is not the intent of individual perpetrators that concerns me here, however, but rather how the mutilations as part of spectacular display killings and torture during interrogations, both deeply sexualized in their practices, can be seen to show the Indonesian state's communicative intent during this period; in essence, the violence in its spectacular and secret forms producing the horror of Michel Foucault's "tortured body" as a sign of power (1977).

THE COMMUNICATIVE INTENT OF TORTURE AND PUBLIC MUTILATION

The violence perpetrated as part of public mutilations during the Indonesian killings can be seen as mirroring the violence committed during torture and interrogation against political detainees rounded up during the anticommunist purges. In both public mutilations and interrogational torture, sexualized violence was a frequent element of these crimes. Given the prevalence of these sexualized forms of violence, we must see this sexualization of torture and mutilation as fundamental to both, in form and in the intent of these acts. It is the intent and, in particular, the communicative elements of both torture and public mutilations that reveals how each becomes a mirror of the other.

Torture is essentially goal-orientated: to obtain information, to punish, to intimidate, and to terrorize (Wisnewski 2010, 3–5). States that practice torture against their citizens exhibit their willingness to create pain to achieve political outcomes. Thus this second part of my argument seeks to reevaluate our understanding of torture in Indonesia during the 1965 killings through the inclusion and evaluation of such practices both within interrogational settings and where such actions were publicly displayed. In both settings, the acts reveal the intentional creation of suffering by state agents as well as the state's willingness to utilize terror as a didactic function. To make this argument, I follow the work of researchers who have examined the spectacular and hidden or secret forms of violence perpetrated by state actors and how these forms of violence are both forms of terror (Foucault 1977; Graziano 1992; Humphrey 2002). In particular, here I make use of Daniel Rothenberg's concept of "public presentational torture" to discuss spectacular forms of violence as terror; that is, "the mangled bodies of victims bearing the signs of torture [that] are purposefully displayed for political ends" (2003–2004, 470), and how this violence is tied to interrogational torture.

For Rothenberg, it is the relationship between the violence done to the individuals whose bodies are destroyed and its impact on society that underpins the "communicative logic of broken bodies" through torture; both are interrogational and presentational as public spectacles of violence. The communicative logic of this violence serves many purposes. It is essential to the type of "terror warfare" that destabilizes communal life, infecting everyday interactions and activities with fear, as Carolyn Nordstrom (1998) shows. This profound destabilization through terror brings on Michael Taussig's "doubleness" of living with pervasive violence, whereby the normalcy of everyday life can never be safe again (1989). Moreover, there is an instructive function to this terror, made real in communal life through the rounding up and disappearance of so many, and through the reappearance of some victims, sometimes those people known in the community, displayed on roads and in front of guard posts, bodies torn or ripped apart. The physical and mental trauma perpetrated against individual victims reverberates through their communities (see also the chapters by Anastario and Cosgrove in this volume). In many ways, the terror of mass violence, such as during the mid-1960s in Indonesia, communicates the state's attempt to establish control and its demand for acquiescence from the population under that control (see Sluka 2000).

The spectacular, purposeful, and forcefully visible violence on the roads and in the towns, which invoke "body horror" in mutilation and display (Taylor 1997), and the mostly invisible but well-known violence done to hundreds of thousands who disappeared into the detention centers across Indonesia, were intimately connected forms of terror. The two faces of torture, the secret and the spectacular, during these years of mass social unrest and violence in Indonesia were inseparable and essential means by which this terror was spread and inculcated (see Pohlman 2012). In many ways, both functioned as terror by destabilizing social bonds and spaces, and both showed, as Rothenberg interprets it, the state's willingness to use violence against bodies to achieve political ends. In this way, both the spectacular and secret forms of torture were also constitutive of bare life; life that was marked and captured by the military state that emerged during the 1965–1966 massacres in Indonesia but which was also excluded from all forms of social, legal, or other protection. In Giorgio Agamben's terms, each of the people tortured in the detention camps and each person tortured and mutilated on the roads and in front of homes was made *homo sacer*, one whose rights and social place has been stripped away, whose life is without significance or protection and who therefore can be killed with impunity (Agamben 1998). The public killings, the display of corpses and parts of corpses, and the fetishized trophy-taking not only functioned to terrorize, this violence also created the bare life, so crucial to the founding of the Indonesian state, which must be subjugated and exterminated. The military state that rose during the massacres created a nation in which the PKI and its supporters were the enemy, which justified and necessitated their eradication; as *homo sacer*, each suspected communist supporter was bare life that, while utterly excluded from the new society, was also fundamental to the creation of the new Indonesian state (Agamben 1998). As Teresa Macias explains, *homo sacer* "is the life, not excluded from, but actually captured in, the grip of power, that authorizes the constitution of the nation, the subjectification of the citizen and the design and implementation of those institutional procedures and practices that render the power of the state over life thinkable and practicable" (2013, 118).

The bare life of those accused of communist sympathies was also clear for those who disappeared from their families and communities in the mass arrests. While the corpses of victims were terrifyingly visible spectacles of bare life that could be eradicated with impunity, those who were taken and disappeared were frighteningly unseen. As Frank Graziano (1992) puts it, the disappeared were made into an "absent spectacle," which also served to terrorize communities. The people taken into the detention centers were frequently tortured and starved and many did not survive. Such places became "public secrets" (*"rahasia umum"*) within their local communities. In my interviews with survivors of the detention centers across various regions of Sumatra and Java since the early 2000s, they were described as places that local people avoided because they were *angker* (Javanese for "uncanny") or haunted, violent places where people went to die. "People knew what happened there," as Ibu Nana said during one of our interviews together with Ibu Lani, "Everyone knew. . . . [People were] tortured, killed there, taken away in trucks and executed in the night. How could [they] not know?"[6] As Graziano explains, in relation to the disappeared during the

Argentine Dirty War years, "Instead of cheering or gasping or screaming beside the gallows, the public voice reached only a hushed whisper risked in the shadows, a mumble of rumors diffusing the spectacle by word of mouth through a population that was itself diffused, confused, frightened" (1992, 73). The terror is in not seeing but knowing what happened to those disappeared into the detention camps. The camps are spaces of exception and impunity where individuals are reduced to bare life.

The mass violence that spread across Indonesia, perpetrated by soldiers and policemen and the many civilian militia groups who worked closely with state forces, forever changed Indonesia. The terror of those months that followed the October 1965 coup never really ended. As other researchers, such as Ariel Heryanto (2006) and Michael van Langenberg (1990) have argued, the violence of 1965–1966 both established and perpetuated General Suharto's New Order regime. The Indonesian military, by so completely eradicating its main political rival, the PKI, ensured both the emergence and consolidation of its power. Furthermore, by using the killings of 1965–1966 as legitimation for their authoritarian rule, and by creating and re-creating the fallacy of a resurgent "communist threat" in the subsequent thirty-three years of rule, the regime created an "almost unstoppable mechanical reproduction and elaboration of fear and intimidation surrounding the possible re-occurrence of such major violence" (Heryanto 2006, 4).

This continuing legacy of the 1965 violence on Indonesian society was an issue raised numerous times during my interviews with mainly women survivors over the past decade. Once again, I return to the interview with Ibu Sri, Ibu Lani, and Ibu Nana, and reflect on their interpretation of this legacy. In their joint testimony, they very clearly linked the terror of those months following the coup with how this violence affected communities. Notably, they specifically linked the spectacular forms of public presentation torture, and the threat of arrest and disappearance, with these pedagogical functions of terror. At the beginning of this chapter, I quoted parts of my interview with these three women in which they described various acts of public mutilation and torture. This quote directly follows their story of how victims' heads were cut off, impaled on long bamboo spears, and paraded about the village.

ANNIE: Why would they do that?

IBU LANI: Because they wanted to be in power for a long time. In order to terrify the public. By showing off like that, by making others watch this decapitated head, carried around here and there, that was scary. Terrifying. If you frighten people, you make them stupid. If they're stupid, of course they won't criticize you. That was the aim of it. Because if you want to have power, you terrify people with these immoral acts.

IBU NANA: If you spoke out, then the same thing would happen to you. You'd be killed, taken [arrested], gone. [Your head] on a spear. That's what it was like. You'd better watch it, if you spoke out, because the same thing would happen to you. So everyone was afraid . . . our lips were sealed by that event. By that savagery.

CONCLUSION: COMMUNICATIVE INTENT THROUGH SEXUALIZED TORTURE AND PUBLIC MUTILATION

In those months of terror following the October 1965 coup in Indonesia, an estimated half a million people were killed, leftist politics were erased from the Indonesian polity, and the foundations were laid for the following thirty-three years of the New Order's militarist, authoritarian regime. Key to the terror of these months was the torture perpetrated by Indonesian state security services and their co-opted civilian counterparts, both in the streets and in the marketplaces through public presentational forms and in the interrogation rooms across Indonesia in which hundreds of thousands were tortured during political detention.

As I have argued in this chapter, the violence of public mutilations in many ways mirrored the violence of the interrogations. In this analysis, I have emphasized that in both public mutilations and interrogational torture the violence and intent of torture cannot be understood to "lie simply in the pain that is associated with the act, but in the intentional creation of this pain in the service of state interests" (Rothenberg 2003–2004, 496–497). When we examine the torture perpetrated in 1965–1966 in both its spectacular and secret forms, it is essential that we examine how both functioned as communicative acts to horrify, subdue, and inculcate fear among the population. Those taken, tortured, and killed were made into Agamben's *homo sacer*, life that was justifiably eradicated (1998).

Furthermore, when examining not only the intents of these acts but also their forms, it is clear that sexualized violence was fundamental to both public mutilation and interrogational torture. Given the prevalence of these sexualized forms of violence, we must see this sexualization as essential to the intent of these acts. By examining these two faces of torture, I argue that we must understand these acts as interconnected, requiring an engagement with and recognition of both the different forms of torture and their communicative elements. By highlighting how these acts of torture and dismemberment in the interrogation centers and as part of public mutilations were sexualized, I argue that these acts are profoundly gendered in both their intent and form.

NOTES

1. "Ibu" is an Indonesian term meaning "mother/wife." All names of informants are pseud-onyms. This particular interview was recorded on voice recorder and took place in West Sumatra, September 2005.

2. The military regime that rose to power during the massacres, under General Suharto, was known as the "New Order" and lasted from 1966 until 1998. The regime was an authoritarian, militarist government that used anticommunism, and the threat of a communist resurgence, to maintain legitimacy (Heryanto 2006).

3. The recent 2012 film *The Act of Killing* teases out some of the complexities of remembering and celebrating mass murder in Indonesia.

4. The interview took place in West Sumatra, September 2005.

5. For example, interviews with Ibu Moeliek (Sumatra, September 2005); Ibu Lis (Sumatra, September 2005); and Ibu Astuti (Sumatra, September 2005).

6. Interview with Ibu Nana and Ibu Lani, together with Narny Yenny, Sumatra, September 2005. The word used by Ibu Nana was "*dibon,*" which literally means "borrowed" but was a common euphemism for being taken away from a detention center and executed, often in groups, and then the victims' bodies disposed of in mass graves.

REFERENCES

The Act of Killing. 2012. A film directed by Joshua Oppenheimer and anonymous (listed this way for the safety of the other directors). Denmark: Final Cut For Real Productions.

Agamben, Giorgio. 1998. *Homo Sacer: Sovereign Power and Bare Life.* Translated by Daniel Heller-Roazen. Stanford: Stanford University Press.

Anonymous. 1990. "Additional Data on Counter-revolutionary Cruelty in Indonesia, Especially in East Java." In *The Indonesian Killings 1965–1966: Studies from Java and Bali,* edited and translated by Robert Cribb. Clayton, Victoria: Centre of Southeast Asia Studies, Monash University.

Bunster-Burotto, Ximena. 1994. "Surviving beyond Fear: Women and Torture in Latin America." In *Women and Violence,* edited by Miranda Davis. London: Zed Books.

Cribb, Robert. 1990. "Introduction: Problems in the Historiography of the Killings in Indonesia." In *The Indonesian Killings 1965–1966: Studies from Java and Bali,* edited by Robert Cribb. Clayton, Victoria: Centre of Southeast Asia Studies, Monash University.

Feldman, Allen. 1991. *Formations of Violence: The Narrative of the Body and Political Terror in Northern Ireland.* Chicago: University of Chicago Press.

Foucault, Michel. 1977. *Discipline and Punish: The Birth of the Prison.* New York: Pantheon.

Graziano, Frank. 1992. *Divine Violence: Spectacle, Psychosexuality, and Radical Christianity in the Argentine "Dirty War".* Boulder, CO: Westview Press.

Harrison, Simon. 2012. *Dark Trophies: Hunting and the Enemy Body in Modern War.* New York: Berghahn Books.

Heryanto, Ariel. 2006. *State Terrorism and Political Identity in Indonesia: Fatally Belonging.* London: Routledge.

Humphrey, Michael. 2002. *The Politics of Atrocity and Reconciliation: From Terror to Trauma.* London: Routledge.

Komnas Perempuan. 2007. *Kejahatan Terhadap Kemanusiaan Berbasis Jender: Mendengarkan Suara Perempuan Korban Peristiwa 1965.* Jakarta: Komnas Perempuan.

Macias, Teresa. 2013. "'Torture Bodies': The Biopolitics of Torture and Truth in Chile." *International Journal of Human Rights* 17: 113–132.

Margiyono and K. Tri Yunanto. 2007. *Neraka Rezim Soeharto Misteri Tempat Penyiksaan Orde Baru.* Jakarta: Spasi and VHR Book.

Nordstrom, Carolyn. 1998. "Terror Warfare and the Medicine of Peace." *Medical Anthropology Quarterly* 12: 103–121.

Pohlman, Annie. 2012. "Spectacular Atrocities: Making Enemies during the 1965–1966 Massacres in Indonesia." In *Theatres of Violence: Massacre, Mass Killing and Atrocity throughout History*, edited by Philip G. Dwyer and Lyndall Ryan. New York: Berghahn Books.

———. 2015. *Women, Sexual Violence, and the Indonesian Killings of 1965–1966.* New York: Routledge.

Roosa, John. 2008. "The Truths of Torture: Victims' Memories and State Histories in Indonesia." *Indonesia* 85: 31–50.

Rothenberg, Daniel. 2003–2004. "'What We Have Seen Has Been Terrible': Public Presentational Torture and the Communicative Logic of State Terror." *Albany Law Review* 67: 465–499.

Siregar, M. R. 1993. *Tragedi Manusia Dan Kemanusiaan: Kasus Indonesia, Sebuah Holokaus Yang Diterima Sesudah Perang Dunia Dedua.* The Hague: Tapol.

Sluka, Jeffrey A. 2000. "Introduction: State Terror and Anthropology." In *Death Squad: The Anthropology of State Terror*, edited by Jeffrey A. Sluka. Philadelphia: University of Pennsylvania Press.

Taussig, Michael. 1989. "Terror as Usual: Walter Benjamin's Theory of History as State of Siege." *Social Text* 23: 3–20.

Taylor, Diana. 1997. *Disappearing Acts: Spectacles of Gender and Nationalism in Argentina's "Dirty War."* Durham, NC: Duke University Press.

Treacy, Mary Jane. 1996. "Double Binds: Latin American Women's Prison Memories." *Hypatia* 11: 130–145.

van Langenberg, Michael. 1990. "Gestapu and State Power in Indonesia." In *The Indonesian Killings 1965–1966: Studies from Java and Bali*, edited by Robert Cribb. Clayton, Victoria: Centre of Southeast Asian Studies, Monash University.

Wisnewski, J. Jeremy. 2010. *Understanding Torture.* Edinburgh: Edinburgh University Press.

PART III STATE RESPONSES
TO GENDER VIOLENCE

8 · ADVANCES AND LIMITS OF POLICING AND HUMAN SECURITY FOR WOMEN

Nicaragua in Comparative Perspective

SHANNON DRYSDALE WALSH

Recent scholarship has called for the gendering of security to specifically include women in the assessment of what constitutes insecurity. Women's police stations are significant for advancing security for women in several ways: they are specialized for women, staffed entirely by women, much more approachable than nonspecialized police units, and visible to victims and survivors as security resources. They also help to increase gender consciousness, and their institutional form transforms incentives so that women's security does not "compete" with other types of security. However, there are multiple limitations to using the state and the police—which have often been the perpetrators of or accomplices to violence—in order to address violence against women. These limitations include having an incomplete toolkit for addressing broader forms of marginalization that put women at risk for violence. Also, women's police stations tend to be institutionally marginalized and underfunded. In order to provide a type of security that fully embodies the principles of human security, women's policing must be part of broader programs addressing underlying issues that make women more vulnerable to becoming victims of violence in the first place—such as inequality, structural violence, poverty, and lack of access to education and healthcare.

A SURVIVOR'S STORY

Managua, Nicaragua, has more the feel of a small town than a large city. People are generally easygoing and love to chat. I found the early morning hours were a temporary respite from the blistering heat and humidity that usually strike with the late-morning sun. Despite the mild weather, it was not the beginning of a relaxing day. Security alarms were ringing everywhere and people were briskly passing by as I waited on a large rock outside the entrance to one of the women's police stations. The officers told me that there was something wrong with the alarm system and that the station would open up once they got it fixed.

Rosa (a pseudonym) walked up and took a seat beside me as others started to gather and wait for the station to open. We struck up a friendly conversation and she told me she had come for another visit to the women's police station to have them help process her domestic violence case. With a tone of resignation, she noted that her husband had beaten her repeatedly, a replay of the victimization she and her mother had endured earlier in life. Rosa, who was on her way to work, and trying to support her children now as a single mother, was anxious for the station to open. She was glad that she had been assigned a pro bono lawyer. However, she doubted it would help very much because her husband had money and could afford to hire three different private lawyers.

I asked if the police had been helpful. She replied that she was glad they were there, but that it was difficult to wait for service when you have children and work, and that the police station was always very busy. Rosa decided to leave about five minutes before they fixed the alarm system. The station opened about an hour late. Although this was not a typical day, with the broken alarms and the station opening much later than usual, Rosa was experiencing some of the many typical frustrations with the police and the justice system. The police were always very busy. In part, this was a perverse outcome of their good public relations encouraging women to contact them for services. In my multiple trips to police stations in and around Managua, the small waiting areas were almost always standing room only with lots of children there missing out on the chance to play or learn. Women generally had to make multiple trips in order to process their cases.

This process can be revictimizing because women are inevitably asked to visit the women's police stations multiple times and repeatedly tell the story of their victimization to different people. Though the state is supposed to be empowering women through this process, it is, in fact, disempowering them by requiring them to use the precious few resources they have (time and money) when they are already in an extraordinarily vulnerable position, forcing them to seek help in the first place. Even though free legal assistance is made available through most women's police stations, women have had to pay for it with their sheer effort under difficult circumstances.[1]

The first women's police station was established in Nicaragua in 1993, and now there are over 135 stations throughout the country. Women's police stations are staffed entirely by women, and established with this specialized structure in part to create a place where women feel safe reporting violence. Prior to the establishment of women's police stations, police often dissuaded women from pressing charges, ignoring them or even making them feel guilty about the violence perpetrated against them (Jubb et al. 2008, 30). Police officers had also been known to turn victims away and tell them to behave themselves in order to avoid violence (see Jäppinen and Johnson, this volume).

In response to this widespread discrimination, women's and feminist movements demanded institutional reforms, the provision of comprehensive services for victims, and state provision of access to justice and a commitment to prevent, punish, and eliminate violence against women (Jubb 2008 et al., 22–25). While pressure from women's movement actors was a catalyst for the creation of women's police stations, there was resistance from within the state and the police themselves that required a long period of negotiations and seed funding from international donors before they took root.[2] Women's police stations offer a wide range of prevention and direct services, including receiving complaints, providing psychological services, investigating cases, making arrests, and conducting community outreach and training (Jubb et al. 2010, 247–248).

While there is a need and demand for services to help women victims and survivors of violence, there are multifaceted issues with trying to address violence against women within the security apparatus of the state. Women in general report that they feel more comfortable going to the women's police stations and that this is a big improvement over the old system where there were not specialized officers and women were treated with dismissive attitudes toward victims of domestic violence. However, even though the women's police stations have teams of officers, psychologists, and legal advisers, police have an incomplete toolkit and can only help women in limited ways to live a life free of violent victimization.

Women's police stations can provide a gateway to access the justice system, but they cannot address the broader systemic structural violence that women experience. Paul Farmer describes the concept of structural violence as violence that is "exerted systematically—that is, indirectly—by everyone who belongs to a certain social order" (2004, 307). In Nicaragua, the social and economic structures that disproportionately marginalize women and make them dependent upon their male partners make women particularly vulnerable to sustained violence. This is a worldwide pattern (True 2012). Finally, despite the fact that Nicaragua has the only network of women's police stations in Central America, many do not view violence against women as a security priority, and the stations tend to be underfunded, understaffed, and barely able to meet the demand for their services.

Women's police stations and women's policing units have become more common throughout the world (Pruitt 2013). There has been some research on how women's police stations provide security for women (for example, Hautzinger 2002; Jubb and Pasinato 2002; Jubb et al. 2010; MacDowell Santos 2004), but none that explicitly examine their advances and limitations for providing *human* security. In this chapter, I focus on women's police stations in Nicaragua. Even though they are an improvement over traditional policing, I demonstrate how providing human security for women in the robust sense requires broad institutional and cultural transformation beyond what can be provided for by women's policing.

WOMEN'S POLICE STATIONS AND HUMAN SECURITY

Over the past two decades, scholars have adopted the concept of "human security" to focus on security within borders. This is an appropriate and useful theoretical lens through which to understand the limits and advances of state-based attempts to gender security, since women can lack security even in a country that is secure in the more traditional sense of lacking external or internal threats to national security (Ballaeva 2007; United Nations Development Program 1994). Several scholars have also called for the gendering of security to specifically include women in the assessment of what constitutes insecurity (Blanchard 2003; Chenoy 2005; Hoogensen and Stuvøy 2006; Hudson 2005, 2009; Hudson et al. 2009; Shepherd 2010; Sjoberg and Martin 2010; Tickner 1992, 1995, 2004; Wibben 2011). Women's police stations have become increasingly popular worldwide as an attempt to meet states' obligations to respond to the security threats that are disproportionately faced by women (such as sexual violence and intimate partner violence). Nicaragua has one of the more extensive systems of women's police stations in Latin America, which are operated by women for women and children.

The early 1990s marked a transition from thinking of security almost exclusively in terms of "state security" or "national security" focused on securing national borders to a "human security" framework, as widely disseminated in the 1994 Human Development Report (United Nations Development Program 1994). This report argued that a "secure state" with secure borders could still be inhabited by "insecure people." There has been extensive academic debate among those who favor a narrower versus wider definition of security.[3] However, considering the shockingly high rates of violence against women in Central America, it is evident that women in the region are insecure by even a more narrow definition of human security.

In a 2006–2007 survey, 48 percent of Nicaraguan women who had once had a partner (married or unmarried) reported that they had been a victim of verbal or psychological abuse. In addition, 27 percent reported that they had been subjected to physical abuse, and 13 percent reported sexual abuse by their partner or ex-partner (ENDESA 2006–2007, 29). Other surveys in Nicaragua report even higher levels of violence against women. An older study of domestic violence against women in Nicaragua found that 52 percent of ever-married women reported having experienced physical partner abuse at some point in their lives, with a median duration of abuse lasting five years. Twenty-one percent of ever-married women reported physical, sexual, *and* emotional abuse, and the likelihood of abuse increased while women were pregnant (Ellsberg et al. 2000). In addition, women are at risk of violent victimization for a broad range of reasons, suggesting that the human security approach that focuses on multidimensional ways to address security problems is necessary.

What is human security? The 2000 UN Millennium Summit agreed on the importance of both "freedom from want" and "freedom from fear" as security concerns (Commission on Human Security 2003). In 2003, the UN's Commission on Human Security rearticulated the importance of shifting to a new paradigm of security that centers on people, not states. It conceptualizes human security broadly: enhancement of human freedoms and human fulfillment; protection from threats; and, the creation of systems that provide people with the building blocks of survival, livelihood, and dignity, offering individuals opportunities and choices to fulfill their own potential (Commission on Human Security 2003). The Commission on Human Security argued that human security complements, but is distinct from, state security in four respects. In terms of human security, (1) the concern is the individual and the community rather than the state; (2) menaces to security include threats and conditions that have not always been classified as threats to state security; (3) the range of actors is expanded beyond just the state; and (4) achieving human security includes empowering people to fend for themselves, and not simply protecting people.

Women's police stations are examples of institutional forms that embody these principles of human security. They are concerned with the individual and community, rather than the state, by focusing on victimization of women and children within state borders. Perpetrators of violence against women and children are recognized as security threats and criminals by women's police stations.[4] Women's police stations, situated within the state, coordinate with non-state actors in order to improve women's security. Women's police stations can and do empower women in significant ways, though the tools for doing so are relatively limited, and local or uneven institutional implementation often deviates from institutional design.

The kinds of security risks that women face in their daily lives are different from those of men. For example, women are at higher risk for being victimized within the home, and are at higher risk than men for sexualized violence. Since the security risks for women are specialized, a justice system that ignores gender-specific differences will inevitably fail to protect women from crimes to which they are disproportionately vulnerable. Although women's movements have at times resisted engaging the state out of legitimate concerns about co-optation, feminist political scientists increasingly recognize that it is necessary for women's movements to intervene, monitor, provide training, and have an increased presence within state bureaucracies in order to appropriately address women's issues (Franceschet 2010; Medie 2013; Staudt 1998, 56; Weldon 2002). In part, women's police stations were constructed in order to improve human security for women. In the following section, I briefly discuss the advantages of this specialized form of policing as well as some key limitations.

ADVANCES AND PRECARIOUS POSITIONING OF WOMEN'S POLICE STATIONS

The state is in a precarious position to provide security for women, given that states have at times been a source of threat to their own people. Before the 1979 Sandinista Revolution in Nicaragua, the police (then, the National Guard) worked for the Somoza dictatorship to "maintain order" through violent and coercive means and committed massive human rights violations against real and perceived revolutionaries. Despite the fact that the police were restructured after the Revolution, which dismantled the National Guard, the population at large remained wary of police as a provider of public security. Even after undergoing police reforms and bringing more women into the force, the police as a whole were not providing adequate security for abused women. Specialized women's policing was proposed by women across different sectors in the state and civil society as necessary for improving security and police responsiveness for women victims of violence (Jubb et al. 2008). Women's police stations are precariously situated as a part of the police, which functions as the coercive and repressive arm of the state.

At the same time, specialized institutions that focus on mitigating violence against women help to improve responsiveness to victims in significant ways. Specialization on the structural level helps to reshape institutional incentives such that attending to women victims is an explicit aim of officers within the women's police stations. S. Laurel Weldon (2002) notes that these institutions can help to transform unequal relations of power between men and women and correct for existing gender biases. For example, while far from ideal, women's police stations in Brazil have resulted in a vast improvement in police responsiveness to violence against women (MacDowell Santos 2005). While these institutions are no guarantee of improving women's security, the lack of them is a virtual guarantee that improvements will not be made and an indicator that the state is failing to secure one of the most basic rights for its women citizens: the right to live a life free of violence. As one interviewee in Nicaragua states: "Violence [against women] is worldwide. There should be women's police stations throughout Central America, because people come and people go and the attention [to victims] should be specialized for women. It is very important that women do not feel alone in the moment that they encounter aggression and violence. If they feel 'if you hit me, I am going to report you to the police,' that already earns them a little respect."[5]

Some of the scenarios that compelled women to advocate for women's police stations include a historical lack of services for women, widespread lack of gender consciousness within the police, and incidents of women being turned away when seeking police protection. Gender consciousness emerged in part through practices of consciousness-raising efforts by Latin American feminists (Jubb and Izumino 2002). As is most relevant to the work of the police, having gender consciousness, at a minimum, would mean viewing violence against women as an expression of male domination or patriarchy (MacDowell Santos 2005, 49). One interviewee recounts the stark differences between regular police stations and the women's police stations in the late 1990s:[6]

> [In a regular police station] ... there were times that you would go and spend the entire day waiting. And they would prioritize robbery or something else that was a priority ... the usual reaction was that "she deserves it." ... The women's police stations, just getting inside the buildings, was a friendlier environment.... It was a place that was nice and clean, where people donated some toys so that children could stay entertained. And there was also some coordination so that someone could look after the children at the time that the mother was with the officer. This was another point: there was privacy. There was an office. You could go inside and close the door and talk with the officer or psychologist or social worker.

HUMAN SECURITY AND THE LIMITATIONS OF WOMEN'S POLICE STATIONS

Although women's police stations advance human security in significant ways, they have several limitations for advancing security within the human security framework. Women's police stations and officers treat violence against women within a narrow justice system framework of response to security threats. They are limited by this role and their institutionally limited toolkit so that they cannot address broader structural forms of violence that make women vulnerable to physical and emotional violence. In addition, women's policing is still not taken as seriously as other forms of policing and goes underresourced. There are also several other limitations regarding the culture, practice, and relationships between the police and civil society. In order to provide a type of security that fulfills broader principles of human security, women's policing must be a part of more comprehensive (state and nonstate) programs that address underlying and interconnected issues of structural violence, women's inequality, poverty, lack of access to education, lack of access to healthcare, and other risks for women's security that make them more vulnerable to becoming victims of violence in the first place. Women's police stations are designed to be a gateway to the justice system. The readily available tools for police officers are to facilitate obtaining restraining orders and facilitating the advancement of legal cases against aggressors through the court system. However, few victims of violence follow through with cases. They often want and need something different that women's police stations can only provide indirectly. It is not practical for most women to simply leave their aggressors because they (and their children) are economically dependent upon them and they have no safe place to go or they are in love with them (which can be a result of traumatic bonding similar to the Stockholm syndrome). In response, women often express a desire to have police help "fix" their relationships. If they were not so physically and economically vulnerable, women might be empowered to effectively demand their abusers leave or negotiate community intervention. However, the institutional design of women's police stations fails to meet the complex needs of women victims.

Scholarship on women's police stations is rooted in feminism and spans sociology, anthropology, and political science. Critiques of women's police stations focus in part on their failure to implement the feminist goals that were a catalyst for their creation (Hautzinger 2002; Jubb and Pasinato Izumino 2002; Jubb et al. 2010; MacDowell Santos 2005). Scholarship on Brazil notes that a lack of gender consciousness among male and female police officers is a serious limitation (Hautzinger 2002; MacDowell Santos 2005). The reality in Nicaragua is different from that in Brazil: Nicaraguan female police in general demonstrate a higher degree of gender consciousness than is apparent in the accounts of Brazilian female officers. I agree with these scholars that a lack of gender consciousness is an obstacle to empowering women and engendering justice. However, I interpret the instances of lack of sensitivity toward victims in Nicaragua primarily as an outcome of fatigue and frustration from having to apply a limited toolkit for the provision of justice. Women victims of violence need far more comprehensive services and resources than the justice system can provide, such as a way to take care of their children if they are to even consider transitioning away from living in a situation of violence. While victims may request reconciliation, it is not always or even usually because women really want to stay in their relationships. They just want the abuse to stop. However, the police and justice system provide them with no viable alternative that other institutions (such as child protection services) might be able to provide if resources were available.

Focusing on the ways in which women's police stations do and do not implement human security ideals (in addition to feminist ones) highlights the problems that are rooted in an institutionally limited toolkit. It also suggests some avenues for improvement. Women's human security cannot be delivered holistically by the police, but rather must be delivered by the police working in close coordination with nonstate actors who are not limited by the institutional structure of the police. Close coordination between the police and nonstate actors has enabled the women's police stations in Nicaragua to make many more advances than would have otherwise been possible. This coordination helps to explain the improved performance of the women's police force, despite having relatively little funding.

For example, the women's movement, with the financial support of several international donors, constructed several women's clinics, including the Ixchen Women's Center, the Association for the Assistance of the New Family in Nicaragua (ANFAM, Asociación para el Apoyo de la Nueva Familia en Nicaragua) and the Sí Mujer Foundation. These clinics have coordinated with women's police stations to provide additional services for victims seeking policing services. For many years, ANFAM performed forensic medical evaluations for women victims of violence and had the only forensic medicine specialist on staff that was recognized by the state.[7] Since 1998, the state has had forensic medicine specialists. These specialists and many others within the state (such as psychologists, lawyers, and judges) who now provide services to victims of violence began their work at the women's health centers. Although coordination between the state and women's movement organizations has been necessary in order to compensate for a lack of state services, the coordination itself made it possible to improve them. However, advances are no guarantee of sustained success. As the political and economic climate changes, so does the capacity of the state to coordinate with civil society, as do the resources that donors have available to sustain state institutions. The current president in 2016 is Daniel Ortega, himself accused of violence against women and protected from potential charges through political immunity. Thus, Nicaragua faces at least two serious challenges for the capacity of state institutions to address violence against women: the global economic downturn and opposition from powerful state actors that include the president.[8]

CONCLUSION

Women's police stations in Nicaragua have improved security in significant ways. However, they have neither the mandate nor the institutional capacity to improve security for women in the most substantial ways by providing pathways to other forms of security. Women's police stations have limited resources and incentives to implement a broader human security agenda. In order to provide a sense of security that fulfills the principles of human security in the robust sense, they must become part of more comprehensive (state and nonstate) programs that address underlying and interrelated risks to women's security, including structural violence, women's inequality, and poverty, as well as lack of access to education and healthcare. Addressing these broader issues would contribute to preventing abuse since these are factors that make women more vulnerable to becoming victims of violence. The institutional design of women's police stations seems premised on the idea that violence against women is the most significant security risk for women seeking services. However, there are significant security risks to following through with filing and following up on a police complaint and eventually leaving an aggressor. These include falling deeper into poverty and hunger or angering an aggressor who may violently retaliate.

Women's police stations are an advance in many ways, but also have many drawbacks. They are much better than nonspecialized police forces, which traditionally have not addressed violence against women as a crime and have generally refused to implement the law even after domestic violence was criminalized. Having state institutions that address violence against women through a justice system that is not integrated with broader development institutions is problematic for improving women's security. Because women are disproportionately poor and economically dependent upon abusive partners, women's policing alone will be unlikely to provide them with a viable pathway out of a violent household. It is imperative that international donors focus on gendered forms of development such as education and job training programs for women, access to affordable healthcare, state subsidies for child care, enforceable regulations for child support, and temporary or permanent housing for women. Small, local NGOs are often the most capable institutions to implement these programs and can help to both strengthen and monitor the state. Broad-based development programs are not as popular in the modern era of international donor agendas. However, these programs are necessary for providing human security for women who need viable pathways to economic and other forms of security *in order to* achieve bodily security.

NOTES

I give my heartfelt thanks to the many women in Nicaragua who shared their time and knowledge. I am grateful for comments and suggestions from the book editors and from Christina Ewig, Terry MacDonald, Lesley Pruitt, Joseph Staats, Aili Mari Tripp, Jaqui True, and Jeremy Youde. This research was funded by the Fulbright-Hays Foundation, Mellon/American Council of Learned Societies, American Political Science Association Fund for the Study of Women and Politics, and the National Endowment for the Humanities.

1. See Dána-Ain Davis's discussion of institutional time, "Knowledge in the Service of a Vision: Politically Engaged Anthropology," in *Engaged Observer: Anthropology, Advocacy, and Activism,* edited by Victoria Sanford and Asale Angel-Ajani (New Jersey: Rutgers University Press, 2006), 228–238.

2. Anonymous interview from Managua, Nicaragua, with women's advocate. Interview conducted by the author on February 29, 2008.

3. See reviews of these debates in Bellamy and McDonald 2002; Hoogensen and Stuvøy 2006; King and Murray 2001; Thomas and Tow 2002.

4. This undermines recent and still-prevalent norms that violence against women is a private family matter rather than a public security issue.

5. Anonymous interview from Managua, Nicaragua. Interview conducted by the author on July 24, 2006.

6. Anonymous interview from Managua, Nicaragua. Interview conducted by the author on October 29, 2013.

7. Anonymous interview from Managua, Nicaragua. Interview conducted by the author on February 26, 2008.

8. International donors supporting women's police stations have been withdrawing from Central America. There is evidence that Daniel Ortega continually sexually abused his stepdaughter Zoilamérica Narváez, who revealed this in 1998 (Ojito 1998). Ortega has maintained political immunity from his crimes. Even though he was a leftist leader of the revolution, he has since posed obstacles for coordination between the state and women's organizations in Nicaragua, reportedly fearing that women's organizations were helping Zoilamérica Narváez (Meléndez 20013; Narváez 2002).

REFERENCES

Ballaeva, E. A. 2007. "Gender-Related Aspects of Security." *Anthropology and Archeology of Eurasia* 45 (4): 56–66.

Bellamy, Alex J., and Matt McDonald. 2002. "'The Utility of Human Security': Which Humans? What Security? A Reply to Thomas & Tow." *Security Dialogue* 33 (3): 373–377.

Blanchard, Eric M. 2003. "Gender, International Relations, and the Development of Feminist Security Theory." *Signs: Journal of Women in Culture and Society* 23 (4): 1289–1312.

Boesten, Jelke. 2006. "Pushing Back the Boundaries: Social Policy, Domestic Violence, and Women's Organizations in Peru." *Journal of Latin American Studies* 38 (2): 355–378.

Chenoy, Anuradha M. 2005. "A Plea for Engendering Human Security." *International Studies* 42 (2): 167–179.

Commission on Human Security. 2003. "Human Security Now." New York: Commission on Human Security/United Nations Office for Project Services.

Ellsberg, Mary, Rodolfo Peña, Andrés Herrera, Jerker Liljestrand, and Anna Winkvist. 2000. "Candies in Hell: Women's Experiences of Violence in Nicaragua." *Social Science and Medicine* 51: 1595–1610.

ENDESA (Encuesta Nicaragüense de Demografía y Salud). 2006–2007. *Informe Preliminar: Encuesta Nicaragüense de Demografía y Salud ENDESA 2006/07*. Managua: Instituto Nacional de Información de Desarrollo and Ministerio de Salud.

Farmer, Paul. 2004. "An Anthropology of Structural Violence." *Current Anthropology* 45 (3): 305–325.

Franceschet, Susan. 2010. "Explaining Domestic Violence Policy Outcomes in Chile and Argentina." *Latin American Politics and Society* 52 (3): 1–29.

Hautzinger, Sarah. 2002. "Criminalising Male Violence in Brazil's Women's Police Stations: From Flawed Essentialism to Imagined Communities." *Journal of Gender Studies* 11 (3): 243–251.

Hoogensen, Gunhild, and Kirsti Stuvøy. 2006. "Gender, Resistance, and Human Security." *Security Dialogue* 37 (2): 207–228.

Hudson, Heidi. 2005. "'Doing' Security as though Humans Matter: A Feminist Perspective on Gender and the Politics of Human Security." *Security Dialogue* 36 (2): 155–174.

Hudson, Natalie Florea. 2009. *Gender, Human Security, and the United Nations: Security Language as a Political Framework for Women.* London: Routledge.

Hudson, Valerie M., Mary Caprioli, Bonnie Ballif-Spanvill, Rose McDermott, and Chad F. Emmett. 2009. "The Heart of the Matter: The Security of Women and the Security of States." *International Security* 33 (3): 7–45.

Jubb, Nadine, and Wânia Pasinato Izumino. 2002. "Women and Policing in Latin America: A Revised Background Paper." *CERLAC Occasional Paper.* Toronto: Centre for Research on Latin America and the Caribbean at York University. Accessed February 14, 2011. http://www.yorku.ca/cerlac/documents/jubb.background.pdf.

Jubb, Nadine, Gloria Camacho, Almachiara D'Angelo, Bina Yáñez de la Borda, Kattya Hernández, Ivonne Macassi León, Cecília MacDowell Santos, Yamileth Molina, and Wânia Pasinato. 2008. *Regional Mapping Study of Women's Police Stations in Latin America.* Project: Access to Justice for Women in Situations of Violence: A Comparative Study of Women's Police Stations in Latin America (Brazil, Ecuador, Nicaragua, Peru). Quito, Ecuador: Centre for Planning and Social Studies.

Jubb, Nadine, Gloria Camacho, Almachiara D'Angelo, Kattya Hernández, Ivonne Macassi, Liz Meléndez, Yamileth Molina, Wânia Pasinato, Verónica Redrobán, Claudia Rosas, and Gina Yáñez. 2010. *Women's Police Stations in Latin America: An Entry Point for Stopping Violence and Gaining Access to Justice.* Quito, Ecuador: Centre for Planning and Social Studies.

King, Gary, and Christopher J. L. Murray. 2001. "Rethinking Human Security." *Political Science Quarterly* 116 (4): 585–610.

Medie, Peace A. 2013. "Fighting Gender-Based Violence: The Women's Movement and the Enforcement of Rape Law in Liberia." *African Affairs* 112 (448): 377–397.

Meléndez, José. 2013. "'Daniel Ortega es un Abusador Sexual,' Insiste su Hijstra." *CRHoy: Noticias 24/7. Costa Rica.* August 15. Accessed June 26, 2014. http://www.crhoy.com/daniel-ortega-es-un-abusador-sexual-insiste-su-hija/.

Narváez, Zoilamérica. 2002. "Case 12,230: Zoilamériza Narváez vs. the Nicaraguan State." *Envío: Política, Sociedad, Cultura, Economía.* March. Accessed June 26, 2014. http://www.envio.org.ni/articulo/1567.

Ojito, Mitra. 1998. "Conversations/Zoilamerica Narvaez: A Victim of Sexual Abuse in a Prison of Political Ideals." *New York Times*, March 29. Accessed June 25, 2014. http://www.nytimes.com/1998/03/29/weekinreview/conversations-zoilamerica-narvaez-victim-sexual-abuse-prison-political-ideals.html.

Pruitt, Lesley. 2013. "All-Female Police Contingents: Feminism and the Discourse of Armed Protection." *International Peacekeeping* 20 (1): 67–79.

Santos, Cecília MacDowell. 2004. "En-Gendering the Police: Women's Police Stations and Feminism in Sao Paulo." *Latin American Research Review* 39 (3): 29–55.

———. 2005. *Women's Police Stations: Gender, Violence, and Justice in São Paulo, Brazil.* New York: Palgrave Macmillan.

Shepherd, Laura J. 2010. "Feminist Security Studies." In *The International Studies Encyclopedia*, edited by Robert A. Denemark. Malden, MA: Wiley Blackwell.

Sjoberg, Laura, and Jillian Martin. 2010. "Feminist Security Theorizing." In *The International Studies Encyclopedia*, edited by Robert A. Denemark. Malden, MA: Wiley Blackwell.

Staudt, Kathleen A. 1998. *Policy, Politics, and Gender: Women Gaining Ground.* West Hartford, CT: Kumarian Press.

Thomas, Nicholas, and William T. Tow. 2002. "The Utility of Human Security: Sovereignty and Humanitarian Intervention." *Security Dialogue* 33 (2): 177–192.

Tickner, Ann J. 1992. *Gender in International Relations: Feminist Perspectives on Achieving Global Security.* New York: Columbia University Press.

———. 1995. "Re-visioning Security." In *International Relations Theory Today*, edited by Ken Booth and Steve Smith. Cambridge: Polity Press.

———. 2004. "Feminist Responses to International Security Studies." *Peace Review* 16 (1): 43–48.

True, Jacqui. 2012. *The Political Economy of Violence against Women.* Oxford: Oxford University Press.

United Nations Development Program. 1994. *Human Development Report.* Oxford: Oxford University Press.

Weldon, S. Laurel. 2002. *Protest, Policy, and the Problem of Violence against Women: A Cross-National Comparison.* Pittsburgh, PA: University of Pittsburgh Press.

Wibben, Annick T. R. 2011. *Feminist Security Studies: A Narrative Approach.* London: Routledge.

9 · THE STATE TO THE RESCUE?

The Contested Terrain of Domestic Violence in Postcommunist Russia

MAIJA JÄPPINEN AND JANET ELISE JOHNSON

In the early 1990s, if an average person on the street in Russia was asked about domestic violence (*domashnee nasilie*), she or he would probably have responded by asking what was meant by domestic violence. Over the following decade—with links to global women's activism to stop violence against women—women's organizations have worked valiantly to bring domestic violence to public discussion, naming and conceptualizing it as a social problem and linking it to gender equality. As of 2015, the same question would elicit more understanding; however, the typical Russian would probably focus the conversation on the vulnerability of children abused by their parents. As the current public debate constructs the traditional family as the nation's core, violence against women has been eclipsed by a gender-blind discussion of violence in the family.

In this chapter, we examine the changing response to domestic violence in the Russian Federation since the collapse of the Soviet Union in 1991. The last two and half decades have been tumultuous for Russian citizens, beginning with a devastating depression that left most households on an unending financial roller-coaster ride, made worse by the loss of the country's superpower status. The promise of democracy rang hollow as society became more violent and political elites joined the oligarchs in stealing from the state. By the 2000s, when Vladimir Putin came to power, his promise of a more muscular state, even if more authoritarian, seemed like a good deal for many people, especially as the Russian economy grew phenomenally until the 2008 global economic crisis. We argue that the attempts at liberalization as communist control over society collapsed gave officials more excuses to ignore domestic violence. Building on the global critiques of violence against women, women's nongovernmental organizations in Russia made inroads just as the state began to consolidate a more authoritarian regime. The result is some limited responsibility-taking by the Russian state, but the response is more about rescuing than about empowering women. We illustrate these developments with case examples based on our extensive fieldwork in Russian civic and public organizations from our disparate backgrounds in political science and social work.

While extensive anecdotal evidence suggests that domestic violence got worse in the 1990s, there is unfortunately little credible data to document the problem (ANNA 2010; CEDAW Committee 2010; Johnson 2005). The Ministry of Interior has no separate category for either intimate partner violence or family violence, with all violent acts within the private sphere treated under the category of "violence in everyday life." Because of women's rational mistrust of the police in this post-Soviet society, especially when it comes to domestic violence, even if there were police counts the vast majority of all domestic violence cases remain outside the official statistics (see Walsh in this volume).[1]

The best estimates available come from a more than a decade-old survey that found that every second married woman had experienced physical violence from her husband at least once, with almost one out of five experiencing regular or severe violence (Gorshkova and Shurygina 2003). Psychological violence was used in most relationships. Sexual violence in marriage, although common, was not even regarded as violence by most survey respondents. Some 13 percent of the female respondents reported having husbands forbid them to work or study or refuse (or threaten to refuse) them use of the family money on account of their alleged bad behavior. Anecdotal evidence suggests that violence against women, including abductions and honor killings, are higher in the North Caucasus, shaped by Russia's brutal campaigns in the region and the radicalization of the resistance (ANNA 2010, 37–41). This data, while limited, suggest that domestic violence is widespread in Russia, more prevalent than the world average lifetime estimate of 35 percent (World Health Organization 2013).

THE RUSSIAN HISTORY OF SELECTIVE
INTERVENTION AND PRIVATIZATION

Domestic violence has a different history in Russia than in the United States. In prerevolutionary Russia and then the Soviet Union, the assumption has been that domestic violence was taboo (Attwood 1997, 99; Beschetnova 2003, 8; Muravyeva 2012, 56). This is only partly true, as there had never been a private sphere as it is conceived in the West. Court cases from the eighteenth century show that intimate partner violence, although a part of the life of Russian families, was not regarded as normal and acceptable by women experiencing it (Muravyeva

2008, 2012). Both the state and the Orthodox Church responded to severe cases of violence by punishing the perpetrator, allowing divorce, and providing shelter for women in monasteries. In the years following the Bolshevik Revolution, wife beating was handled disapprovingly in meetings of the women's sections of the central committee of the Communist Party and in state-sponsored women's magazines (Gradskova, Romanov, and Iarskaia-Smirnova 2005, 15). Later, when the state reverted to more conventional notions of gender, incidents of domestic violence were sometimes regulated under the criminal statue of hooliganism or addressed by the state as a part of antialcohol campaigns (Johnson 2009, 23, 25; Muravyeva 2014; Sperling 1990, 19). Women's councils and comrade courts also handled complaints of "improper behavior of husbands in the family," while local branches of trade unions intervened by criticizing a perpetrator's behavior or sending him to coercive detoxification (Zhidkova 2008, 21–22). The Soviet state's commitment to women's employment, equal pay, daycare, and universal healthcare lessened women's economic dependency on their husbands and provided exit options (Johnson 2009, 24).

Yet the cases were not named as domestic violence nor seen as gender violence. Soviet police treated cases of domestic violence as "family scandals," and the goal of police prevention was reconciliation (Johnson 2009, 24). By the 1970s, "difficult life situation" served as a euphemism for domestic violence. As with other social problems, domestic violence was seen as a relic of bourgeois morals, which would vanish as the socialist state developed toward communism. Violence was explained by the individual perpetrator's abnormal personality combined with alcohol abuse (Voigt and Thornton 2002, 98). Gender roles emphasizing strong men and vulnerable women and their interconnections to violence were not acknowledged (Attwood 1997, 100–101).

As communism collapsed, people's lives became more private, and domestic violence was privatized. Entering one's family life and prosecuting domestic violence through laws against hooliganism became less justifiable (Johnson 2009, 30), and the police started to ignore cases of domestic violence or to refuse to help victims (Human Rights Watch 1995). The new societal order called for more traditional gender roles, and domestic violence was sometimes seen as a counterreaction to gender equality, a disruption to the "natural" order of things (Attwood 1997; Johnson 2009, 31). All this was made worse by the economic depression and collapse of the welfare state, leaving women newly vulnerable to domestic violence.

THE RISE AND DECLINE OF AN NGO
WOMEN'S CRISIS CENTER MOVEMENT

The end of communist control—occurring at approximately the same time as the Fourth World Conference on Women (Beijing, 1995) declared the goal of

preventing and eliminating all forms of violence against women and girls—
also created opportunities for independent women's groups to raise the issue
of violence against women, and it became a key theme of an emerging Russian
women's movement (Hemment 2004). The first crisis centers were established
by women's NGOs in the early 1990s, with the assistance of foreign donors and
based on collaborations between Russian women's activists and Western feminists (Hemment 2004; Johnson 2009, 44). Transnational collaborations also
offered them a model for organizing their activities (Hemment 2004). The goal
of the first crisis centers was twofold: to help victims of violence with crisis hot-
lines and in-person counseling and to change attitudes toward the problem in
society and the state (Pashina 2003, 77–79; Zabelina 1999, 36).

By the 2000s, there was a respectable network of crisis centers spread around
Russia. There were successful NGO crisis centers in Moscow and St. Petersburg
as well as in several regional capitals (e.g., Kazan, Barnaul, Saratov, Tver, Arkhangelsk, and Murmansk). There were also some public crisis centers, for example
in St. Petersburg and Izhevsk, which applied a gender-sensitive focus in their
work and collaborated with the NGO network.

However, this heyday for women's crisis centers was followed by a period
of decreasing funding from abroad as donors were pulled or pushed out. In
the beginning of the 2010s, activist crisis centers were on life support, lacking
funding or a sufficient constituency (Johnson and Saarinen 2011, 2013; Saarinen
2009). Like many NGOs in Russia, these autonomous women's crisis centers
were also faced with increasing restrictions, most notably a 2006 NGO law
imposing new registration burdens and a 2012 law requiring NGOs engaged in
political activities and receiving foreign funds to register as "foreign agents."[2] By
2015, of the hundred or so centers, only a handful were still functioning, while
others have had to significantly curtail their activities or struggle with intermittent funding. In Moscow, the one center (Yaroslavna) that provided psychological support vanished, while a leaner ANNA (National Center for Prevention of
Violence), funded by the international cosmetics company Avon, managed a
national hotline for domestic violence survivors. In St. Petersburg, Aleksandra
had closed while the Institute of Nondiscriminatory Gender Interrelations Crisis Center for Women, having been raided as a "foreign agent" in 2013, struggled
to continue its feminist advocacy, including providing help in court cases to a
small number of individual women. Many strong centers outside of these big cities have disappeared; others, struggling with intermittent funding, have had to
significantly reduce staff, programs, and services.

The movement's biggest achievement has been transforming public consciousness about domestic violence. In the late 1990s to the early 2000s, the crisis
centers achieved remarkable media coverage of their cause (Johnson 2009, 101).
By the new millennium, surveys show that most, if not virtually all, Russians

see domestic violence as a problem, and most reject the old justifications for it, such as infidelity (2008 Gallup survey cited in ANNA 2010, 47; Gorshkova and Shurygina 2003; Stickley et al. 2008, 451). Domestic violence has become a common subject of talk shows and dramas on television, and Russians activists express the general sense that the recognition of domestic violence has changed. This is not to say that most Russians see the problem as rooted in patriarchal norms, but the issue has become more prominent and the public has moved toward disapproval.

EVOLVING RESPONSE OF STATE WELFARE SERVICES IN THE 2000S

The Russian activists' advocacy, reinforced by international pressure, also proved successful enough to get the state's attention, even as it moved toward authoritarianism. Since 1999, based on a national social service law, the Russian government has gradually taken responsibility for providing help to violence survivors, setting up crisis departments for women "in difficult life situations" inside public social service centers.[3] The aim of the crisis departments is "to provide psychological, juridical, pedagogical, social, and other forms of help to women and children, whose situation is dangerous for their physical or mental health or who have experienced psychological and physical violence."[4] Women and children experiencing violence are a special target group of the departments, but the departments also address homelessness, health problems, and other difficult life situations. The services differ, but usually they provide consultations with psychologists, social workers, and lawyers. As of 2010, there were some 120 crisis departments, nineteen crisis centers for women and three for men, and twenty-three shelters, which is of great importance to survivors of violence (ANNA 2010).

While the largest shelter in the country—with eighty beds—was opened in 2014 in Moscow, the most successful state program is in St. Petersburg (Johnson, Kulmala, and Jäppinen 2015). Even before the national legislation, in 1996, feminist activists sought and found government support for a citywide shelter. By 2005—as a result of pressure from feminist and other domestic violence activists—the city also made a commitment to establish crisis departments for women across the city. In 2013, each of eighteen municipal districts within the city had a crisis department. Six of them included shelter space for women, with the others obligated to create such accommodation in the near future.

The strength of these public crisis departments is that they have stable—though scarce—resources for the work that provide for premises and shelters that few NGOs have been able to sustain (Johnson and Saarinen 2013). The shelter capacity is still quite limited, with only eighty-five beds in St. Petersburg (approximately 0.7 beds per 10,000 people compared to the Council of Europe's recommendations of one per 10,000 citizens [European Commission 2010]).[5]

The challenges these public crisis departments confront relate to the wide scope of their work. First, as these departments deal with a variety of issues, staff members have not necessarily received specialized training on how to work with violence survivors. In these conditions, domestic violence is sometimes treated by drawing on old stereotypes, such as the assumption that women provoke the violence used against them. Second, as is typical in public social services in Russia, staff turnover is high. Without specialized training or long-term experience, service providers treat domestic violence as an issue related to the perpetrator's personal problems or alcohol abuse and view it as a conflict between spouses with both parties equally responsible (Jäppinen 2015; Johnson, Kulmala, and Jäppinen 2015). Gender-sensitive conceptualizations of domestic violence, which emphasize violence against women, are eclipsed by a gender-blind treatment through the lens of violence in the family. This broadens the scope from intimate partner violence to include child abuse, and talking about protecting the family is required to justify the services to women survivors of violence. In the gender-sensitive approach, women's safety and right to live without violence is prioritized, while the family-centered approach emphasizes keeping the family together and may treat women mainly as wives and mothers. State social services do not conduct big informational campaigns to change society's view of domestic violence; thus responsibility for preventing future violence is laid on the shoulders of women survivors of violence (Jäppinen 2015; Johnson and Saarinen 2013; Virkki and Jäppinen 2016). Because government officials have used the existence of public crisis centers to argue that NGO crisis centers are no longer necessary, there is little opportunity to emphasize the gendered nature of domestic violence and its connections to gender inequality in society.

On the other hand, the focus on keeping families together has led to the development of work practices with male perpetrators of violence. In contrast to ambivalence among Western feminists about working with men, Russian activists have long believed that working with men is essential (Saarinen 2004), and they struggle to change the cultural presentation of a Russian man not seeking help from professionals for their personal problems (Kay 2006). Many public crisis departments routinely contact the perpetrator or visit their home to find out his version. Without legislation requiring batterers to get treatment, very few men volunteer even to try to change their behavior (Jäppinen 2015). There are some encouraging examples of successful work with men. In St. Petersburg, a civic organization called Men of the XXI Century works with a handful of self-identified perpetrators (Johnson, Kulmala, and Jäppinen 2014). In the small town of Sortavala near the Finnish border, staff members and male volunteers have been trained to work with men, and remarkable informational efforts have been made to reach male clients (Jäppinen 2009, 2015).

NO COMPREHENSIVE LEGISLATION ON DOMESTIC VIOLENCE, BUT SMALL IMPROVEMENTS IN LAW ENFORCEMENT

According to activists (ANNA 2010), the biggest problem facing women seeking exit from violent relationships is the lack of comprehensive legislation on domestic violence, which most other postcommunist states have passed (Fábián 2010).[6] National legislation on domestic violence was proposed twice in the legislature (the Duma) in the late 1990s, but met substantial resistance, with some lawmakers concerned that shelters would be akin to brothels (Johnson 2009). Pressure from the United Nations and agreement from Putin put legislation back on the table in 2012, with the establishment of a working group of lawmakers and feminist activists. According to interviews with those involved in the working group, the draft legislation—based on the UN's model legislation, the legislation of Russia's neighbors, and the particularities of Russia's experience—calls for increased services for women and children, mandates the state's involvement with prosecuting domestic violence, would require batterers to get treatment, and establishes mechanisms for collecting good data on the extent of the problem. The plan was to schedule hearings in the national legislature in September 2013, but the Russian Orthodox Church and a leading parents' group claimed that it would contribute to the destruction of the family (Baczynska 2013). The support of those with conservative views about the family has become incredibly important to Putin following the widespread 2011 and 2012 protests against the government from the more moderate middle class. As of January 2016, the legislation remains stalled.

Without such reform, there are few legal mechanisms for addressing domestic violence. There are no restraining, protection, or barring orders. Acts of domestic violence, as any violent crime against a person, are punishable under the criminal code, but there is no consideration of the special characteristics of domestic violence, such as the cycle of violence and appeasement. In the rare event that acts of domestic violence are prosecuted, they tend to be prosecuted under articles requiring private prosecution (ANNA 2010, 10–11; Johnson 2005; Open Society Institute 2007). In such cases, the victim must bring the charges herself and provide the necessary evidence—in contrast, the accused has the right to obtain free legal aid. If the victim reconciles with the batterer, the case is dropped. These legal practices reinforce widespread beliefs among law enforcement that domestic violence is a private matter and that women reporting violence should reconcile with their husbands. These laws and practices not only affect the lives of violence survivors, but signal that domestic violence is condoned. One of the most important tasks of women's crisis centers has been to assist clients through the legal process.

Police attitudes toward domestic violence have improved some. In 2006, the Ministry of the Interior launched a campaign, including posters at bus stops, encouraging people to contact a beat cop if they experience violence in the family, a symbolic change from previous years when officials declared that domestic violence was not their concern. More meaningfully, several crisis centers (for example, in Sortavala and Saratov) have carried out projects to develop collaboration with the police, train police officers to work with domestic violence cases, and create interagency models for violence prevention.

DOMESTIC VIOLENCE UNDER AUTHORITARIANISM, ECONOMIC CRISIS, AND MILITARISM

As part of the increased attention to violence against women around the world, a handful of feminists in Russia started women's crisis center activism soon after the collapse of the Soviet system, and during the 1990s it grew into a nationwide movement. While the transnational funding dried up over the next decade, the civic organizations were successful enough to bring the issue of domestic violence to the agenda of public social services, which then started to establish services for violence survivors. The state's increased responsibility for helping the victims, and thus more stable resources for domestic violence services, are remarkable improvements, especially since these public crisis departments often have shelter space to provide temporary housing. These small steps toward addressing the problem, though, come at a cost. The inclusion of domestic violence into the broader work of the crisis department may blur departments' expertise on domestic violence issues, staff members are not always trained specifically to work with violence survivors, and as state agencies they do little advocacy work or public information campaigns.

Over the same period, the focus of public debate has shifted from violence against women to family violence to child abuse. Russia is not an exception in this. Most domestic violence work is done within the tensions between gender-sensitive and family-centered approaches in societies that do not recognize the gendered roots of the problem. The tension between these two can sometimes even be fruitful, as their flexible use can help to undermine the traditional gender order (Johnson and Zaynullina 2010). But the shrinking of the most feminist-oriented, NGO part of domestic violence work in Russia runs the risk of leaving only the family-centered discourse.

The attention to violence against women by transnational women's activists and donors in the 1990s helped increase the state's responsiveness, but the current response is shaped by increasing authoritarianism, continuing economic crisis, and a resurgent militarism. Regulations on the autonomous crisis centers are part of a broader campaign to co-opt and control civic organizations. The blurring of once feminist approaches into family-oriented responses to domestic violence relate to the regime's reliance on conservative family values and traditional gender norms, as manifested in the campaigns to play up Putin's manliness, the severe punishment of the feminist punk band Pussy Riot, and antigay legislation. The increased responsiveness of social services, while partly a democratic maneuver recognizing people's needs, is more a policy of state paternalism designed to blind people to increasing repression. The recent global economic crisis has taken a toll on Russia's economy, which may not be able to afford its promised social policy. The 2008 war with Georgia and the 2014 conflicts with Ukraine demonstrate Russia's more aggressive foreign policy, creating an atmosphere for further moves away from feminist ways of addressing domestic violence. For women in Russia to live free from domestic violence requires not just more specialized services with trained staff, a legal framework to respond effectively to the problem of domestic violence, and significant changes in the perceptions of gender roles in family and society, but also marked changes in Russia's patriarchal regime, political culture, and economy.

NOTES

The research and thinking for this project was furthered by our participation in the project Welfare, Gender and Agency in Russia in the 2000s (2008–2010/2012), led by Aino Saarinen, through the Aleksanteri Institute at the University of Helsinki (http://www.helsinki.fi/aleksanteri/english/ projects/wga.htm). We thank in particular Olga Liapounova and Meri Kulmala for their participation in our 2013 trip to St. Petersburg and, for providing the necessary financing, the Academy of Finland-funded Finnish Centre of Excellence in Russian Studies—Choices of Russian Modernisation coordinated by the Aleksanteri Institute at the University of Helsinki (http://www.helsinki .fi/aleksanteri/crm/index.html) as well as a PSC-CUNY Award (# 65055–00 43), jointly funded by The Professional Staff Congress and The City University of New York. Corresponding author: Maija Jäppinen (maija.jappinen@helsinki.fi).

1. Statistics on the number of women killed by their current or former intimate partners each year are contradictory and unreliable.

2. See also Kulmala 2013; Saarinen, Ekonen, and Uspenskaya 2014.

3. Federal Law No. 195-FZ of December 10, 1995, "On the Fundamentals of Social Services for the Populace in the Russian Federation"; see also ANNA 2010.

4. Statute of the Ministry of Labor of the Russian Federation of June 27, 1999, number 32, "On Confirming the Methodological Recommendations for Organizing the Functions of State (Municipal) Institution 'Complex Center of Social Services for the Populace.'"

5. Not all other European countries have succeeded in providing enough shelter places, though. In Finland, for example, the figure was only 0.23 per ten thousand in 2009, compared, e.g., to 1.64 in Norway or 1.47 in the Netherlands.

6. In some regions of Russia, such as in Arkhangelsk, there are regional laws on domestic violence, but as with many such laws in this centralized state, they have little impact.

REFERENCES

ANNA (National Center for the Prevention of Violence). 2010. "Violence against Women in the Russian Federation: Alternative Report to the United Nations Committee on the Elimination of Discrimination against Women." July. Accessed January 28, 2014. http://www2.ohchr .org/english/bodies/cedaw/docs/ngos/ANNANCPV_RussianFederation46.pdf.

Attwood, Lynne. 1997. "'She Was Asking for It': Rape and Domestic Violence against Women." In *Post-Soviet Women: From the Baltic to Central Asia*, edited by Mary Buckley. New York: Cambridge University Press.

Baczynska, Gabriela. 2013. "Victims of Domestic Violence Face Uphill Battle for Protection in Russia." Reuters, August 20. Accessed January 28, 2014. http://www.reuters.com/ article/2013/08/20/us-russia-women-violence-idUSBRE97J0CX20130820.

Beschetnova, O. V. 2003. *Sotsialnaya rabota s zhenshchinami, postradavshimi ot nasiliya v sem'ye*. Balashov: Balashovskiy filial SGU.

CEDAW Committee. 2010. "Conclusion Observations of the Committee on the Elimination of Discrimination against Women: Russian Federation." United Nations Convention on the Elimination of All Forms of Discrimination Against Women /C/USR/ CO/7. Accessed January 28, 2014. http://daccess-dds-ny.un.org/doc/UNDOC/GEN/ N10/485/54/PDF/ N1048554.pdf?OpenElement.

European Commission. 2010. *Violence against Women and the Role of Gender Equality, Social Inclusion, and Health Strategies*. European Commission, Directorate-General for Employment, Social Affairs and Equal Opportunities.

Fábián, Katalin, ed. 2010. *Domestic Violence in Postcommunist States: Local Activism, National Policies, and Global Forces*. Bloomington: Indiana University Press.

Gorshkova, I. D., and I. I. Shurygina. 2003. *Nasilie nad zhenami v sovremennykh rossiyskikh sem'yakh*. Moscow: Maks Press.

Gradskova, Yulia, Pavel Romanov, and Elena Iarskaia-Smirnova. 2005. *History of Social Work in Russia*. Accessed January 28, 2014. http://www.sweep.uni-siegen.de/content/Results/ Final_Reports_PDFs /FinalReportRus.pdf.

Hemment, Julie. 2004. "Global Civil Society and the Local Costs of Belonging: Defining Violence against Women in Russia." *Signs: Journal of Women in Culture and Society* 29 (3): 815–840.

Human Rights Watch. 1995. *The Human Rights Watch Global Report on Women's Human Rights*. New York: Human Rights Watch.

Jäppinen, Maija. 2009. *Turvakotityön menestystarina Sortavalassa: Arviointi Solidaarisuuden ja Sortavalan kaupungin toteuttamista lähialueyhteistyöhankkeista vuosina 2004–2008*. Evaluation report for International Solidarity Foundation. Helsinki: Solidaarisuus. Accessed January 28, 2014. http://www.solidaarisuus.fi/@Bin/119303/Evaluaatio%20Sortavalan%20 hankkeista.pdf.

———. 2015. "Väkivaltatyön käytännöt, sukupuoli ja toimijuus: Etnografinen tutkimus lähisuhdeväkivaltaa kokeneiden naisten auttamistyöstä Venäjällä." Helsinki: University of Helsinki, Department of Social Research.

Johnson, Janet Elise. 2005. "Violence against Women in Russia." In *Ruling Russia: Law, Crime, and Justice in a Changing Society*, edited by William Axel Pridemore. Lanham, MD: Rowman & Littlefield.

———. 2009. *Gender Violence in Russia: The Global Campaign against Gender Violence in the New Russia*. Bloomington: Indiana University Press.

Johnson, Janet Elise, Meri Kulmala, and Maija Jäppinen. 2015. "Street-Level Practice of Russia's Social Policymaking in Saint Petersburg: Federalism, Informal Politics, and Domestic Violence." *Journal of Social Policy*, published online in November.

Johnson, Janet Elise, and Aino Saarinen. 2011. "Assessing Civil Society in Putin's Russia: The Plight of Women's Crisis Centers." *Communist and Post-Communist Studies* 44: 41–52.

———. 2013. "Twenty-First-Century Feminisms under Repression: Gender Regime Change and the Women's Crisis Center Movement in Russia." *Signs: Journal of Women in Culture and Society* 38 (3): 543–567.

Johnson, Janet Elise, and Gulnara Zaynullina. 2010. "Global Feminism, Foreign Funding, and Russian Writing about Domestic Violence." In *Domestic Violence in Postcommunist States*, edited by Katalin Fábián. Bloomington: Indiana University Press.

Kay, Rebecca. 2006. *Men in Contemporary Russia: The Fallen Heroes of Post-Soviet Change?* Aldershot, UK: Ashgate.

Kulmala, Meri. 2013. *State and Society in Small-Town Russia: A Feminist-Ethnographic Inquiry into the Boundaries of Society in the Finnish-Russian Borderland.* Department of Social Research 2013, book 14. Helsinki: University of Helsinki.

Muravyeva, Marianna. 2008. "Obliki nasiliya: Formy i metody nasiliya nad zhenshchinami v Rossii XVIII veka." In *Gendernoe ravnopravie v Rossii*, edited by N. L. Pushkareva, M. G. Muravyeva, and N. V. Novikova. St. Petersburg: Aleteiya.

———. 2012. "Povsednevnye praktiki nasiliya: Supruzheskoe nasilie v rossiyskikh sem'yakh v XVIII v." In *Bytovoe nasilie v istorii rossiyskoy povsednevnosti (XI–XXI vv.)*, edited by M. G. Muravyeva and N. L. Pushkareva. St. Petersburg: European University.

———. 2014. "Bytovukha: Family Violence in Soviet Russia." *Aspasia* 8: 90–124.

Open Society Institute. 2007. *Violence against Women: Does the Government Care in Russia?* Open Society Institute, Network Women's Program, VAW Monitoring Program. Budapest: Open Society Institute.

Pashina, Albina. 2003. "The Movement of Crisis Centres in Russia: Features, Success, and Problems." In *NCRB: A Network for Crisis Centres for Women in the Barents Region. Report of the Nordic-Russian Development Project, 1999–2002*, edited by Aino Saarinen. Arkhangelsk: Pomor State University.

Saarinen, Aino. 2004. "Tensions in Combating Violence against Women in the East-West Transregion of Barents—the 'Man Question.'" In *Crisis Centres and Violence against Women: Dialogue in the Barents Region*, edited by Aino Saarinen and Elaine Carey-Bélanger. Arkhangelsk: Center for Women's Studies and Gender Research, Pomor State University, and Oulu University Press.

———. 2009. "A Circumpolar Case: Networking against Gender Violence across the East-West Border in the European North." *Signs: Journal of Women in Culture and Society* 38 (1): 519–523.

Saarinen, Aino, Kirsti Ekonen, and Valentina Uspenskaya. 2014. "Breaks and Continuities of Two 'Great Transformations.'" In *Women and Transformation in Russia*, edited by Aino Saarinen, Kirsti Ekonen, and Valentina Uspenskaya. London: Routledge.

Sperling, Valerie. 1990. "Rape and Domestic Violence in the USSR." *Response to the Victimization of Women and Children: Journal of the Center of Women Policy Studies* 13 (3): 16–22.

Stickley, Andrew, Olga Kislytsina, Irina Timofeeva, and Denny Vågerö. 2008. "Attitudes toward Partner Violence against Women in Moscow, Russia." *Journal of Family Violence* 23: 447–456.

Virkki, Tuija, and Maija Jäppinen. 2016. "Gendering Responsibility: Finnish and Russian Helping Professionals' Views on Responsible Agency in the Context of Intimate Partner

Violence." In *Interpersonal Violence: Differences and Connections*, edited by Marita Husso, Tuija Virkki, Marianne Notko, and Jari Eilola. London: Routledge.

Voigt, Lydia, and William E. Thornton. 2002. "Russia." In *Domestic Violence: A Global View*, edited by Randal W. Summers and Allan M. Hoffman. Westport, CT: Greenwood Press.

World Health Organization. 2013. "Global and Regional Estimates of Violence against Women: Prevalence and Health Effects of Intimate Partner Violence and Non-partner Sexual Violence." Accessed January 28, 2014. http://www.who.int/reproductivehealth/publications/violence/9789241564625/en/.

Zabelina, Tatyana. 1999. "Rossiya i SNG: Krizisnye tsentry v deystvii." In *Dozhtizheniya i nakhodki: Krizisnye tsentry Rossii*, edited by Tatyana Zabelina and Evgeniya Israelyan. Moscow: Press-Solo.

Zhidkova, E. M. 2008. "Sem'ya, razvod, tovarishcheskiy sud: Pravovoe polozhenie sovetskoy sem'i i zhenshchin v gody 'ottepeli.'" In *Gendernoe ravnopravie v Rossii*, edited by N. L. Pushkareva, M. G. Muravyeva, and N. V. Novikova. St. Petersburg: Aleteiya.

10 · THE ABSENT STATE

Teen Mothers and New Patriarchal Forms of Gender Subordination in the Democratic Republic of Congo

SERENA COSGROVE

This chapter explores how state institutions, families, and communities often abandon teenage single mothers in the eastern part of the Democratic Republic of Congo if they have gotten pregnant out of wedlock, been raped, or become pregnant through transactional sex. It is sobering the extent to which state institutions—particularly the justice system—not only do not protect young mothers but exacerbate their exclusion and vulnerability, often revictimizing them in the process. In a country still struggling to emerge from decades of civil war, sexual violence and gender-based violence have become prevalent in the region, even in cities outside of active war zones.

Since the early 1990s over five million people have died and a million people have been displaced by the conflict that has consumed much of the Great Lakes region of central Africa, in particular the eastern part of the Democratic Republic of Congo (DRC). Armies from multiple countries, including the army of the DRC itself and rebel groups, have often targeted women and young girls, using their bodies to send messages of retribution and anger to the local community, military leaders, tribal chiefs, and political leaders. "Women in the eastern Democratic Republic of the Congo have faced what many say are the worst instances of sexual and gender-based violence in the world" (Kelly 2011, 1). Research in conflict and postconflict areas shows that when sexual violence and other forms of gender-based violence are used during war, these same practices can become normalized not just in war zones but outside of war zones (see Immigration and Refugee Board of Canada 2006; Cosgrove 2014; Jones 2010; Kelly et al. 2011; Sanford 2008). In regions where violence against women has become normalized during times of conflict and where gender hierarchies are entrenched, the same practices bleed into postconflict communities when fighting lessens or ceases, due to wartime trauma, patriarchal values, poverty, impunity, and fragile state institutions. In the DRC, in fact, all types of sexual violence are higher in the eastern province of North Kivu than in the capital, Kinshasa (Peterman, Palermo, and Bredenkamp 2011, 1060).[1] Goma, the capital of North Kivu in eastern Congo, hasn't experienced active warfare within the city limits since November 2012 when the M23 rebels took over the city for ten days,[2] but rape, sexual exploitation, and sporadic fighting and violence remain epidemic in the city.

Young poor women are particularly vulnerable because often the state, their families, and their communities shun them rather than seek to address what has happened to them. Families punish young pregnant women because of the stigma of pregnancy out of wedlock by ostracizing them, restricting their movements, or refusing to cover their school or medical costs. Community institutions such as schools and churches often expel or shun young women when they get pregnant. And after giving birth, mothers often can't go back to school because families refuse to pay school fees or allow them to attend church because of their status. This shunning or "what the World Health Organization calls 'social murder'" (cited by Immigration and Refugee Board of Canada 2006, 2) has severe consequences for these young women. This chapter draws on interviews and focus groups with teen mothers in Goma, North Kivu, to understand better the lack of protection provided to these women by their communities and government.[3]

It is hard to come up with exact figures about sexual violence because it is believed underreporting is prevalent due to social stigma and lack of incentives to speak out (Peterson, Palermo, and Bredenkamp 2011). As made clear in multiple testimonies gathered for this research project, the cycle of discrimination and exclusion only intensifies when women try to take their cases to court. Given the extreme limitations of the Congolese state, judges and other judicial employees—who are owed back salaries and seldom if ever paid for their jobs—are paid off or susceptible to the strong-arm tactics of wealthier or politically connected stakeholders; seldom do officials or family members ask the woman what her needs and wants are in the situation. In Goma, these teen mothers' only support comes from nongovernmental organizations trying to provide them with some support services and human rights and vocational training.

CONTEXTUALIZING THE GOMA CASE

Goma is a city of approximately one million inhabitants in the province of North Kivu, DRC. Since the first massacres in Masisi in 1991–1992, the arrival of refugees from Rwanda after the 1994 genocide, and then Congo's own civil wars in 1997–2002, Goma has received up to a million refugees at a time as well as successive waves of internally displaced people fleeing violence from armed combat in and around their communities. This has created a patchwork of camps around Goma, with some people having moved (and lost all their possessions) numerous times in the past twenty years. Mount Nyiragongo erupted in 2002 and one-third of Goma was covered in lava, which resulted in further displacement and economic disaster, as it cut off one-third of the airstrip, reduced air traffic, and destroyed the main downtown commercial section as well as thousands of homes. Fighting between armed groups in surrounding agricultural areas has reduced agricultural production; roads have been cut off or become unusable or simply unsafe, reducing movement of agricultural produce. Goma, which formerly exported agricultural products to the country and region, has become an importer of foodstuffs.

Seen as a safer place than their communities of origin, internally displaced peoples and refugees from nearby countries (Rwanda and Burundi) have sought shelter and safety in Goma when conflict has forced them to leave their homes. Goma has become a hub for humanitarian organizations due to the presence of international NGOs, the emergence of local civil society organizations, and the different agencies of the United Nations, including the peace-enforcement military presence of the United Nations Organization Stabilization Mission in Democratic Republic of the Congo. Presently, most refugees from other countries have returned to their countries of origin or have joined Congolese communities. The most vulnerable population around Goma at this time are the camps composed of over one hundred thousand internally displaced peoples and the marginalized communities of extremely poor Congolese who have moved into Goma seeking safety from conflict in their communities.

Though recently fighting has diminished due to the fact that the United Nations has upgraded troops there from a peace-keeping to a peace-enforcing presence, the eastern part of the DRC still has a number of rebel groups and local militias fighting the armed forces of the Congolese government and often fighting each other. From local self-defense groups called "Mai Mai" to larger armed groups fighting for different leaders and political agendas, the results of the fighting have had severe repercussions for local populations, especially women, children, and other vulnerable groups such as the elderly, the ill, and the disabled. "Increasingly, wars take place not on the front line but in the middle of communities, including soldiers and civilians alike" (Coulter 2008, 57). Soldiers have frequently sexually assaulted and killed women and men, stolen household goods and crops, and killed farm animals. The conflict has forced these people to flee their communities of origin, seeking a place where they can find safety, food, and medical attention; this situation is why the Democratic Republic of Congo is currently one of the poorest countries in the world according to the Human Development Index. "Government and healthcare infrastructure in the region has been decimated, creating some of the worst health and development indicators in the world" (Kelly et al. 2011, 6).

PREVALENCE OF SEXUAL VIOLENCE AND GENDER-BASED VIOLENCE OUTSIDE OF WAR ZONES

Research has been carried out about why sexual violence became so prevalent in the war zones of the DRC (Ericksson Baaz and Stern 2009, 2010, and 2013). When soldiers receive orders to sexually assault and mistreat women, men, girls, and boys in war zones, rape has become a weapon of war; the responsibility lies with the commander who ordered it and the perpetrator who enacted it (Sanford, Duyos Álvarez-Arenas, and Dill, this volume). Additionally, the hypermasculinity of the military and soldiers' exposure themselves to sexual violence leads soldiers and rebels alike to use drugs and women's bodies to feel better about themselves and escape fear and resentment due to harsh conditions, lack of pay, contempt for their superiors, and corruption (Ericksson Baaz and Stern 2009, 2010, and 2013). This is especially pertinent for boys (and girls) abducted into the different armed groups and forced to carry out violent acts. As Maria Ericksson Baaz and Maria Stern note: "Failing to recognize the rights and needs of men and boys connected to a violent experience and performed masculinity will surely manifest itself in a perpetuation of cycles of violence. Combatants (and others) who have experienced trauma and humiliation by being subjected to violence themselves, or been forced or encouraged to inflict violence on others, tend to be more prone—in the short term and when proper countermeasures are lacking—to perpetrate new violent acts. This is especially true of the juvenile combatants integrated into the national army and police force" (2010, 46).

Unless there are institutional responses to prevent and punish sexual violence, it continues, perpetuating an ever-widening set of ripples that extends from victims to entire families and communities. "Widespread sexual violence . . . not only traumatizes individuals, it fractures families and communities" (Kelly et al. 2011, 2). Sexual violence—especially as it has been used as a weapon of war in the eastern DRC—does not solely involve a perpetrator and a victim: often commanders have authorized it and other soldiers, family members, and community members are forced to observe and participate in the violence.

The physical, psychological, and economic effects of sexual violence have greatly hindered women's livelihoods and traditional contributions to the local economy as traders and farmers. Often left wounded or with long-term physical ailments as well as the psychological symptoms of trauma, these women face multiple barriers to earning a living. Now they are often too afraid to leave home to tend crops or sell items at nearby markets. Women who have lost their husbands and families in the war and cannot earn their living through farming and trading sometimes turn to other income-generating activities, "for example, when women must trade sex for food and money" (Kelly et al. 2011, 2).

This chapter is a contribution to postconflict literature, which tracks how sexual violence and gender-based violence grow even as the fighting lessens. Why are sexual violence and other forms of gender-based violence such as domestic violence growing in the cities even as the conflict diminishes in the countryside? Belligerent forces often become habituated to using violence to feed, clothe, and take care of themselves, but former soldiers who have been ordered or encouraged to carry out violent practices during the conflict are supposed to abandon them during peace. Dr. Margaret Agama, the United Nations Population Fund representative, comments on this phenomenon, saying, "Initially, rape was used as a tool of war by all the belligerent forces involved in the country's recent conflicts, but now sexual violence is unfortunately not only perpetrated by armed factions but also by ordinary people occupying positions of authority, neighbours, friends, and family members" (UN Population Fund 2008).

Violence and sexual abuse have become normalized to the extent that "rape becomes a habit taken up by civilian men and carried seamlessly from wartime into the troubled 'post-conflict' time beyond that is labeled 'peace'" (Jones 2010, 8). Not only have these practices become part of the social fabric, but their perpetuation reinforces impunity and the state's lack of accountability. Correspondingly, local economies stagnate due to lack of production, and destruction associated with war often means there are few employment opportunities. For men used to being providers, unemployment can generate low self-esteem and frustration, which can manifest in drug and alcohol abuse and violence in the home. Patriarchal structures retrench due to wartime practices and economic pressures, and women—especially young women and girls—find themselves at the mercy of angry fathers and men in general. Women's rights to bodily integrity and other human rights are threatened while men's positions are privileged. The structural nature of this heightened gendered subordination requires that the state respond to prevent gendered violence, protect victims, and prosecute perpetrators. Research participants from a study on the impacts of sexual violence led by the Harvard Humanitarian Initiative's Women in War program "attributed the rise in violence to a culture of impunity in which people can steal from those who are more successful and carry out reprisals for perceived wrongs" (Kelly et al. 2011, 28). In postconflict settings—as in the eastern region of the DRC—state institutions are weak, if they are functional at all, and tend to preference the needs of elites and those with power, often men, and seldom teen mothers.

In the case of Goma, the perpetrators of the increased numbers of rape and sexual exploitation are seldom brought to justice. Because the Congolese government has had so little control over the region for decades, justice institutions are fragile: laws exist that would protect the rights of all citizens, but these laws are rarely enforced. Research sponsored by international agencies use the following terms to describe the Congolese state: "considerably weakened" (Immigration and Refugee Board of Canada 2006, 3), "decaying legal system," "collapsed," and "suffers from chronic staff shortage" (Global Rights 2005). In the east and particularly in rural communities, there is not sufficient infrastructure, financial resources, support, or police to implement laws that protect women. And sadly for the eastern part of the country, "there is such a severe shortage of judicial personnel that courts can no longer hear cases, public prosecutor offices cannot conduct investigations" (Global Rights 2005, 6). In the few cases that do make it to court, judges and judicial employees are vulnerable to manipulation by wealthier patrons or strong-arm politics by thugs, gangs, or other stakeholder groups existing in the gray areas of illicit activities enabled by war. This is exacerbated by the fact that many public sector employees—including judges—seldom get paid regularly, making them even more susceptible to corruption and bribes: "all judicial personnel are forced to live off the backs of victims" (Global Rights 2005, 8).

Given the poverty of the region, many of the people who have moved into urban marginalized communities or been relocated to the displaced people camps around Goma do not have sufficient resources to cover their basic needs; in some cases, parents must decide whether they will feed their children or send them to school (Kelly et al. 2011, 37–39). Also, many families have been split up due to displacement and war, and many young children are either alone without family or are responsible for caring for their families. This puts more pressure on them and makes them vulnerable to sexual violence and exploitation. Girls under the age of eighteen are among the most vulnerable. In the following section, the experiences of teen mothers will serve to illuminate the challenges they face. In the final section, I will briefly discuss signs of hope for giving these women voice and power to challenge the discrimination they face.

TEEN MOTHERS CONFRONT NEW FORMS OF PATRIARCHAL CONTROL

The resiliency of teen girls in postconflict Goma is constantly challenged because often they are alone; having been separated from family, they have few financial resources because they are internally displaced people or poor, and they are vulnerable to perpetrators demanding sex in exchange for providing food and shelter. Teen mothers—in the city, nearby communities, and the surrounding internally displaced people camps—are socially ostracized by their families and communities, seldom served by the judicial system of their country, yet are responsible for the well-being of their children. Whether from rape or having sex with men in exchange for small gifts to help their families, teen pregnancy in the DRC is at 135 births/1,000 women compared to neighboring Rwanda at 34.[4] In eastern Congo, rates are even higher than the DRC average.

Similar to other conflict settings in which the international peace-building community has been very involved, the inability of the local state to enforce laws protecting women and other groups raises the question of whether or not this is actually a postconflict situation. If state institutions are barely functional, is there a state? Is there peace? In Congo, the rush to declare the war over also masks ongoing violence (Autesserre 2010) and leaves many citizens vulnerable to the whims of local strongmen and elites. As in the case of Congo, there is a legal framework that on paper very much protects young women's rights, but in practice rape kits have run out, the attitudes of the police are more often supportive of the perpetrators than the victims, perpetrators and their supporters pay off judges, and women cannot afford lawyers to represent their interests. Extreme poverty exacerbates women's situations, especially in a country that "ranks second to last on the Human Development Index (186 out of 187 countries), and its per capita income, which stood at US$220 in 2012, is among the lowest in the world."[5] In a country that can hardly be labeled postconflict, with one of the highest levels of poverty in the world, and with limited resources for state offices, the justice system, when it works, attends more to those who can pay than to those who most need protection.

The young mothers I interviewed and heard from in focus groups talked about all of these challenges they face, from their own families to the society they inhabit. Many got pregnant through rape or not knowing they could say no. Gabrielle,[6] a seventeen year old with a son, recounts: "The other boy took my school bag away from me; I had all my school fees in it because the principal had not been at school that day to receive it. He took the bag into the room. He pulled me from behind and the buttons popped off my shirt. I was ashamed to cry out because I was known there."[7] In Gabrielle's case, her family did help her to take her case to court: "There was a court decision. The boy went to prison. Then the rebels took over Goma and released all the prisoners. He fled."[8] Gabrielle's family has been more supportive than others, but still she has not been able to go back to school: "If my father could find money, I could keep studying. He is a cook and was trained; he used to work for the priests but has not worked for two years."[9] Young mothers have trouble finding employment because of lack of skills and networks and no one to take care of their children. Their families' poverty becomes a cycle they cannot break out of: little family income means teen mothers can't finish their studies and not finishing their studies means they cannot get jobs.

Once they are mothers, young, unmarried women with babies are stigmatized, marginalized at school and in their faith communities. They are either forbidden to continue studying by their families, the schools don't let them in, or they can't afford to continue studying. Marie is now twenty-two years old and has a two-year-old daughter. "I was a junior in high school when I met the father of my daughter."[10] At first he seemed like the answer to her dreams and her family's financial problems, but then he left. "My parents have had to cover expenses [they weren't interested in covering]. . . . I've been rejected by my family: my brothers and sisters and my parents . . . my mother doesn't even want to see me. I was supposed to be the smart one, the one who would get schooling and be able to support my family. . . . In the neighborhood, no one talks to me either because they say I will contaminate the other girls."[11] Because of the ostracism, young single mothers often experience low self-esteem; in many cases, teen mothers experience depression and psychological symptoms related to the conditions under which they got pregnant.

Neema was drugged and raped by the older brother of a girlfriend from school. Today she is twenty years old and has a four-year-old daughter. The family of her attacker and the men of her family have colluded with the state to put Neema's custody of her child in question.

> "This year 'my inlaws,'" Neema says derisively, "came to take my daughter away from me. Culturally here in Congo, children belong to the father, not the mother. They came to the house to take the baby. They brought my maternal and paternal uncles and brothers together. They all agreed 'my inlaws' would pay US$800 to take my daughter. I was told they'd agreed my daughter would go. She'd be taken care of and I could continue going to school. I said that I didn't agree with this, I told them they had no right to take my child. My family knew I loved going to school. They said if I didn't give away my baby, they would quit paying for my schooling. I said OK. I will keep my daughter and stay out of school. The day came that they had agreed to. I said my signature was not on the documents they had signed."[12]

Dealing with sexual violence out of court is common because this is "often more effective than legal procedures for obtaining compensation, at least for the family. However, out-of-court settlements are negotiated between families and rarely take into account the victim's opinion or the prejudice they suffer" (Global Rights 2005, 9). Indeed, this exemplifies what happened to Neema's case. However, for her, the situation escalated even more. Neema's case ended up in court. According to Neema: "[The court] said to me, 'women don't give birth, men are the creators of life and you have no way to support your child.' It should go to her 'legitimate' father. At the court they tried to convince me so they could pronounce a judgment. They told me to go home with my kid but told my family to keep trying to convince me to give up the child. This case continues. . . . My father said to me, 'This is finished. See what you have done to your family? You and your child don't have anything to do with us anymore.'"[13] Neema's situation demonstrates how the state and families collude to punish and limit young women's capabilities. The absent state has merged with patriarchal norms, which are heightened due to war and insecurity because it is unable to enforce women's rights.

These in-depth interviews were complemented by the input of thirty other young mothers who participated in the focus groups.[14] Similar to Gabrielle, Marie, and Neema, many of them were unable to continue with their studies after getting pregnant: "There are many of us who quit school when we had our babies. We need to learn how to read and write Swahili." "When I was pregnant, I had to stay at home. My parents said I'd never go back to school." Throughout the 2000s the literacy rate of Congolese women (age 15–24) dropped in comparison to men from 0.87 to 0.67 in 2007 according to Millennium Development Goals indicators; educational attainment, as measured by having started first grade and reached the last grade of primary school, was 62.1 percent for girls and 83.5 for boys as of 2012.[15] Furthermore, many women are shunned, mistreated, and disrespected at home by family members, within their faith communities, or in their neighborhoods: "People didn't talk to me, but whispered about me when I walked in the neighborhood. I wasn't able to sing in the choir at church." "When I was pregnant, I had to stay at home. My parents said I'd never go back to school."

I met these young women through a local NGO in Goma, HOLD DRC (Humanitarian Organization for Lasting Development, Democratic Republic of the Congo).[16] HOLD DRC was founded in 2012 to improve public health practices, by identifying resources that can be mobilized in communities and both long-term and short-term activities that both empower vulnerable groups of people and respond to humanitarian crises. HOLD has served 322 young mothers through this program. They have come from a wide variety of tribes, ethnic groups, and backgrounds in Congo, Rwanda, and Burundi. They have learned skills that will help them earn income and prevent disease, and then teach those skills. They are sharing this information in their neighborhoods and in the internally displaced people camps surrounding Goma. Among the beneficiaries of HOLD DRC are well over four hundred children, whose lives will be different because their mothers were able to participate in the program and can better provide, protect, and educate them. However, this one NGO's efforts are not enough to address the economic, psychological, cultural, and institutional challenges and limitations that the region faces. Even a hundred civil society organizations like HOLD will not solve the structural problems that create such a hostile environment for women; the Congolese government—with support from the international community and the complete demobilization of rebel groups—must strengthen institutions to address poverty and promote inclusion of women and children. The army, health system, and judicial system need the training, capacity, and resources to serve the needs of the most vulnerable groups in society.

CONCLUSION

The situation that many young women face today in the eastern part of the Democratic Republic of Congo is the convergence of gendered forms of violence perpetuated by commanders and warfare strategies during the conflict, patriarchal forms of control over women that intensified due to economic and social crises, and an incipient state whose weak institutions are unable to prevent sexual violence, protect victims, and hold perpetrators accountable. The grinding structural violence of poverty and war perpetuates the individual violence enacted on women's bodies, and the state remains absent in their defense. However, many of the teen mothers I interviewed described their efforts to educate themselves, generate income, and contribute to the development of their communities. Many women say: "At first I was very discouraged. Before, I shut myself in the room and had no friends and my parents did not speak to me. Now I can stand in front of people and speak up. I have learned how to live with people." "No man can trick me anymore. I have learned about spacing children. I won't be following a boy around asking for things." Their resiliency and fortitude are signs of hope for their own futures and that of their communities and country.

The future of Congo lies in the capacity of its state to create a society where all citizens can have access to education and justice so they can contribute much needed skills and energy to the rebuilding of the country after so much devastation and suffering. Recent signs of positive change at the national level include the appointment of a presidential adviser on sexual violence and child recruitment for former conflict areas, as well as the fact that one of the articles of the Congolese constitution addresses sexual violence and commits public authorities to its elimination (Peterson, Palermo, and Bredenkamp 2011, 1066), but these efforts will only be successful if state institutions are able to follow through with implementation. The challenge remains to see change in state institutions on the local level, particularly in the eastern part of Democratic Republic of Congo where conflict has most affected the country.

NOTES

The author would like to thank Timo Mueller from the Enough Project and Sophia Sanders from the Eastern Congo Initiative for support on this chapter. Any errors are mine.

1. "The disparity between Nord-Kivu and Kinshasa was even greater among women reporting that they had been raped in the preceding 12 months" (Peterman, Palermo, and Bredenkamp 2011, 1064).

2. The March 23 Movement (commonly referred to as the M23 rebels) was a rebel military group active in the eastern part of Congo. With supposed ties to the Rwandan army, most M23 rebels laid down their arms in recent peace negotiations.

3. The interviews and focus groups I cite in this chapter come from an evaluation to assess the initial results of the Congolese nongovernmental organization HOLD DRC and its programming with teen mothers and peer educators. The focus groups occurred in French and Swahili with HOLD staff assisting in translation. Focus group questions were developed in conjunction with HOLD staff and conversations with beneficiaries. The first focus group included ten peer educators out of a total of twenty, the second focus group included ten young mothers trained in job skills out of over two hundred young women, and the third focus group included ten leaders from the Human Development Groups out of 120 leaders. In addition to the focus groups, three of the teen mothers were individually interviewed with a semistructured interview guide to gather their personal stories and learn more about their income-generating abilities, support structures, and future aspirations. Also, HOLD trainers were interviewed regarding their reflections and observations of the young women they train.

4. Statistics from 2012 United Nations Population Division: http://data.worldbank .org/indicator/SP.ADO.TFRT/countries/RW-CD?display=default.

5. World Bank Democratic Republic of the Congo Overview: http://www.worldbank.org/ en/country/drc/overview.

6. All names are pseudonyms to protect the privacy of women interviewed.

7. Interview carried out November 26, 2013.

8. Ibid.

9. Ibid.

10. Ibid.

11. Ibid.

12. Interview carried out November 27, 2013.

13. Ibid.

14. Three focus groups carried out the week of November 25, 2013.

15. See the United Nations Millennium Development Goals indicators official website: http://mdgs.un.org/unsd/mdg/Default.aspx.

16. HOLD DRC has developed an integrated approach to public health training, vocational skills training, and increased awareness about human rights and women's rights in their first program, Succeeding Together. It has focused on (1) vocational training in culinary arts, sewing, and the beauty arts for young single mothers from the camps and nearby poor communities; (2) leadership development for the students participating in the vocational training; and (3) the selection and formation of peer educators to replicate workshops in the camps and communities about personal hygiene, preventing the spread of malaria and HIV/AIDS, and ending sexual violence against women and girls. Peer educators have committed to sharing information with at least ninety people per month. HOLD's programs promote asset-based development in its beneficiaries so they can support themselves. They have learned about

governance and communication skills and to advocate for themselves, their children, and others in their community.

REFERENCES

Autesserre, Severine. 2010. *The Trouble with the Congo: Local Violence and the Failure of International Peacebuilding*. New York: Cambridge University Press.

Clinton, Hillary Rodham. 2014. Interview by Charlie Rose. Hulu.com, July 17. Accessed July 17, 2014. http://www.hulu.com/watch/662679.

Cosgrove, Serena. 2014. "Development in Reverse: The Effects of War and the Challenges of Peace." Unpublished manuscript.

Coulter, Chris. 2008. "Female Fighters in the Sierra Leone War: Challenging the Assumptions?" *Feminist Review* 88 (1): 54–73.

Eriksson Baaz, Maria, and Maria Stern. 2009. "Why Do Soldiers Rape? Masculinity, Violence, and Sexuality in the Armed Forces in the Congo (DRC)." *International Studies Quarterly* 53 (2): 495–518.

———. 2010. "The Complexity of Violence: A Critical Analysis of Sexual Violence in the DRC." Working Paper on Gender-Based Violence. Uppsala, Sweden: Nordic Africa Institute and Swedish International Development Cooperation Agency. Accessed July 25, 2014. http://nai.diva-portal.org/smash/get/diva2:319527/FULLTEXT02.pdf.

———. 2013. *Sexual Violence as a Weapon of War? Perceptions, Prescriptions, Problems in the Congo and Beyond*. London: Zed Books.

Global Rights. 2005. "SOS Justice: What Justice Is There for Vulnerable Groups in the Eastern DRC? Assessment of the Justice Sector in North and South Kivu, Maniema and North Katanga." August. Accessed July 24, 2014. http://www.globalrights.org/sites/default/files/docs/SOS_ExecutiveSummary_ENG_FIN.pdf.

Immigration and Refugee Board of Canada. 2006. "Democratic Republic of the Congo: Prevalence of Domestic Violence, the Availability of Legal Protection, Methods of Punishing or Deterring Offenders, and Presence of Support Systems for Survivors." March 22. Accessed July 21, 2014. http://www.refworld.org/docid/45f147152d.html.

Jones, Ann. 2010. *War Is Not Over When It's Over*. New York: Henry Holt and Company.

Kelly, Jocelyn. 2011. "Opinion: Rape Traumatizes All Congolese, Not Just Women." Harvard Humanitarian Initiative. Accessed July 25, 2014. http://hhi.harvard.edu/sites/default/files/publications/publications%20-%20women%20-%20opinion.pdf.

Kelly, Jocelyn, Justin Kabanga, Will Cragin, Lys Alcayna-Stevens, Sadia Haider, and Michael J. Vanrooyen. 2012. "'If Your Husband Doesn't Humiliate You, Other People Won't': Gendered Attitudes towards Sexual Violence in Eastern Democratic Republic of Congo." *Global Public Health: An International Journal for Research, Policy, and Practice* 7 (3): 285–298.

Kelly, Jocelyn, Michael VanRooyen, Justin Kabanga, Beth Maclin, and Colleen Mullen. 2011. "Hope for the Future Again: Tracing the Effects of Sexual Violence and Conflict on Families and Communities in Eastern Democratic Republic of the Congo." Harvard Humanitarian Initiative. Accessed July 17, 2014. http://hhi.harvard.edu/sites/default/files/publications/publications%20-%20women%20-%20hope.pdf.

Kumar, Krishna, ed. 2001. *Women and Civil War: Impact, Organizations, and Action*. Boulder, CO: Lynne Rienner.

Peterman, Amber, Tia Palermo, and Caryn Bredenkamp. 2011. "Estimates and Determinants of Sexual Violence against Women in the Democratic Republic of the Congo." *Research and Practice* 101 (6) (June): 1060–1067.

Sanford, Victoria. 2008. "From Genocide to Feminicide: Impunity and Human Rights in Twenty-First-Century Guatemala." *Journal of Human Rights* 7 (2): 104–122.

Stearns, Jason. 2011. *Dancing in the Glory of Monsters: The Collapse of the Congo and the Great War of Africa*. New York: Public Affairs.

Tsongo, Claudine. 2014. "Challenging Injustice for Vulnerable Women." Opinion piece, accessed on the Eastern Congo Initiative's website on July 25, 2014. http://www.easterncongo.org/blog/detail/2014–07-challenging-injustice-for-vulnerable-women.

UN News Centre. 2014. "DR Congo: UN Hails Appointment of Senior Adviser on Sexual Violence, Child Recruitment." July 14. Accessed July 18, 2014. http://www.un.org/apps/news/printnews.asp?nid=48268.

UN Population Fund. 2008. "Campaign Says 'No' to the Sexual Violence That Rages in DRC." Accessed January 30, 2016. http://www.unfpa.org/news/campaign-says-no-sexual-violence-rages-drc.

11 · ANTI-TRAFFICKING LEGISLATION, GENDER VIOLENCE, AND THE STATE

CECILIA M. SALVI

This chapter explores the relationship between the state, human rights law, and gender violence by examining state interventions into the business of human trafficking in the United States. I first give an overview of the history of anti-trafficking legislation by focusing on the anti-trafficking movement that led to the passage of the Victims of Trafficking and Violence Protection Act (VTVPA) in 2000 and highlight the gendered discourses surrounding the creation of that legislation. I then focus on how NGOs have responded to and reinterpreted anti-trafficking legislation in ways that facilitate and increase state power. In responding to human trafficking, NGO interventions strengthen the state's regulatory power rather than weaken it. In contrast, scholars have suggested that NGO practices weaken state power in other areas (such as international aid to Haiti [Schuller 2009] and markets in Cairo [Elyachar 2005]). Finally, I discuss the consequences of anti-trafficking legislation in light of neoliberal policies.

I aim to demonstrate the significance of discourses about gender, victimhood, and morality in creating anti-trafficking legislation and the unintended consequences of making certain categories of people visible, and others invisible, as legal subjects (Coutin 2000; Warren 2007). Scholars of domestic violence (Jäppinen and Johnson, this volume) and women's police stations (Walsh, this volume) have already discussed the effects of recent state intervention into areas of gender violence that were previously considered private. I also engage with current debates in anthropology on human trafficking and the role of the state in perpetrating and facilitating gender violence, demonstrating that gendered violence is experienced in multiple ways by citizen and noncitizen victims of trafficking. Investigating state practices in connection with sexism and hetero-normative patriarchy reveals the intersecting ways that state sovereignty is produced and reproduced in its interactions with nonstate actors such as NGOs.

FEMINIST PERSPECTIVES ON GENDER VIOLENCE

Catherine MacKinnon's seminal *Toward a Feminist Theory of the State* (1989) enabled feminist scholarship to reconceptualize the state in gendered terms and to emphasize the role of power structures and patriarchal norms in reproducing gender inequality. In this same vein, Christa Craven and Dána-Ain Davis "highlight the potential of feminist activist ethnography to respond to and dislodge neoliberal politics and policies" (2015, 3). This chapter draws from feminist scholarship to highlight how state and NGO interventions against human trafficking maintain neoliberal policies by (1) creating pathways to citizenship for certain victims, while denying it to others, and (2) shifting focus away from the link between labor exploitation (of which human trafficking is a specific form) and deregulation and privatization of industries.

While gender violence has been a central theme in feminist scholarship, what actually constitutes "gender violence" remains contentious. Sally Engle Merry (2006) demonstrates how the "vernacularization" of human rights, and specifically women's rights, is a complex process in which concepts about gender violence are produced at the international level by the United Nations, NGOs, and other transnational groups and turned into specific practices by activist and governments at the local level. Merry and Susan Coutin (2014) demonstrate, for example, how statistical measurements of violence called indicators "produce general knowledge for various publics and, at the same time, directly or indirectly enter into political decision making" (4). In this way, "violence against women" becomes a significant topic in which various state and nonstate actors can intervene.

Relatedly, the debate on human trafficking is subject to debates about its representation as a global phenomenon of human rights abuse. Many researchers and activists argue that anti-trafficking campaigns are in fact campaigns against the sex work industry (Agustín 2008; Soderlund 2005), which resonate closely with colonial discourses about women "out of place" (Levine 2003) and too easily conflate sex work and sex trafficking (Limoncelli 2009; Musto 2009). Anthropological investigations by Thaddeus Blanchette and Ana Paula da Silva (2012), Nandita Sharma (2006), and Tiantian Zhang (2010) underscore how anti-trafficking legislation is deployed to regulate sex workers and irregular migrants in ways that reproduce harmful racialized, gendered, and xenophobic discourses about particular social groups that become "objects of State interest" (Blanchette and da Silva 2012, 108) through the intervention of NGOs.

ANTI-TRAFFICKING LEGISLATION IN THE UNITED STATES

Human trafficking[1] is believed to be an estimated $32 billion-a-year business involving 161 countries (U.S. Department of State 2014; International Labor Organization 2014). It is legally defined in international law as a specific form of labor exploitation, which "shall include, at a minimum, the exploitation of the prostitution of others or other forms of sexual exploitation, forced [labor] or services, slavery or practices similar to slavery, servitude or the removal of organs" (Palermo Protocol 2000, Article 3). In the United States, which is both a destination and source country, both the primary and secondary economy are subject to exploitative labor practices in such industries as care and hospitality, commercial sex work, and agriculture, and informal sectors such as sweatshops, street vending and peddling, and drug smuggling. Legally, this exploitation rises to the level of trafficking when a person is obligated to perform sexual or physical labor through "force, fraud, or coercion" (Victims of Trafficking and Violence Protection Act 2000) exerted upon that person by another.

The Trafficking Victims Protection Act (TVPA), the subsection of the VTVPA that directly refers to trafficking, and its subsequent reauthorizations over the years, define "severe forms of trafficking in persons in the United States" as

> Sex trafficking in which a commercial sex act is induced by force, fraud, or coercion, or in which the person induced to perform such act has not attained eighteen years of age;
>
> and
>
> The recruitment, harboring, transportation, provision, or obtaining of a person for labor or services, through the use of force, fraud, or coercion for the purpose of subjection to involuntary servitude, peonage, debt bondage, or slavery (H.R. 3244).

The law established a method by which the federal and local governments could protect survivors, prosecute traffickers, and prevent trafficking. These "3 Ps"—protection, prosecution, and prevention—form the backbone of the U.S. government's criminal justice approach, an often contentious modus operandi that NGOs argue should instead focus on prevention, protection, and partnerships. The Act also created a special T-visa for foreign survivors whose trafficking occurred in the United States. This definition, however, is not set in stone. The reauthorization acts of the VTVPA—in 2003, 2005, 2008, 2011 (when it failed to pass), 2013, and 2015—provided an avenue of intervention for NGOs and the state to continue to redefine trafficking, as I explain below.

ANTI-TRAFFICKING LEGISLATION AS A
RESPONSE TO GENDER VIOLENCE

In the latter half of the nineteenth century in Europe and the Americas, fear of the enslavement of women and girls of European descent gave rise to international movements to combat the "white slave trade," leading to the first antislavery conventions such as the International Agreement for Suppression of White Slave Traffic (1904, 1910) and the Slavery Convention (1926). In the United States, the passage of the White-Slave Traffic Act (1910), better known as the Mann Act, aimed to allay social panic over their presumed kidnapping into prostitution. It is clear from these conventions that slavery meant the prostitution or involvement in the commercial sex trade of European and European-descended women and girls, without consideration of "force, fraud, or coercion" that is now central to the term; their involvement in the sex trade was presumed to be involuntary.

As Carol Vance (2013) has argued, it is by means of an "analogic stretch" that current anti-trafficking activists have been able to claim historical continuity with these earlier movements and that various forms of extreme labor exploitation have come to be incorporated in the current legal definition of human trafficking. This analogic stretch is central to the construction of "modern-day slavery" as a gendered form of violence against women and to their construction as "innocent victims." It creates a binary in which "good" moral women are privileged over less "innocent" victims, such as irregular migrants, undocumented workers, and those who willingly engage in sex work.

The concerted efforts by activists, NGOs, international organizations, and governments that is now known as the global anti-trafficking movement came about in the 1990s as a response to increasing worldwide concern by human rights activists over the "disappearances" of migrant women, especially in Eastern Europe and Russia (Loar and Ardito 2010, 273) in the aftermath of the fall of communism. As Gail Kligman and Stephanie Limoncelli note, "one of the most striking images of the changes in Eastern Europe . . . was that of women lining the highways across the region, offering sex for sale" (2005, 120). Because of the visibility of the women, support for and awareness of international anti-trafficking laws were garnered "within the context of violence against women" (Loar and Ardito 2010, 264) at two specific events: the 1993 Vienna World Conference on Human Rights and the 1995 UN Fourth World Conference of Women in Beijing. Birgit Locher argues that framing human trafficking as violence against women "revitalized" a long-standing movement against slavery and "[was] of major importance in gaining support for the issue and making it comprehensible to both politicians and a broader audience" (2007, 28; see also Askola 2007).

This growing international awareness influenced the burgeoning anti-trafficking movement in the United States, which had begun in the mid-1980s as a response to violence against women, focusing almost exclusively on sexual violence. National and foreign experts, particularly from women's rights organizations, testified before Congress. At the federal level, Hillary Clinton and Madeline Albright worked with an "unlikely alliance" (Soderlund 2005, 73) of NGOs, feminists, and religious conservatives. With bipartisan support, their activism culminated in the passage of the VTVPA, signed into law on October 28, 2000, by President Bill Clinton.

Scholars have demonstrated that the framework and language of the VTVPA were chosen "in close consultation with NGOs" (Loar and Ardito 2010, 263). Precisely because there were many different actors involved, Gretchen Soderlund notes: "Reflecting the fractious context in which they were conceived, [UN and U.S. anti-trafficking legislation] offer multiple definitions of trafficking" (2005, 74). Brenda Oude Breuil and colleagues' work in Europe demonstrates that "the emphasis on women and children reflects a gendered stereotype; women are supposed to be victims, men are perceived as perpetrators" (2011, 34). This gendered stereotype is evident, for example, in the rationale that "[t]raffickers primarily target women and girls, who are disproportionately affected by poverty, the lack of access to education, chronic unemployment, discrimination, and the lack of economic opportunities in countries of origin" (TVPA 2000, 102.b.4). Along the same line, when the TVPA failed to be reauthorized in 2011, it was reauthorized in 2013 under Title XII of the Violence Against Women Act.

LAW AND NGO INTERVENTION: FEDERAL AND STATE ANTI-TRAFFICKING LEGISLATION

NGO networks have been moderately successful in incorporating key legislative changes into the subsequent reauthorizations of the TVPA (or the Trafficking Victims Protection Reauthorization Acts, TVPRAs). For example, the TVPRA of 2003 (section 1595) allows victims to sue their traffickers in civil court. The TVPRA of 2008 includes a number of exceptions to T-visa requirements, granting exceptions to cooperation with law enforcement to victims who would suffer physically or mentally for doing so. The most successful of these legislative campaigns came after almost a decade of lobbying. While T-visas and U-visas (visas for victims of violent crimes such as domestic violence, kidnapping, rape, or trafficking) are pathways to citizenship, more than eight years after the passage of the TVPA, the federal government had not issued the regulations to allow visa holders to apply for legal permanent residency. After their visas expired, they were left in a state of legal limbo: technically deportable but unable to leave the country because they would be denied reentry. It was only after intense pressure from activists and NGOs that the government issued the regulations. Finally, throughout the subsequent reauthorizations there has been an increase in state action, both nationally and internationally, against human trafficking, with particular attention paid to extending a criminal justice approach. For example, the TVPRA of 2013 reinforces cooperation between state and federal law enforcement. The 2015 Justice for Victims of Trafficking Act expands the capacity of the Department of Justice to monitor suspected cases of child pornography and labor exploitation.

NGOs have been more successful in lobbying for legislation at the state level and consequently readily supported increasing the scope of government intervention into human trafficking. State representatives are more accessible to lobbyists, and passage of legislation is much easier. Moreover, the most contentious provisions of anti-trafficking laws, such as mandated cooperation with law enforcement agencies, a focus on domestic sex trafficking victims, and funding allocations, are federal ones. Therefore, NGOs have been largely supportive of increased local state intervention into human trafficking. In California, the Coalition to Abolish Slavery and Trafficking supported and coauthored AB 22, the California Trafficking Victims Protection Act; ACR 28, the National Day of Human Trafficking Awareness Act; and SB 657, the California Transparency in Supply Chains Act of 2010. The Coalition to Abolish Slavery and Trafficking was one of the key authors of SB 1569, the Human Service for Immigrant Survivors of Human Trafficking and Other Crimes Act, the 2006 bill that granted human trafficking victims the same state benefits as refugees.

HUMAN TRAFFICKING ASYLUM CASES

As Aiwha Ong argues when discussing neoslavery in the context of migrant workers, in order to make claims on behalf of marginalized and exploited people, "NGOs define and sort out different categories of excluded humanity, in order to give them resources that *may* be convertible into entitlement and rights" (2006, 198). Although the TVPA excludes many categories of trafficked or exploited persons from receiving benefits (for example, those whose trafficking occurred outside of the United States are not eligible for T-visas or U-visas), activist lawyers at human rights organizations work to expand the categories of those who are entitled to receive immigration relief and services.

Lawyers face several challenges when applying for immigration relief for their clients. The two most established forms of immigration relief for foreign-born victims of human trafficking are the T-visa and the U-visa. Many victims choose not to apply for either because they are ineligible or because they would be required to cooperate with law enforcement officers in the prosecution of a trafficker, including giving a statement to the FBI and testifying in court. They are often fearful of retaliation from their traffickers or hesitant to work with law enforcement agents. In addition, in 2010 the cap of five thousand U-visas granted was reached for the first time, so applicants were wait-listed until the following year. As Human Rights USA, an NGO that developed the use of human-trafficking asylum cases in the United States, has stated: "Broader forms of protection are needed to adequately protect the many trafficked persons who do not qualify" for the visas (2011, 3).

An asylum petition must be based on persecution or "a well-founded fear of persecution on account of race, religion, nationality, membership in a particular social group, or political opinion" (Refugee Act of 1980, 201.42). As Tina Javaherian argues, given both the challenges and opportunities noted above, "The most viable route for a female [not male or transgender] victim of human trafficking to attain asylum is to establish that she was targeted for persecution due to her gender, or in other words, her membership in the particular social group of 'women in (her specified country)'" (2013, 423). She argues that "women from (a given country) . . . [is a] valid social [group]" (425).

Although they represent a fraction of asylum claims, human trafficking asylum case law has developed that addresses gender-based social groups. While some authorities even suggest that gender alone can make up a social group, court responses are "subject to inconsistent and arbitrary determinations" (McGregor 2014, 223–224). More commonly, gender has been recognized along with nationality, tribe/ethnicity, region, age, marital status, and other characteristics as forming the basis for a cognizable social group, such as:

"young Albanian women without the protection of male relatives"
"rural-born Guatemalan women who were forced into a marriage and resisted
    both the marriage and social norms of female subservience"
"Cameroonian women sold into polygamous marriage who resisted that mar-
    riage and treatment as property"
"Chinese women who have been forced into marriage by physical and/or sexual
abuse, and live in a part of China where forced marriage is considered valid and
enforceable." (Human Rights USA 2011, 37)

"While most countries now recognize that 'private' harm [such as trafficking] can constitute persecution and that non-state actors can perpetrate harm where the state fails to provide protection, asylum cases brought by women still raise complex questions" (Marouf 2008, 51). Rather than a "particular social group," asylum case law has been expanded to create a particular "subset of vulnerable women." As human trafficking asylum petitions become a more established means of securing rights, male and transgender victims of trafficking become excluded from this protection. Although it is a resourceful strategy employed by lawyers, the example cases listed above highlight the continued gendering of trafficking as specifically or only pertaining to female victims and in ways that resonate with anti-trafficking discourses about their "vulnerability." Moreover, the documents lawyers rely on to demonstrate that the fear of return is well founded are often government reports (such as the Trafficking in Persons annual reports) that emphasize that women who resist cultural norms do so at grave risk, echoing patriarchal ideas about "women out of place" with overtly racialized connotations.

SERVICE PROVISION

Funded by both private donors and government grants, NGOs provide services to certified victims of trafficking, which include male, female, and transgender victims. However, this service provision is not unproblematic. First, many NGOs only have the capacity or funding to provide services to female victims. Relatedly, dependence on federal funding often influences and can even determine the course of service provision. NGOs that receive federal funding are now mandated to create a comprehensive plan to identify and serve U.S. citizen victims. In response, many anti-trafficking NGOs have revised their public awareness campaigns, and have hired lawyers and social work staff to work exclusively with U.S. citizen victims.

Finally, despite the focus on sex trafficking, anti-sex-work sentiments often pervade legislation. The Bush administration, in the 2002 National Security Presidential Directive (and language adopted into the TVPRA of 2003), enacted policies that focus on domestic rather than foreign-born victims, especially sex trafficking victims who are minors; NGOs were required to sign a pledge stating that they do "not promote, support, or advocate the legalization or practice of prostitution." Although President Barack Obama rescinded this requirement in 2011, trafficking victims who knowingly engage in sex work either before or after being trafficked are ineligible for certification by the U.S. Department of Health and Human Services as recognized victims of trafficking and thus lose access to benefits (which are often administered by an NGO). Still, in 2011 Los Angeles County established the STAR (Succeeding Through Achievement and Resilience) Court to provide victim-centered specialized services for minor sex-trafficking victims. No such services exist for commercially exploited minors within the labor sector, again demonstrating the centrality of sexual exploitation to the general understanding of trafficking. Additionally, as opposed to those who are trafficked into the labor sector, immigrant minors who are trafficked for commercial sexual exploitation do not have to prove "force, fraud or coercion" in their visa applications.

By funding NGOs to carry out the task of providing food, shelter, and medical and mental health services to victims that it "rescues" through law enforcement raids, the state can intercede in the business of human trafficking in a way that limits its responsibility. As Jäppinen and Johnson (this volume) have noted in the case of domestic violence in Russia, the "result is some limited responsibility-taking by the Russian state, but the response is more about rescuing rather than about empowering" victims. Similarly, caring for victims remains the purview of charitable "human rights" workers, while the structural and institutional forms of violence, marginalization, and economic precarity, which make people vulnerable to trafficking in the first place, remain intact.

ADVOCACY

The concerted efforts of NGO advocates in responding to trafficking, in conjunction with the state, increases the number of actors that continue to make "visible" the violence perpetrated against trafficking victims (Warren 2007, 242). This relationship also expands the purview of state and federal governments into new sectors, such as compliance monitoring. Together with local partners and national umbrella networks like the Freedom Network, anti-trafficking NGOs are able to garner support for key legislative changes, such as the reauthorizations of the TVPA and influence the writing of or even coauthor key legislative texts in states with well-developed anti-trafficking legislation, such as California.

Recent laws expand the scope of the understanding of labor trafficking and the actors involved. The Foreign Labor Contractors: Registration Act of 2014 requires foreign labor contractors to disclose specific information in writing and register with the Labor Commissioner's office by 2016. The California Transparency in Supply Chains Act of 2010 requires companies making more than $1 million in profit to report their labor practices so that consumers can make informed choices regarding the origin of the products they buy. Companies must also display their labor practices and efforts to eliminate goods produced through trafficking from supply chains on their websites. The law also established an Interagency Task Force to Monitor and Combat Human Trafficking and grants California's attorney general the authority to monitor and enforce the Act.

By holding businesses accountable, advocates contend that they can significantly reduce trafficking at the source, as well as reduce the demand for cheap goods if conscious consumers are well informed. More important, laws aimed at stopping trafficking at its source also shift responsibility for recognizing and combating trafficking to businesses and consumers, rather than the state. Concomitantly, NGO advocacy for increased state intervention, regulation, and sanction reinforces the legitimacy of the state to regulate businesses and intercede on behalf of potentially exploited workers.

HUMAN TRAFFICKING AND NEOLIBERAL POLICIES

Some scholars have pointed to NGOs as actors that reinforce neoliberal policies at the cost of state sovereignty. Mark Schuller notes that international aid organizations "glue" globalization and buttress neoliberal humanitarian interventions by "contribut[ing] to the weakening or undermining of states" (2009, 97). Similarly, Julia Elyachar demonstrates that, in Cairo, Egypt, dispossession of the poor through "empowerment debt" and the marketizing of social "networks and practices that used to be seen as lying outside the market" (2005, 5) are central to neoliberal agendas and development discourses.

In Tiantian Zheng's reading of Nandita Sharma, "[a]nti-trafficking discourse chooses to focus on [the] suffering of trafficking over other suffering created by state policies on illegal immigration and global capitalist labor markets" (2010, 8; see also Sharma 2005). In an interesting analysis of the meaning of human agency under neoliberalism, Taitu Heron convincingly argues that globalization trends that began in the 1960s continued unabated, and in the 1990s "the subsequent ideological shift that accompanied the collapse of socialism in Eastern Europe suggests that development models based on liberal democracy and capitalist economics" are guided by American, European Union, and world financial institution models (2008, 85–86). She attributes increasing social inequality and poverty to neoliberal policy reforms, arguing instead for policies that promote, among others, "agential capacity" that facilitate rights. Sharma similarly calls for a reevaluating of how anti-trafficking laws can create more precarious situations for those who cannot be legally defined as victims (2005).

As these authors make apparent, capitalist and neoliberal economic practices account for the hyperexploitation that amounts to trafficking. Structural and institutional forms of violence are associated with the state, especially during times of conflict and revolt, while violence that is experienced as personal or individual by the victims, such as human trafficking or domestic violence, is instead associated with criminal actors and becomes a space for state intervention on their behalf. Even as the state regulates and prosecutes these illicit violations, and engages in a global "fight" against trafficking, its own complicity in perpetuating and facilitating personal and individual forms of violence against victims goes unexamined, as child welfare institutions, businesses, and individual consumers come under increasing surveillance.

CONCLUSION

In this chapter, I have explored the gendered characteristics surrounding the creation, passage, and reinterpretation of anti-trafficking legislation in the United States and have shown how the historical context in which anti-trafficking emerged continues to inform the language of legislation and its interpretation. Because it lies at the intersection of gender, migration, legality, and human rights, human trafficking provides a case study for examining the various ways that the state, often through nonstate actors, maintains, reproduces, and extends its power, surveillance, and legitimacy. Drawing from feminist scholarship, I argue that NGO interventions into the business of human trafficking have *increased* the power of the state to intercede in the lives of both citizens and noncitizens in the United States. First, NGOs legitimate the claims that the state is the only institution fully capable of responding to the worldwide phenomenon of human trafficking through expanding legislation increasing the monitoring of borders, businesses, and labor sectors, and funding NGOs to provide services. Second, as human trafficking asylum cases clearly reveal, anti-trafficking legislation continues to reproduce problematic assumptions about deserving and undeserving victims based on gendered and racialized discourses. Women and girls continue to be viewed as the primary (if not the only) victims that deserve rescuing. Services for men and transgender individuals are severely underdeveloped. Additionally, victims of other kinds of violence—irregular and economic migrants, sweatshop workers, and those trafficked outside of the country—remain invisible to the state.

NOTES

Many thanks to Katerina Stefatos and John Raymond for their valuable insights and encouragement.

1. Human trafficking is also known as "modern-day slavery" by groups that underscore a historical continuity with nineteenth-century abolitionists.

REFERENCES

Agustín, Laura María. 2008. *Sex at the Margins: Migration, Labour Markets, and the Rescue Industry.* New York: Zed Books.

Askola, Heli. 2007. *Legal Responses to Trafficking in Women for Sexual Exploitation in the European Union.* Portland, OR: Hart Publishing.

Attorney General, California, 2010. "California Requires Human Trafficking Signs for Certain Businesses." Accessed February 20, 2016. http://oag.ca.gov/human-trafficking/sb1193.

Blanchette, Thaddeus Gregory, and Ana Paula da Silva. 2012. "On Bullshit and the Trafficking of Women: Moral Entrepreneurs and the Invention of Trafficking of Persons in Brazil." *Dialectical Anthropology* 36 (1–2): 107–125.

Coutin, Susan Bibler. 2003. *Legalizing Moves: Salvadoran Immigrants' Struggle for U.S. Residency.* Ann Arbor: University of Michigan Press.

Craven, Christa, and Dána-Ain Davis. 2015. *Feminist Activist Ethnography: Counterpoints to Neoliberalism in North America.* Lanham, MD: Lexington Books.

Elyachar, Julia. 2005. *Markets of Dispossession: NGOs, Economic Development, and the State in Cairo.* Durham, NC: Duke University Press.

Heron, Taitu. 2008. "Globalization, Neoliberalism and the Exercise of Human Agency." *International Journal of Politics, Culture, and Society* 20 (1): 85–101.

International Labor Organization. 2014. *Profits and Poverty: The Economics of Forced Labor.* Geneva: ILO.

Javaherian, Tina. 2013. "Seeking Asylum for Former Child Soldiers and Victims of Human Trafficking." *Pepperdine Law Review* 39 (2): 422–482.

Kligman, Gail, and Stephanie Limoncelli. 2005. "Trafficking Women after Socialism." *Social Politics* 12 (1): 118–140.

Levine, P. 2003. *Prostitution, Race and Politics: Policing Venereal Diseases in the British Empire.* London: Routledge.

Limoncelli, Stephanie A. 2009. "The Trouble with Trafficking: Conceptualizing Women's Sexual Labor and Economic Human Rights." *Women's Studies International Forum* 32: 261–269.

Loar, Theresa, and Laura Ardito. 2010. "Women's Leadership in the Fight against Human Trafficking." In *Gender and Women's Leadership: A Reference Handbook*, edited by Karen O'Connor, 260–269. Washington, DC: Sage.

Locher, Birgit. 2007. *Trafficking in Women in the European Union: Norms, Advocacy-Networks and Policy Change.* Wiesbaden: VS Verlag für Sozialwissenschaften.

MacKinnon, Catharine. 1989. *Toward a Feminist Theory of the State.* Cambridge: Harvard University Press.

Marouf, Fatma E. 2008. "The Emerging Importance of 'Social Visibility' in Defining a 'Particular Social Group' and Its Potential Impact on Asylum Claims Related to Sexual Orientation and Gender." *Yale Law and Policy Review* 27: 47–106.

McGregor, Kelsey M. 2014. "Human Trafficking and U.S. Asylum: Embracing the Seventh Circuit's Approach." *Southern California Law Review* 88: 197–226.

Merry, Sally Engle. 2006. *Human Rights and Gender Violence: Translating International Law into Local Justice.* Chicago: University of Chicago Press.

Merry, Sally Engle, and Susan Bibler Coutin. 2014. "Technologies of Truth in the Anthropology of Conflict." *American Ethnologist* 41 (1): 1–16.

Musto, Jennifer Lynne. 2009. "What's in a Name? Conflations and Contradictions in Contemporary U.S. Discourses of Human Trafficking." *Women's Studies International Forum* 32: 281–287.

Ong, Aiwha. 2006. *Neoliberalism as Exception: Mutations in Citizenship and Sovereignty.* Durham, NC: Duke University Press.

Oude Breuil, Brenda Carina, Dina Siegel, Piet van Reenen, Annemarieke Beijer, and Linda Roos. 2011. "Human Trafficking Revisited: Legal, Enforcement and Ethnographic Narratives on Sex Trafficking to Western Europe." *Trends in Organized Crime* 14 (1): 30–46.

Schuller, Mark. 2009. "Gluing Globalization: NGOs as Intermediaries in Haiti." *PoLAR* 32 (1): 84–104.

———. 2005. "Anti-Trafficking Rhetoric and the Making of a Global Apartheid." *NWSA Journal* 17 (3): 88–111.

Sharma, Nandita. 2006. *Home Economics: Nationalism and the Making of 'Migrant Workers' in Canada.* Toronto: University of Toronto Press.

Soderlund, Gretchen. 2005. "Running from the Rescuers: New U.S. Crusades against Sex Trafficking and the Rhetoric of Abolition." *NWSA Journal* 17 (3): 64–87.

U.S. Department of State. 2014. *Trafficking in Persons Report.* Washington, DC: Department of State.

Vance, Carol. 2013. "What's in a Name? The Sex Slave Next Door." Paper presented to an American Anthropological Association panel, "Analogic Stretch: The Slave and Social Death Concepts in the Moral Order of Crime against Humanity," Denver, November 22.

Warren, Kay. B. 2007. "The 2000 UN Human Trafficking Protocol: Rights, Enforcement, and Vulnerability." In *The Practice of Human Rights: Tracking between the Global and the Local*, edited by Mark Goodale and Sally Merry, 242–269. Cambridge: Cambridge University Press.

World Organization for Human Rights USA. 2011. "Guide to Establishing the Asylum Eligibility of Victims of Human Trafficking and Forced Marriage." Last accessed Feb 22, 2016. http://www.violenceisnotourculture.org/resources/guide-establishing-asylum-eligibility-victims-human-trafficking-and-forced-marriage.

Zheng, Tiantian. 2010. Sex Trafficking, Human Rights, and Social Justice. New York: Routledge.

CONCLUSION

Reflections on the Women, Peace, and Security Agenda

KIMBERLY THEIDON

The United Nations Security Council "notes that rape and other forms of sexual violence can constitute a war crime, a crime against humanity or a constitutive act with respect to genocide ... [and] ... affirms its intention, when establishing and renewing state-specific sanction regimes, to take into consideration the appropriateness of targeted and graduated measures against parties to situations of armed conflict who commit rape and other forms of sexual violence against women and girls in situations of armed conflict."

— Security Council Resolution 1820 (2008)

It is a pleasure to write the conclusion for this engaging and timely edited volume. These chapters challenge researchers and practitioners to engage critically with multiple facets of the state—interventions, policies, actors, and agencies—to further our understanding of the gendered complexities of violence during periods defined as conflict, postconflict, and peace. The authors challenge those tidy categories, understanding that security and peace are intrinsically gendered goods, and that public calm may coexist with private, intimate violence in the home.

Rather than engage with each chapter individually, I wish to consider the broader issues this volume raises. I propose reading against the narrative of feminist progress to address certain silences, absences, and erasures in the Women, Peace, and Security Agenda (WPS Agenda) as it is currently conceived. On a complementary front, a series of UN Security Council resolutions have focused on the important role women play in conflict prevention, resolution, and peace-building efforts, while simultaneously denouncing the use of rape and sexual violence against women and girls in situations of armed conflict. Collectively known as the Women, Peace, and Security Agenda, these resolutions (1325, 1820, 1888, 1889, 1960, 2106, and 2122) demand the complete cessation of all acts of sexual violence by all parties to armed conflicts, with each successive resolution lamenting the slow progress made to date on this issue. To be sure, the Women, Peace, and Security Agenda constitutes a hard-won feminist victory; it is an ambivalent one as well. How does the WPS Agenda reflect the mainstreaming of more radical feminist demands, shifting the focus from gender equality to a more protectionist scaffolding? What understandings of sex, gender, and gender regimes infuse the UN Security resolutions? What does the WPS Agenda bring into focus, and what might it obscure?

Over the past twenty years, there has been increased international attention to conflict-related rape and sexual violence. In March 1994, the United Nations established a Special Rapporteur on Violence Against Women to examine the causes and consequences of gender-based violence, especially rape and sexual violence targeting women and girls.[1] Additionally, the UN's ad hoc International Criminal Tribunals for the former Yugoslavia and Rwanda—countries where conflict-related sexual violence in the early 1990s captured international attention on an unprecedented scale—greatly advanced efforts to codify sexual and reproductive violence. The jurisprudence resulting from these two tribunals classified systematic rape and other sex crimes as war crimes, crimes against humanity, and forms of genocide. The Rome Statute of the International Criminal Court, adopted in 1998, built on and extended these advances, providing a broader basis for prosecuting sexual crimes (including rape, sexual slavery, enforced prostitution, forced pregnancy, enforced sterilization, or any other form of sexual violence of comparable gravity) as violations of international laws on war, genocide, and crimes against humanity. No longer would sexual crimes be considered merely "moral offenses" or "injuries to honor or reputation" as they had been defined in the Geneva Conventions (1949).

The UN resolutions that constitute the WPS Agenda have overwhelmingly focused on women and girls as victims of sexual violence during armed conflict. Strikingly absent in this agenda are men and boys as *victims* of sexual violence, women as *perpetrators* of violence, *children* born as a result of wartime rape and sexual exploitation, and the broader goal of *gender equality*. The focus on "conflict-related sexual violence" also has temporal and geographical implications: the Women, Peace, and Security Agenda draws attention to the front lines of war and to extraordinary forms of sexual violence bracketed in time, which may result in obscuring the less dramatic yet everyday forms of gender-based violence that distort the lives of women and girls, men and boys. It also leaves men and boys as perpetrators hovering in the margins of the resolutions or, at best, as "those secondarily traumatized as forced witnesses of sexual violence against family members."[2]

In what follows, I draw upon research that I have conducted in Peru and Colombia, the Final Report of the Peruvian Truth and Reconciliation Commission (TRC), and relevant comparative research and literature to explore four themes. I begin by discussing how the TRC implemented a "gender focus" in its investigations and in its final report. Influenced by the feminist campaign to "break the silence" around rape as an intrinsically emancipatory project, the TRC actively sought out first-person accounts of rape, with rape understood to be the emblematic womanly wound of war. I will analyze what a focus on rape and sexual violence brings into our field of vision, and what it may obscure. Between the trope of "unspeakable atrocities" and the call to "break the silence," a great deal was being said. A critical rereading of the TRC's 2003 final report reveals that women frequently spoke about the systematic violation of their social, economic, and cultural rights—injuries that cannot be reduced to the violation of bodily integrity, as horrible as that violation may be. I will also discuss what women have talked about with my research team and me. When speaking outside the "victim-centered" space of the TRC, women narrated much more complicated stories about war and its effects, and about the multiple roles they assumed during the armed conflict and its aftermath. In these nuanced stories, women challenged some common-sense notions of gender and war, and provided us with an opportunity to think beyond rights and remedies to a more robust sense of gender and harm, of gender and justice.[3]

I will then discuss how rape of men by other men was a form of establishing relations of power and domination at the nexus of gender, ethnicity, and social class. The literature on male-dominant environments, such as armed groups, indicates that these groups utilize elaborate socialization mechanisms that are especially relevant to understanding the roles some men assume during conflict.[4] From illegal armed groups to state-sponsored militaries, induction into male-dominant groups frequently involves brutal or demeaning rites of passage, which in turn establish hierarchical relationships among the men. Exploring these internal dynamics forces us to reconsider "militarized masculinity" as a uniformly shared identity, and to question its explanatory or predictive value with regard to the use of sexual violence against civilians. I conclude this section by illustrating how men are both perpetrators *and* victims of sexual violence, and what the erasure of the latter means in terms of gender-based violence, essential-isms, and the politics of victimhood.

Taken together, it is my hope that these reflections complement the impor-tant pieces in this edited volume, and respond to their collective call for further research and analysis on gender, violence, and the state.

COMMISSIONING GENDER

On August 28, 2003, the commissioners of the Peruvian Truth and Reconcilia-tion Commission submitted their Final Report to President Alejandro Toledo and the nation. After two years and some seventeen thousand testimonies, the commissioners had completed their task of examining the causes and conse-quences of the internal armed conflict that convulsed the country during the 1980s and 1990s. The TRC determined that almost seventy thousand people had been killed or disappeared, and that 75 percent of the casualties were rural peas-ants who spoke Quechua or some language other than Spanish as their native tongue. Thus, the distribution of deaths and disappearances reflected long-standing class and ethnic divides in Peru.

Although the TRC was given a gender-neutral mandate, feminists were suc-cessful in insisting that the commission think about the importance of gender in its work. Drawing upon previous commissions in Guatemala and South Africa, they argued for proactive efforts to include women's voices in the truth-seeking process. This reflected the desire to write a more "inclusive truth," as well as developments in international jurisprudence with regard to sexual violence. In light of concerns that "[p]erhaps the most commonly underreported abuses are those suffered by women, especially sexual abuse and rape" (Hayner 2001, 77), efforts were made to encourage women to come forward. "Gender sensi-tive" strategies were employed with the goal of soliciting women's testimonies about rape and other forms of sexual violence, with rape understood to be the emblematic womanly wound of war. The results? Of the 16,885 people who gave testimonies to the TRC, 54 percent were women and 46 percent men (TRC, vol. VIII, 64). Thus, many women did come forward to provide their testimonies: they spoke a great deal, but not necessarily about sexual violence—at least not in the first person. The total number of reported cases of rape was 538, of which 527 were committed against women and 11 were crimes against men (TRC, vol. VIII, 89). The commission's effort to provide a "fuller truth" about the use of sexual violence by various armed groups was met overwhelmingly with silence.[5]

Shame is frequently cited as the reason women and men do not speak about sexual violence, and this is certainly one explanatory variable. But to assume shame may inadvertently convey reactionary messages about purity, chastity, and cleanliness—and may imply that a rape survivor is "damaged goods." We should consider the troubling message this sends to the thousands of people who have survived this brutal form of violence. Additionally, survivors may have forged a different relationship with their past, however painful it might have been. Outside the victim-subject position assigned to them by the TRC, women often spoke in my interviews with defiance, courage, pride, or rage about their experiences of sexual violence, narrating heroism in a multitude of guises. These stories are at odds with the abject rape script too frequently foisted upon survivors.

Indeed, in constructing the "Rape Victim" as a transnational phenomenon for activist purposes, international conflict feminism may have unintentionally revived an essentialized notion of "woman," eliding feminist and postcolonial critiques of this monolithic category. Insights regarding intersectionality and the politics of positionality, in this context, seem to have ceded to a victim-centered politics that elides the heterogeneity of women's experiences.[6] As Ratna Kapur has argued, "The victim-subject relies on a universal subject: a subject that resembles the uncomplicated subject of liberal discourse. It is a subject that cannot accommodate a multi-layered experience" (2005, 99). The repeated emphasis on "conflict-related sexual violence against women and girls" risks erasing social context and the cultural meanings assigned to sexual violence and its legacies. Additionally—and ironically, given the tenacious effort to have sexual violence recognized as a war crime and a crime against humanity—sexual violence might not be what women categorize as the worst violation they have endured during times of war.

For example, I found that survivors of sexual violence in Peru may consider the loss of entire families due to brutal massacres, or to the slow grinding death of starvation, to be the most searing aspect of the internal armed conflict. Sexual violence may not be at the top of some women's hierarchy of harms; thus, more emphasis should be placed on discovering local women's priorities, including their views of what constitutes redress and justice. The risk of overemphasizing the sexual and penetrative violation of women's bodies is that women are reduced to sexualized objects to which damage is done, eliding both their protagonism in the face of danger as well as the more complicated stories women tell about war and its effects.

The literature on truth commissions has lamented that women "do not talk about themselves," but rather about the suffering of others.[7] However, in foregrounding the ways in which violence has affected their homes, personal spaces, communities, and their loved ones, women are talking about themselves. They are narrating the violation of what, in many societies, are their areas of expertise, and they often do so in the voice of the witness rather than that of the victim.[8] A feminist theory of harm might begin with understanding the importance of connectivity and interdependence in many women's lives given their roles as caregivers in most societies. I recall the many times women in Peru lamented "we were both mother and father during those years" or insisted "when children are hungry, it is the mother who must respond." These women were clear that when children and families are in danger, it is women who must shoulder the struggle of daily life. Thus we might begin with a more fundamental question: What exactly *is* the injury?

Recall that women provided over half of the testimonies compiled by the TRC. What did they talk about? Women offered tremendous insight into the gendered dimensions of war, and the ways in which violence permeated all spheres of life. They spoke about the challenges of keeping children fed, homes intact, livestock safe, the search for missing loved ones, the lacerating sting of ethnic insults in the very cities in which they sought refuge: women spoke about familial and communal suffering, and about the quotidian aspects of armed conflict. When people go to war, caregiving can become a dangerous occupation. While they did not provide the emblematic rape narrative, these wide-ranging and diffuse harms are precisely how many women experienced this war. While the international focus on conflict-related rape and sexual violence has been a hard-won achievement, it comes at a cost. Even a broad definition of sexual violence results in a narrow understanding of the gendered dimensions of war, and of the full range of harms that women (and men) experience and prioritize.

What do women name as violence? The focus on bodily integrity, while important, flows from a focus on the so-called first-generation human rights (civil and political rights protected by a variety of treaties following World War II). The "second-generation" rights—social, economic, and cultural—have taken longer to be enforceable and remain "soft law" standards in most instances. However, as illustrated by my research in Peru, the emphasis women place on the violation of social, economic, and cultural rights should inform accountability dialogues and transitional justice debates in the aftermath of armed conflict.

Transitional justice is a field of postwar inquiry and intervention focused on addressing the legacies of past human rights violations in the hope that doing so will build a more peaceful and just future; it may include tribunals, war crimes prosecutions, memorials, reparations, and truth commissions (Teitel 2002). Transitional justice imports many elements of the liberal human rights tradition, with its foundation in Enlightenment principles of individual freedom; the autonomous individual and the social contract; the public sphere of secular reason; the rule of law; and the centrality of retributive justice, particularly in the form of criminal justice and prosecutions. Some have referred to this as the "liberal peace-building consensus," and acknowledge the many contributions this approach has made to postconflict reconstruction (Philpott 2007).

Liberal legalism, however, has both strengths and weaknesses. Feminist legal theorists have provided compelling critiques of law and liberalism, underscoring the failure of both to adequately capture the experiences of women. Fionnula Ní Aoláin has referred to this as the "problem of capture" (2009). As she argues, "The idea of harm to women has been central to women's placement in legal discourse. Such placement, however, is not synonymous with status and recognition" (2–3). Indeed, the conceptual and practical consequences of such efforts frequently affirm women's secondary and disjunctive social status, and give rise to regulatory or protectionist legal regimes that may be constraining and paternalist in their application. Thus one caution about the Women, Peace, and Security Agenda is the way in which a broader feminist platform was reduced to a focus on violence against women—particularly sexualized violence—such that the series of UN resolutions are more about protecting women than protecting (and promoting) their rights.[9]

ADD MEN AND STIR?

> Some of the recruits were really young. They were just adolescents. They didn't want to participate [in the rapes]. If someone refused, the rest of the men would take him aside and rape him. All of them would rape him, with the poor guy screaming. They said they were "changing his voice"—with so much screaming, his voice would lower and he wouldn't be a woman anymore. (Former member of the Peruvian navy, cited in Theidon 2012)

I turn now to the men, noting one irony in the UN Security Council resolutions under consideration here. In much of the policy literature—including UN and World Bank documents—"gender" is frequently a code word for "women," leaving men as the unquestioned, unmarked category. When we turn to sexual violence, however, the logic of the default is reversed. As Lara Stemple has noted in her analysis of Resolution 1325, the foundational resolution of the WPS Agenda, "In the perambulatory language, boys are included through the use of the term 'women and children.' But as soon as sexual violence is addressed specifically, the instrument excludes them, switching to the term 'women and girls'" (2009, 622). Men and boys as victims of gender-based and sexual violence are all but erased.

A cursory reading of reports on sexual violence leads to a similar conclusion. There is generally the toss-away line or footnote acknowledging that, of course, men and boys may also be victims of sexual violence—and then the report returns to its main storyline, which I gloss as "womenandgirls." One is reminded of the outmoded and critiqued Women in Development approach that was introduced in the 1970s, and which reached its apex during the UN Decade for Women (1976–1985). Later referred to facetiously as "add women and stir," Women in Development was increasingly criticized for its emphasis on women, rather than on gender relations, and for failing to address systemic gender inequality. As critics argued, Women in Development did not "consider the underlying and often discriminatory gender structures upon which these very projects are often built" (Chant and Gutman 2000, 6). In the new focus on women and girls and conflict-related sexual violence, men and boys figure as potentially violent actors or, at best, "secondary victims" traumatized by witnessing the abuse of their family members. This framework fails to grasp men as vulnerable to sexual violence, and older concerns about female honor and male offense creep back into the conversation.

Clearly, gender-sensitive research should include studying the forms of masculinity forged both during armed conflict and as one component in reconstructing individual identities and collective existence in the aftermath of war. This means incorporating a nuanced gender analysis into our research design and recommendations, and contemplating how our methods and questions would change if we included men and boys as both perpetrators *and* victim-survivors of gender-based and sexual violence. Additionally, given that women survivors of sexual violence are unjustly made to bear the narrative burden for these crimes, involving men in our research on sexual violence is crucial.

There is not just one explanation or motivation for sexual violence during armed conflict. As with any sort of human action, the specificities matter. Indeed, the specificities are key to moving beyond the "boys will be boys" shrug of inevitability to understanding when and where sexual violence occurs; which individuals or groups are targeted and why; who the perpetrators are; and the types of sexual violence practiced, and how these may vary across time, space, and armed groups.

In her comparative research, Elisabeth Wood has employed the concept of a "repertoire of violence" to refer to the range of violent acts an armed group deploys. She then examines whether or not sexual violence figures in to that broader repertoire. Wood has found that different forms of violence do not covary; in other words, even in highly violent conflicts the use of sexual violence may be either very low or virtually nonexistent. This has led her to state that rape is not inevitable in war, a conclusion that leads to a series of important consequences (Wood 2009). Investigating this variation moves beyond essentializing arguments about men, guns, and testosterone: understanding variation allows us to identify those factors that encourage—or may serve to limit—the deployment of sexual violence. It becomes easier to hold perpetrators accountable if we can demonstrate that rape and other forms of sexual violence are not "an unfortunate but inevitable by-product of the necessary game called war" (Brownmiller 1975).

My research and the Peruvian TRC's final report reveal that patterns of sexual violence varied across armed parties to the conflict. Shining Path guerrillas were more inclined toward sexual slavery and mutilation, forced nudity, and coerced abortions; the Peruvian armed forces were more likely to engage in sexual torture and gang rape. Indeed, as my research showed, when women described their experiences of rape, it was never one soldier but rather several. "They raped the women until they could not stand up." The soldiers were mutilating women with their penises, and the women were bloodied. These were blood rituals.[10]

When analyzing gang rape, we should think about why the men raped this way. An instrumentalist explanation would indicate that the soldiers raped in groups in order to overpower a woman, or so that one soldier could stand watch while the others raped. However, it would be a limited reading to attribute this practice to the necessity for pure force or standing watch. When a soldier pressed his machine gun into a woman's chest, he did not need more force. When the soldiers came down from the bases at night to rape, "privacy" was not their primary concern. They operated with impunity.

Clearly there is a ritualistic aspect to gang rape.[11] Many people related that after killing someone, the soldiers drank the blood of their victim, or bathed their faces and chests with the blood. Blood ties were established between soldiers, and bloodied wombs birthed a lethal fraternity. These blood ties united the soldiers, and the bodies of the raped women served as the medium for forging those ties.

In their analysis of rape during the 1992–1994 Bosnian war, Bulent Diken and Carsten Bagge Lausten suggest that gang rape forges a "brotherhood of guilt" based in part upon the abjection of the victim (2005). For the authors, men's guilt is the key emotion: guilt unifies the perpetrators, and rape is the rite of initiation. Additionally, they argue that shame resists verbalization while guilt incites it: "Whereas guilt can be verbalized and can perform as an element in the brotherhood of guilt, shame cannot, which is why it often results in trauma. War thus both creates and destroys communities [of the perpetrators and the victims respectively]" (ibid., 114).

Gang rape not only breaks the moral codes that generally order social life: the practice also serves to eradicate shame. Committing morally abhorrent acts in front of others not only forges bonds between the perpetrators but also forges *sinvergüenzas*—shameless people—capable of tremendous brutality. To lose the sense of shame—a regulatory emotion because shame implies an Other in front of whom one feels ashamed—creates men with a recalibrated capacity for atrocity. Acts that obliterate shame also obliterate a sense of self, contributing to processes aimed at subsuming individuality to create group cohesion and "selflessness" in the service of a collective. Additionally, there is a temporal aspect to understanding these acts and the men who engage in them—and to understanding why the solidarity of guilt may give way to a deep sense of shame over time. In my research, I am struck by the fact that "men don't talk," at least not in the first person, about their participation in rape.

But they certainly do talk during the act itself. Women (and men) emphasize what the soldiers said while raping them: "*Terruca de mierda*" (terrorist of shit; shitty terrorist), "*ahora aguanta India*" (now take it, Indian), "*carajo, terruca de mierda*" (damn it, terrorist of shit), and "*India de mierda*" (shitty Indian). The soldiers were marking their victims with physical and verbal assaults. Importantly, in my conversations as well as in the testimonies provided to the TRC, acts of sexual violence were almost always accompanied by ethnic and racial insults, prompting me to consider the ways in which gender, racial, and military hierarchies converged during the internal armed conflict.

Where did the soldiers learn this behavior, and acquire such virulent disdain for people ethnically similar to themselves? I suggest we look to the barracks. Drawing upon her research in Guatemala, Diane Nelson has written that "[r]eports of brutal barracks training suggest that internalized racism is a tool used to break the boys down so they may be remade as soldiers, in part by promising them marks of ladino identity (modern bourgeois practices like wearing shoes and eating meat) and of masculinity. Mayan men are often feminized in relation to traditional practices and in their limited power vis-à-vis the ladino" (Nelson 1999, 91). Military service, for all of its abuses, is thus a way to become "less Indian" in a context in which "the Indian is often coded as female" (ibid., 182).

This holds true in Peru as well where young rural men swelled the lowest ranks of the army, and were subject to brutal military socialization. "*Los antiguos*" (senior officers and more seasoned soldiers) referred to these young men as "*los perros*" (the dogs); the former soldiers we interviewed summed up their basic training as "*la perrada*"—a dog's life. They recount being forced to lick the floors of filthy latrines, to sleep with dirty flea-infested blankets, to kill dogs, and subsequently drink their blood and eat their raw flesh. These men also described severe beatings and lacerating verbal harassment as punishments for even minor infractions.

Included in the verbal harassment were ethnic insults. The recruits were darker-skinned men from the sierra serving under lighter skinned officers from the coast. Class standing and military rank magnified ethnic difference, which was further enforced by the use of sexual violence, especially rape. In our interviews, former soldiers assured us that "sex was 80 percent of the conversations we had every day." Who could "*tirar*" (rape) another was a determining factor is deciding who was the "*más macho*," and the first one to anally rape another man came out, literally, on top. Just as rank determined who would go first when raping civilians, that same hierarchy was repeated within the barracks. The gang rapes began with the highest-ranking officer and ended with the lowliest recruit. Rape was a means of establishing hierarchies, between armed groups and the population, and within the armed forces themselves. Several former soldiers described the use of sodomy on young recruits who were reluctant to demonstrate the "appropriate" level of aggression vis-à-vis the civilian population. In other instances, we were told that if a recruit refused to participate in the raping, he would be shot and his family told that he died in combat. Thus, I stress again the importance of understanding men as both victims and victimizers during times of conflict, a recognition that need not devolve into a lack of accountability or endless moral elasticity.

Holding people accountable means having a clear understanding of the forms of violence practiced and suffered, by whom and in what context. This may involve listening differently to male victims, as I have suggested, which could change what we think we know about sexual violence. Across the board in Peru, Quechua-speakers frequently used veiled speech when talking about rape and other forms of sexual violence. The verbs I heard most often (in translation) were *fastidiar* (to bother), *molestar* (to harass), *abusar* (to abuse), and *burlar* (to make fun of or to take advantage of someone). Context is crucial to understanding the meaning of what an individual was actually communicating, and we now know that the gender of the speaker also influenced what was heard and how it was coded by the TRC.

Political scientist Michelle Leiby reviewed a sample of 2,500 testimonies given to the Peruvian TRC, examining what people had said and how the acts they described were coded into the database. When she analyzed the original testimonies (and worked with native Quechua speakers to capture the nuances of language), Leiby found that 22 percent of the victims of sexual violence were men (2009, 82). In the TRC's coding, "The rape of men is treated inconsistently—coded as either sexual violence or torture, and sometimes not recorded at all" (ibid.).[12] Evidently, what determined whether a particular act was coded as sexual violence versus torture often depended not on the act itself, but on the gender of the body upon which the act was performed. The erasure of sexualized violence against men yields stereotypical victim-perpetrator binaries, and reinforces the image of women as persons to whom sexual crimes essentially occur. Women get raped; men, apparently, do not.[13]

For certain testimony takers and database designers in Peru, men as victims of sexual violence was "unthinkable," and the stories men told about being raped, sexually tortured, mutilated, or humiliated were largely erased. Thus, an important silence entered into and molded the archive. Statistics have powerful knowledge effects, and archives are more than a mere collection of documents that define a culture at a particular moment. As Michel Foucault argued, archives are more than institutions neutrally established to preserve texts. Rather, the archive is "the law of what can be said," and the law of how what is said is transformed, used, and preserved (1982). In this instance, the archive leaves us with essentialized notions of victims and perpetrators, categories too frequently assumed to map seamlessly onto gendered dichotomies as well. Gender is reduced to women; gender-based violence reduced to rape; and the more complicated stories people tell about war are at risk of becoming unthinkable and, therefore, erased.

NOTES

1. For an excellent analysis of the violence against women movement, international human rights, and their "vernacularization," see Merry 2006.
2. UN Security Council Resolution 2016 (2013).
3. See Theidon 2016 for a fuller discussion of these issues.
4. The classic work on male fraternities is Peggy Sanday's *Fraternity Gang Rape: Sex, Brotherhood, and Privilege on the College Campus* (1990). On military socialization, the literature is vast; a good place to start is with Joshua Goldstein's *War and Gender: How Gender Shapes the War System and Vice Versa* (2001); Lt. Col. Dave Grossman's *The Psychological Cost of Learning to Kill in War and Society* (1996); and Richard Holmes's *Acts of War: The Behavior of Men in Battle* (1985). For a fascinating analysis of how torture may be resignified by its victims/survivors as a source of pride and a route to male authority, see Peteet (1994). In addition to academic and practitioner texts and documents, some of the finest work has been authored by former soldiers themselves. For an overview of key texts, see Brown and Lutz (2007).
5. For a detailed discussion of these issues, see Theidon 2007 and 2012.
6. I invoke, of course, Kimberlé Crenshaw's concept of intersectionality (1989), as well as the abundant postcolonial critiques, including Anzaldúa 2012; Kapur 2005; and Mohanty 1988.
7. For example, see Hayner 2010 and Ross 2003.
8. See Fiona Ross for her insightful analysis of women's testimonies to the South African TRC (2003).
9. For an interesting critique, see Miller 2004.
10. In this section I draw upon my book *Intimate Enemies: Violence and Reconciliation in Peru* (2012).
11. For her discussion of war rape and male bonding, see Enloe 1988.
12. The most frequent form of sexual abuse suffered by men was sexual humiliation (46%) followed by sexual mutilation (20%), sexual torture (15%), and rape (15%) (Leiby 2009).
13. Space limitations do not allow me to adequately address certain domestic legal systems and the gendered pronouns used in the rape laws. In some countries men cannot "legally" be raped because the law only recognizes female victims. In other cases, "sodomy" may be illegal, and thus a man who comes forward to denounce having been raped is a criminal, not a victim.

REFERENCES

Anzaldúa, Gloria. 2012. *Borderlands/La frontera: The New Mestiza*. New York: Aunt Lute Books.

Brown, Keith, and Catherine Lutz. 2007. "Grunt Lit: The Participant Observers of Empire." *American Ethnologist* 34 (2): 322–328.

Brownmiller, Susan. 1975. *Against Our Will: Men, Women, and Rape.* New York: Simon and Schuster.

Chant, Sylvia, and Matthew C. Gutman. 2000. *Mainstreaming Men into Gender and Development: Debates, Reflections, and Experiences.* London: Oxfam.

Crenshaw, Kimberlé. 1989. "Demarginalizing the Intersection of Race and Sex: A Black Feminist Critique of Antidiscrimination Doctrine, Feminist Theory, and Antiracist Politics." *University of Chicago Legal Forum* 140: 139–167.

Diken, Bulent, and Carsten Bagge Lausten. 2005. "Becoming Abject: Rape as a Weapon of War." *Body and Society* 11 (1): 111–128.

Engle, Karen. 2005. "Feminism and Its (Dis)contents: Criminalizing Wartime Rape in Bosnia and Herzegovina." *American Journal of International Law* 99: 778–816.

Enloe, Cynthia. 1988. *Does Khaki Become You? The Militarization of Women's Lives.* London: Pandora Press.

Foucault, Michel. 1982. *The Archeology of Knowledge.* New York: Pantheon.

Goldstein, Joshua. 2001. *War and Gender: How Gender Shapes the War System and Vice Versa.* Cambridge: Cambridge University Press.

Grossman, Dave. 1996. *The Psychological Cost of Learning to Kill in War and Society.* Boston: Little, Brown.

Hayner, Priscilla. (2001) 2010. *Unspeakable Truths: Facing the Challenge of Truth Commissions.* New York: Routledge.

Holmes, Richard. 1985. *Acts of War: The Behavior of Men in Battle.* New York: Free Press.

Kapur, Ratna. 2002. "The Tragedy of Victimization Rhetoric: Resurrecting the 'Native' Subject in International/Post-Colonial Feminist Legal Politics." *Harvard Human Rights Journal* 15 (1): 1–37.

———. 2005. *Erotic Justice: Law and the New Politics of Postcolonialism.* London: Glass House Press.

Leiby, Michelle. 2009. "Wartime Sexual Violence in Guatemala and Peru." *International Studies Quarterly* 53: 445–468.

Merry, Sally Engle. 2006. *Human Rights and Gender Violence: Translating International Law into Local Justice.* Chicago: University of Chicago Press.

Miller, Alice. 2004. "Sexuality, Violence against Women, and Human Rights: Women Make Demands and Ladies Get Protection." *Health and Human Rights* 7 (2): 16–47.

Mohanty, Chandra Talpade. 1988. "Under Western Eyes: Feminist Scholarship and Colonial Discourses." *Feminist Review* 30: 61–88.

Nelson, Diane M. 1999. *A Finger in the Wound: Body Politics in Quincentennial Guatemala.* Berkeley: University of California Press.

Ní Aoláin, Fionnuala. 2000. "Sex-Based Violence and the Holocaust: A Reevaluation of Harms and Rights in International Law." *Yale Journal of Law and Feminism* 12 (43): 43–84.

Peteet, Julie. 1994. "Male Gender and Rituals of Resistance in the Palestinian 'Intifada': A Cultural Politics of Violence." *American Ethnologist* 21: 31–49.

Philpott, Daniel. 2007. "Religion, Reconciliation, and Transitional Justice: The State of the Field." *Social Science Research Council Working Papers.* New York: Social Science Research Council.

Ross, Fiona. 2003. *Bearing Witness: Women and the Truth and Reconciliation Commission in South Africa.* London: Pluto Press.

Sanday, Peggy. 1990. *Fraternity Gang Rape: Sex, Brotherhood, and Privilege on the College Campus.* New York: New York University Press.

Sivakumaran, Sandesh. 2005. "Male/Male Rape and the 'Taint' of Homosexuality." *Human Rights Quarterly* 27 (4): 1274–1306.

———. 2007. "Sexual Violence against Men in Armed Conflict." *European Journal of International Law* 18 (2): 253–276.

Stemple, Lara. 2009. "Male Rape and Human Rights." *Hastings Law Journal* 60: 605–645.

Teitel, Ruti. 2002. "Transitional Justice as Liberal Narrative." In *Transnational Legal Processes: Globalisation and Power Disparities,* edited by Michael Likosky. London: Butterworths.

Theidon, Kimberly. 2007. "Género en transición: Sentido común, mujeres y guerra." *Analasis Politico* 20 (60): 3–30.

———. 2012. *Intimate Enemies: Violence and Reconciliation in Peru.* Philadelphia: University of Pennsylvania Press.

———.2016. "A Greater Measure of Justice: Gender, Violence and Reparations." In *Mapping Feminist Anthropology in the 21st Century,* edited by Leni Silverstein and Ellen Lewin. New Brunswick, NJ: Rutgers University Press.

TRC (Truth and Reconciliation Commission). 2003. *Informe Final de la Comisión de Verdad y Reconciliación.* 9 vols. Lima: Truth and Reconciliation Commission.

Wood, Elisabeth Jean. 2009. "Armed Groups and Sexual Violence: When Is Wartime Rape Rare?" *Politics & Society* 37 (1): 131–162.

NOTES ON CONTRIBUTORS

MIKE ANASTARIO received his PhD in sociology from Boston College in 2007. He conducts applied research on sexual risk behaviors and on systems for investigating sexual assault.

SERENA COSGROVE, PhD, is an anthropologist and sociologist compelled by the challenges that arise in postconflict settings. She carries out fieldwork in Central America and sub-Saharan Africa. Her book, *Leadership from the Margins: Women and Civil Society Organizations in Argentina, Chile, and El Salvador* (Rutgers 2010), examines women's contributions to societies after war and dictatorship through their civil society organizing. She is an assistant professor at Seattle University.

KATHLEEN DILL is a sociocultural anthropologist. In Guatemala she conducted research on local forms of transitional justice and postwar social reconstruction. Her multifaceted collaboration with Achi-Maya human rights advocates in Rabinal, Baja Verapaz, spanned a decade. In Nicaragua, as part of a team of scientists from King's College London, Dill facilitated the implementation of a satellite-based volcano monitoring system across Central America, and conducted research on the politics of natural disasters and humanitarian aid. Dill has taught at the University of Texas at Austin, Cornell University, and Mills College. She is currently working on a book based on her research in Guatemala.

SOFÍA DUYOS ÁLVAREZ-ARENAS is a lawyer who specializes in human rights and received her degree from the Universidad Complutense (Spain). Since 2000, she has been working in the Human Rights Office of the Archbishop of Guatemala, where she has conducted research on human rights violations, advocacy, and awareness. She is one of the lawyers litigating the case of genocide in Guatemala and has advised the Legal Action Center in Human Rights.

MELANIE HOEWER, PhD, is a lecturer in the School of Politics and International Relations in University College Dublin. Her primary areas of research are women, peace and security, identity in conflict and settlement processes, intersectionality, Latin American politics, and Northern Ireland. Her monograph *Crossing Boundaries during Peace and Conflict: Transforming Identity in Chiapas and in Northern Ireland* (2014) explores the gender and ethnic identity shifts of women during and after episodes of armed conflict. She has several publications on women, peace, and security in Northern Ireland, Colombia, and Liberia, gender violence, and social change in Northern Ireland and Chiapas, among others.

MAIJA JÄPPINEN holds a PhD from the University of Helsinki in social work and is a postdoctoral researcher at the Department of Social Research in the University of Helsinki. Her doctoral dissertation is an ethnographic study about domestic violence and the working practices of women's crisis centers in Russia. She is a member of the Finnish Center of Excellence in Russian Studies "Choices of Russian Modernization" coordinated by the Aleksanteri Institute, University of Helsinki.

JANET ELISE JOHNSON is an associate professor of political science and women's studies at Brooklyn College, City University of New York, and a visiting scholar at the Center for European and Mediterranean Studies, New York University. She holds a BA from Duke University in public policy and a PhD in political science from Indiana University. She has written extensively on gender and politics, including *Gender Violence in Russia: The Politics of Feminist Intervention* (2009) and recent articles published in the journals *Nationalities Papers, Politics & Gender, Communist and Post-Communist Studies,* and *Signs: Journal of Women in Culture and Society.*

LAURA McATACKNEY is an associate professor in sustainable heritage management at Aarhus University, Denmark, having been based at the School of Social Justice, University College Dublin, until 2015. An archaeologist by training, she has previously researched the material remnants of the Troubles that persist into the peace process in Northern Ireland, with a special focus on Long Kesh/Maze prison. She has published a monograph on the subject, *An Archaeology of the Troubles: The Dark Heritage of Long Kesh/Maze* (2014).

FAZIL MORADI is completing his doctoral dissertation at the Max Planck Institute for Social Anthropology in Halle, Germany, and is working on a coedited book on art, memory, and genocide. Moradi conducted the first anthropological study of the Iraqi Ba'thi state's genocide (al-Anfāl operations, 1987–1991), focusing on modern state bureaucracy and archive, and questions of memory, remembrance, monuments, symbols of everyday mourning, justice, forgiveness, forgetting, and modes of representation in the aftermath of genocide in the post-Ba'th Kurdistan region of Iraq. He has taught Anthropography of Genocide at the Institute for Social and Cultural Anthropology, Martin Luther University Halle-Wittenberg.

ANNIE POHLMAN is a lecturer in Indonesian studies at the University of Queensland, Australia. She is author of *Women, Sexual Violence, and the Indonesian Killings of 1965–1966* (2015) and coeditor of *Genocide and Mass Atrocities in Asia: Legacies and Prevention* (2013). Her research areas include Indonesian history and politics, comparative genocide studies, torture, gendered experiences of violence, and oral testimony. Her current research maps forms of torture perpetrated by state agents during Indonesia's New Order regime (1965–1998) across various regions of Indonesia and Timor Leste.

CECILIA M. SALVI is a doctoral student in the Anthropology Department at the Graduate Center, City University of New York, and adjunct lecturer at Baruch College. She is a Chancellor's Doctoral Incentive Program scholar and a Dean K. Harrison fellow.

VICTORIA SANFORD is a professor and chair of anthropology and founding director of the Center for Human Rights and Peace Studies at Lehman College, City University of New York, and doctoral faculty at the Graduate Center. She is the author of *Buried Secrets: Truth and Human Rights in Guatemala* (2003), *Violencia y Genocidio en Guatemala* (2003), *Guatemala: Del Genocidio al Feminicidio* (2008), *La Masacre de Panzos: Etnicidad, Tierra y Violencia en Guatemala* (2009), *Genocidio en la Area Ixil* (2016), and coeditor (with Asale Angel-Ajani) of *Engaged Observer: Activism, Advocacy, and Anthropology* (2006), among others.

KATERINA STEFATOS holds a PhD in politics from Goldsmiths, University of London, and an MSc in gender and the media from the London School of Economics. She has studied politics and international relations in Greece and the United States. She is an adjunct assistant professor in the Department of Anthropology and the Women's Studies Program at Lehman College, City University of New York, and is the Hellenic Studies Program coordinator at Columbia University. She has published papers in international journals, and has contributed book chapters for edited volumes.

KIMBERLY THEIDON is a medical anthropologist focusing on Latin America. Her research interests include political violence, transitional justice, reconciliation, and the politics of postwar reparations. She is the author of many articles, and *Entre Prójimos: El conflicto armado interno y la política de la reconciliación en el Perú* (2004; 2nd edition, 2009) and *Intimate Enemies: Violence and Reconciliation in Peru* (2012). *Intimate Enemies* was awarded the 2013 Honorable Mention from the Washington Office on Latin America–Duke University Libraries Book Award for Human Rights in Latin America, and the 2013 Honorable Mention for the Eileen Basker Prize from the Society for Medical Anthropology for research on gender and health. She is the Henry J. Leir Professor of International Humanitarian Studies at the Fletcher School, Tufts University.

SHANNON DRYSDALE WALSH is an assistant professor and McKnight Land-Grant Professor at the University of Minnesota Duluth. Her research helps explain variation in justice system responses to violence against women in Latin America. In addition, she produces scholarship on crime, sex trafficking, and women's policy making. She has been awarded fellowships and funding from the American Association of University Women, the National Endowment for the Humanities, Fulbright-Hays, and the Andrew W. Mellon/American Council of Learned Societies. She is the author of several articles and was awarded the 2015 Helen Safa Paper Prize by the Latin American Studies Association Gender and Feminist Studies Section. She completed her PhD and MA at the University of Notre Dame and holds a BA from the University of North Carolina at Chapel Hill.

INDEX

abductions, 107, 161

Abdūl-khāleq (Kurdish sibling), 110–111

activists: and activist interventions, 5; anti-trafficking, 174; in Chiapas, Mexico, 64–77; collective narratives of indigenous women, 66–68; domestic violence/gender inequality link in Russia, 11; gendering of experiences of violence by females, 68–70; and gender violence definitions, 172; in Greek military junta, 31n29; indigenous women, 8, 70–71, 72–76, 77; *mestiza* women, 70–72, 76; political, 20, 28; Russian women's, 149–150; women as, 62. *See also* dissidents, female; dissidents, male; political prisoners, male; political prisoners, women

'Aflaq, Michel, 104

Agama, Margaret, 162

Agamben, Giorgio, 28, 125, 127

agency, 5, 20, 28, 58, 62

agency, women's: collective, 9, 66–68; and political resistance, 9, 53, 58–61, 62; possibility of, 8

al-Anfāl operations, 102–113; al-Anfāl trial, 110–111; camps, 107; captured women, 108–110; chemical weapons use by, 106, 107; executions, 107; extermination orders, 105–106, 110; as genocide, 10, 111; human trafficking, 112; Kurdish collaborators with, 107, 113; secret documents of, 108; statistics on, 107; survivors, 108, 112

Albright, Madeline, 175

Aldana, Thelma, 44

al-Djundī, Sāmi, 104

alienation, 22, 28, 44n8

Alivizatos, Nikos, 29n1

al-Majid, 'Ali Hassan, 105, 111

Alston, Philip, 4

Álvarez-Arenas, Sofía Duyos, 34–44

Amnesty International, 20, 21, 29n2

Ana (Tseltal female activist), 68

Anastario, Mike, 6, 10, 85–100

Angelaki, Maria, 23

ANNA (National Center for Prevention of Violence), Russia, 149

anticommunism: in Greece, 9, 26; in Guatemala, 36; in Indonesia, 9, 116, 123, 125, 128n2; and torture, 21, 25, 26

anti-trafficking legislation, 171–181; anti-slavery conventions, 174; history of, 171, 180, 181n1; and NGO advocacy, 179; as a response to gender violence, 174; unintended consequences of, 172; in United States, 12, 173, 175–176

Antonia (indigenous female activist), 70, 72

archival research, 7, 8, 20

Aretxaga, Begoña, 57

Argentina: Dirty War, 11, 13n1, 23, 29n4, 126; domestic violence cases, 3; ESMA detention and torture camp, 13n1, 21, 23, 28

armed conflict contexts: and dimensions of violence, 65, 68, 185; and patriarchal practice, 64; women's participation in, 65. *See also* warfare

Arseni, Kitty, 24

asylum cases, 176–178

autograph books: as documentation methodology, 7, 57, 58; of women political prisoners in Ireland, 9, 30n24, 51, 52, 54–55, 56, 60, 62

Ayress, Nieves, 23–24

Baaz, Maria Ericksson, 161

Barríos, Yasmin, 34, 44

Barzani, Nechirvan, 111

Ba'thi state, Iraqi, 10, 104

Bauman, Zygmunt, 103

Becket, James, 20